EMERGENT TECHNOLOGIES: NEW MEDIA AND URBAN LIFE

Edited by
Bhakti More

EMERGENT TECHNOLOGIES: NEW MEDIA AND URBAN LIFE

Edited by
Bhakti More

COMMON GROUND RESEARCH NETWORKS 2020

First published in 2020
as part of the Technology, Knowledge, and Society Book Imprint
http://doi.org/10.18848/978-1-86335-219-2/CGP (Full Book)

Common Ground Research Networks
2001 South First Street, Suite 202
University of Illinois Research Park
Champaign, IL
61820

Library of Congress Cataloging-in-Publication Data

Names: More, Bhakti, editor.
Title: Emergent technologies : new media and urban life / [edited by]
    Bhakti More.
Description: Champaign : Common Ground Research Networks, 2020. | Includes
    bibliographical references. | Summary: "Contemporary cities are
    witnessing a transformation with the advent of new technologies and
    their impact on the built environment and socio-cultural aspects of
    urban living. We, as academicians from the fields of media sociology and
    urban planning, are keen to explore how the underlying dynamics of
    emerging technologies will impact urban planning, design, and living.
    This edited volume puts together seminal contributions from researchers
    and academicians to establish the context for understanding and
    reflecing on the impact of emergent technologies on the socio-spatial
    and socio-cultural aspects of urban living through cases and insights on
    neighborhood planning, design, and urban digital governance. Moreover,
    this volume will help academicians, professionals, policymakers and
    other key stakeholders explore and create a new urban agenda that
    applies emergent technologies that will engage, connect, and build
    sustainable cities. Cities are the melting pots of communicative actions
    between people and cultures. Contemporary cities are the emerging nodal
    centers of communication that convey a distinct civic experience through
    urban living, forms, patterns, and the built environment. This volume
    examines the impact of the advent of new communication technologies on
    urban living. This book seeks to explore the implications of new
    communication methods and their effects on urban life including changing
    patterns of social interactions"-- Provided by publisher.
Identifiers: LCCN 2020022746 (print) | LCCN 2020022747 (ebook) | ISBN
    9780949313607 (hardback) | ISBN 9781863352185 (paperback) | ISBN
    9781863352192 (pdf)
Subjects: LCSH: City planning--Technological innovations. | Mass
    media--Social aspects. | Architecture and technology. | Urban policy. |
    Community development.
Classification: LCC HT166 .E4674 2020 (print) | LCC HT166 (ebook) | DDC
    307.1/216--dc23
LC record available at https://lccn.loc.gov/2020022746
LC ebook record available at https://lccn.loc.gov/2020022747

Cover Photo Credit: Phillip Kalantzis-Cope

TABLE OF CONTENTS

ACKNOWLEDGEMENTS

This book is a contribution of scholarly articles from researchers on emergent technologies in new media in cities from India, the United States of America, Brazil, Portugal, Pakistan, Malaysia, Ghana, Indonesia, and Bangladesh. I thank the authors for their patience and valuable contributions that made it possible to have various themes and focus areas in the book. Each author has their perspective on the impact of emergent technologies and the new media on urban life.

I thank Dr Mohammed Firoz, Dr Buroshiva Dasgupta, Saayan Chattopadhyay, Dr S.Arulchelvan, Dr Madhavi Reddy, Dr Shilpa Kalyan, Deborah Ryan, Dr Sreetama Mishra, Dr Mohammed Alsam Ansari, Anna Cornaro, Malvika Kaul, Robert Hassan, Dr Senthil Kumaran P, Somali Chowdhary for their guidance, reviewing the chapters, and all their support.

It is my pleasure to thank the team from Common Ground Research Networks, Phillip Kisubika, who was involved in the initial stages of the publication process and Kerry Dixon who gave it a final shape. The book was possible with their constant guidance and co-operation. Thank you to the team at Common Ground Research Networks.

I thank Manipal Academy of Higher Education Dubai Campus for encouraging a research culture at the University, which motivated me for the project and to all my colleagues for their support.

Finally, I thank my family and friends who have always encouraged me in my academic endeavor.

CHAPTER SUMMARIES

Chapter 1
New Media Technologies and the Urban Condition: Changing Socio-Spatial Relations and Emerging Geographies
by Dr. Kapil Kumar Gavsker

The world is urbanizing at an unprecedented pace, and more than half of the population already lives in urban areas. Technological innovations, information flow and expansion of personal space all have changed the conventional understanding of the city. With the emergence of hybrid towns: public space becomes layered with digital and wireless networks which lead to the public sphere as part "mediated" and partly physical. The chapter examines the changing socio-spatial relations in the context of new media technologies and their part in generating multiple experiences of urban space.

Chapter 2
Making or Destroying the City?: American Corporate Culture in Network Neutrality
by Marcus Breen

Neutrality in the United States exposes the political economy of public policy debates and their implications for urban communication. The power struggles between private and public interests overlapping with regulatory models of provisioning are explored in this case study. The chapter proposes a progressive institutional model of government regulation in which "the public interest" acts as a normative standard by which to assess communication systems for urban development. Drawing on Victor Pickard's concept of "corporate libertarianism," the chapter identifies significant implications for information flows within urban landscapes and the national communication infrastructure, in a critical exploration of Network Neutrality.

Chapter 3
The Multiple Layers of Information Communication Technologies and Their Use in Urban Public Space: A Case Study of New York City
by Pierre Depaz and Nicolas Grefenstette

The pervasiveness of digital communication technology transpires in our everyday lives partly because of its multi-layered nature. From connected home devices to wireless hotspots in public spaces, to neighborhood-wide access points and international fiber optics cable, new telecommunications operate on multiple, interconnected scales. Similarly, the planning of urban environments is also one of the different geographies: including the design of living in cities, which takes place at the level of the building, the street, the public square, the neighborhood, the municipality and the region. This chapter aims to provide a new understanding of urban planning practices by examining initiatives taken at different geographical and physical levels in New York City, and analyzing how different technological infrastructures operate and affect us.

Chapter 4
Ghost Cities: Augmented Heritage
by Rodrigo Cury Paraizo and Marina Lima Medeiros

Based on examples of the authors' laboratory and from other researchers and artists' experiences, this chapter argues how the experience of urban cultural heritage through augmented reality transforms those models and images in digital spatialized ghosts. Within the theoretical framework of augmented space and hybrid space, the chapter focus on augmented experiences of art and culture. The authors state that the user engagement - and its relation to urban augmented heritage changes of our relationship with collective memory and the understanding of urban space itself, that is now understood as a medium.

Chapter 5
Anonymous City, Anonymous Talking: Sarahah
by Dr Surhita Basu

The intellectual history of urban anonymity and urban isolation originates from a sense of loss in the conflict between Gemeinschaft and Gesellschaft and the alienation between the communities than within. While theories of urban living post-second world war placed a higher emphasis on economic activities as cities became the centre of consumption, theories on urban cultural transformation gradually came to the forefront. In this neo-Marxist evaluation of urban living was added the information and communication technology revolution that launched network society. This chapter presents a study which however stands unique in its approach towards 'anonymity' as an increasing urban reality, that is, how the digital communication platform is changing and re-establishing the preexisting culture of urban anonymity among the youths of India.

Chapter 6
Urban Walls and Virtual Bridges: Social Capital and the Internet in Divided Cities
by Dr. Francesca Savoldi

Based on the premise that the Internet is a tool that can enable new "walls" or "bridges" between separated communities and can have an influence on the urban transition of the city, this chapter analyses the impact of Internet use on "divided cities" –partitioned spaces characterized by community-based social contestation and segregation, whose nature depends on an ethnic-nationalistic conflict. This investigation used as its case study the city of Belfast, where a fractured urban fabric, characterized by defensive artefacts and eroded social cohesion (both consequences of conflict) coexist with a contemporary process of reunification. The chapter focuses on how emergent communication technologies are influencing social capital in this specific partitioned urban context, impacting its patterns of social interaction, which are conditioned by the high levels of urban segregation inherited from the conflict.

Chapter 7
Karachi's Urbanization: Challenges and Prospects for a Thriving Digital Culture in Urban Life
by Dr.Sadia Jamil

The penetration of Information and Communication Technology (ICT) infrastructure, the proliferation of the Internet and digital technologies in Karachi and its suburb are remarkable developments despite challenges associated with the city's messy urbanization. Karachi's technological developments can be viewed as potential drivers of progress and its growth as a smart city, based on the assumption that thriving digital culture can have a positive impact on almost all aspects of public spheres. Drawing on the 'modernization theory of urbanization' and the 'theory of technological determinism,' this chapter explores the key challenges and issues relating to the penetration of digital culture in Karachi. The chapter also reflects on thriving digital culture in transforming Karachi's city life.

Chapter 8
Living a Watched Life in Kuala Lumpur: Normalization of Surveillance in Urban Living
by Yvonne Hoh Jgin Jit and Amira Firdaus

Technology research firm, IHS, reported that in 2014, there are approximately up to 245 million professionally installed surveillance cameras around the world and Asia is set to take up 68% of the forecasted surveillance camera market. In this chapter, the discussion will track the trajectories of surveillance from being tools of the state to social capital in the hands' social media users and influencers in Malaysia, with Kuala Lumpur as the center of discussion. The chapter will discuss the impact of normalization of surveillance and comfort level around cameras through the post-9-11 rationalization of surveillance.

Chapter 9
Digital Governance and Digital Literacy: Examining the Portuguese Case
by Lucinda Caetano, José Crespo, and Rodrigo Cury Paraizo

In a globalized world, our daily lives are increasingly visible and lived in social networks. There is a worldwide trend to adopt digital technologies by public administration in the form of mobile, web-based applications, digital modeling and simulations, and various other interactive platforms. Portugal is no exception, and the country's legislation contemplates the use of collaborative territorial management platforms. This chapter seeks to discuss and explore the various facets of digital governance in Portugal with a focus on the increasing public participation levels for the collective construction of cities and also analyses mechanisms used by the Portuguese Public Administration to overcome the digital divide.

Chapter 10
The Potato We Need: Public Space, Social Media and Participation in São Paulo's Batata Square
by Fernanda Castilho and Richard Romancini

This chapter aims to analyze and reflect on social movement organizations and their role in the collective occupation of an important public space in São Paulo: the so-called Potato Square. This place is a large and historic space that was recently renewed by the public power and also acquired a new identity through active participation and citizen engagement in the change to this urban space (e.g., planting trees, organizing protests, fairs, and educational booklets). Based on the theoretical framework of placemaking, this chapter aims to observe the strategies of grassroots social movements, especially in the social media.

Chapter 11
Cities as Capitals of Innovation: The Study of Media Organizations and Emerging Digital Culture in Ghana
by Africanus Lewil Diedong

The need for introducing digital technologies into newsrooms is not merely driven by the fact that Ghanaian newsrooms must catch up with their counterparts elsewhere but more importantly, increasingly urban residents' tastes for digitized news is a reality facing media outlets. Drawing on key informant interviews of leaders in print journalism, this exploratory study investigates shifts in newsrooms environments and its implications on news work and trends in urban living, and how the changes can engender participatory communication among urban dwellers and rural residents. Ghana has experienced a checkered press history. The post independent press in Africa was subjected to varying degrees of control by authoritarian regimes, which impacted on news media outlets.

Many news outlets in Ghana operate with limited budgets and slim readership in urban areas, yet they are pressured by trends in modern news practice to adopt new media technologies to stay in business. Investment of scarce resources in new media technologies should consider the current reading culture of Ghanaians, especially urban youth, who are more attracted to using digital technologies. High cost of digital equipment and problems with internet connectivity add to challenges that newspaper organisations must surmount in order to be relevant to an emerging urban readership that is characterized by the desire to acquire the most current information speedily. Despite changes in modes of news production yet little is known about the nature of changes triggered by digital revolution. This emerging digital culture in cities appears to create a gap in communication for rural communities, whereby events and matters of interests to rural dwellers do not get the needed attention in digitization process because they may be of little economic and cultural value. This suggests unique peculiarities that require the attention of stakeholders in media and ICT to isolate what is relevant.

Chapter 12
Social Media Usage Within the Smart City initiative: The Case of the Creative Village in Bandung
by Eni Maryani and Detta Rahmawan

The concept of 'creative village' in the city of Bandung (Indonesia) is an effort to bring in qualitative changes in the slums through cultural and artistic approach. A variety of creative endeavors has transformed the village into a tourist destination and is attracting tourists, observers, and activists from different cities of the world. Visitors use digital technology and social media to share creative village information to broad audiences which helped in building a broader network. However, the sustainability of social media usage is not optimal. This chapter identifies and analyzes the existing obstacles and attempts to answer questions such as why despite being good internet connectivity creative village is failing to take the digital edge to reach out to the broader public.

Chapter 13
Living Culture of Today's Apartment Dwellers: Social Interactions, Social Media and Urban Living in Bangladesh
by Md. Aminul Islam and Naziat Choudhury

In the past three decades, the pattern of social relations has gone through massive transformations in Bangladesh. Within such reality, this study explores how social media are being used to shape and reshape interpersonal relationships within real-life social networks of neighbors in urban areas in the country. It sets out not only the changing patterns of interpersonal relationships among individuals on social networks, but also helps to understand the role social media play in this process. Drawing upon Barry Wellman's networked individualism theoretical framework, data are collected from residents of eight high-rise buildings using a semi-structured questionnaire. The participants of this study are selected through snowball sampling method. The findings indicate that while the urbanization and modernization process in Bangladesh is changing relationship patterns, as seen in other parts of the world, the residents here were limiting their connections to traditional methods of interaction. Social media seem to be contributing to the maintenance of weaker ties here.

CHAPTER 1

New Media Technologies and the Urban Condition: Changing Socio-Spatial Relations and Emerging Geographies

Kapil Kumar Gavsker, Ph.D.
Department of Applied Geography
School of Regional Studies and Earth Sciences
Ravenshaw University, Cuttack, India

ABSTRACT

The world is urbanizing at an unprecedented pace, and more than half of the population already live in urban areas. Technological innovations, information flow, and the expansion of personal space have all changed the conventional understanding of the city. With the emergence of hybrid towns, public space becomes layered with digital and wireless networks, which leads to the public sphere as part-"mediated" and part-physical. The chapter examines the changing socio-spatial relations in the context of new media technologies and their role in shaping social networks, connections, and values across socio-cultural settings leading to newer urban transition.

INTRODUCTION

Contemporary studies in social sciences offer a perspective on changing form and communication relations in the society as framed in expressions such as we live in "a connected age," a "human web," and a "web society". This is to be seen in the context of individualization, social fragmentation, and independent way of life of contemporary modern world. This kind of change seems inevitable with the increasing advancements in technological sector like information, communication and telecommunications and its use by the growing contemporary society, largely by the urban society. Present society is urbanizing faster than its counterpart rural, contributing to the wider access to information and communication technologies and growth in gadgets systems. However, there are regional disparities in urbanization and social and economic change in the world, leading to spatial-digital variation. A growing urbanizing class, wider dependence on use of digital internet connectivity and its applications to the kind of way people live in modern world is a spatially variable phenomenon. The interpretation of this phenomenon depends upon how and through which framework one perceives changes in the contemporary world. There is an unprecedented increase in transnational and global connectivity, which brings people close to each other through new information and communication technology (ICT) in social and economic arena. This change is largely an urban phenomenon, very much induced by technological developments. Thus, the growing urban citizen classes aspire, desire, and are more involved in the present *Internet Revolution* in the post-World War II period. This revolution has played a major role in not only enabling people to have access to updated information, but also in mobility to urban areas, particularly in the developing world experiencing a transition. According to the United Nations' (UN) World Urbanization Prospects report that, "the urban population of the world has grown rapidly since 1950, from 746 million to 3.9 billion in 2014. Asia, despite its lower level of urbanization, is home to 53 percent of the world's urban population, followed by Europe (14 percent) and Latin America and Caribbean (13 percent)" (2014: 1). There is great number of cities in Asia which are growing faster and expanding out caused by economic changes and spatial transformations. Carr (1987) noted that, "increasingly urbanization is also being seen as a dynamic force in society whereby values and behaviour patterns recognised as 'urban'are propagated and cultural change take place" (28).

However, this trend of technology driven society in is not making the world a "flat" surface. Historically, states Alaa Gharbawi, "The Internet, a very complex and revolutionary invention of 1965, has changed our world. The Internet can be defined as a global communications network consisting of thousands of networks typically interconnected by fiber-optic cabling. The Internet is always transforming into new complex hardware and software, in addition to the services it offers" (*Revolution of the Internet*). This effect has played a major role in information dissemination and connecting in the world, but only in urban areas or regions where politico-economic circumstances have favored the internet's installation and growth. However, there has been its spill over effects in the countryside later. Therefore, the internet is a *network of networks*, which is highly sophisticated, advanced, and well managed compared with the telephone network. Thus, unlike the telephone network, the internet uses packet switching. In fact, the Internet Revolution had its beginning in the United States (US) in the early years of 1990s. This was a by product of proliferation and internetworking of computers and their widespread application in the various sectors. The Internet Revolution introduced a different type of mechanization which was distinct from that anchored by the Industrial Revolution. It has become broad and far reaching in its impact, causing the mechanization of information and communication. Hinshaw and Stearns stated that, "what made industrialization revolutionary was that it harnessed new forms of energy, namely fossil fuels that enabled people to accelerate the creation of new tools, trades, and trading relationships. Like [these] other revolutions, industrialization has changed the way humans work, think, relate to each other and think" (2013:xxix). Whereas internet revolution changed the conventional system of working, thinking and organization.

Calling this phenomenon the *Internet Revolution* means it has transformed, influenced, and affected the significant proportion of the population of the contemporary world. Socio-cultural change seems inevitable and sometimes visible in terms of the internet's influence on children's education, connectivity with families and friends, purchasing goods and, above all, individuals' behavior. Without doubt, technology is continuously changing. These growing changes in the communication environment bring social and economic consequences to different aspects of everyday life. It is true that globalization and the spread of ICTs is closely related, as transnational communication and transaction play a key role in the whole process. Therefore, as ever more economic activities become concerned with differential application of ICTs, and the latest technical developments that affect new activity are thought to be of potentially far-reaching significance. In such circumstances, urban life seems unimaginable without the internet and telecommunication connectivity of our modern times. Graham states that, "[the] speculation and hype around 'multimedia', the 'communications revolution', the emergence of the 'information' or 'cyber' society, and the growing importance of the new 'electronic spaces' within computer networks have proliferated" (1997: 105). However, urban space at any point in time is the result of processes that play role in its production. Morphology of urban settlements exhibits the kind of combination of use of land and functions carried out and prevail in urban space. A basic fact is that socio-spatial disparities and inequalities are intrinsic to urban space as they are product of socio-economic changes and spatial processes and factors.

Thus making sense of urban geography do matters to a great deal in knowing nature of social and economic interaction, spatial distribution of income, inclusion in the economy and overall development processes. Furthermore, new media have a potential role in making sense of public space for the public and in infusing the technocratic conception of the city. Ampatzidou and Molenda suggested that, "new media give rise to a new set of spatial strategies and tactics that can be employed either to increase a centralised technocratic view of the city, or may lead to the definition of a new type of public" (2015: 110). This should be seen in the context of newer conceptualization of urban development such as smart cities and digital cities.

The major thrust of discussion in this paper is as follows: i) to examine the changing socio-spatial relations in the context of new media technologies and their part in generating myriad experiences of urban space; ii) to interpret critically the very access to and powerful nature of new media technologies in shaping existing social networks, connections, and values across socio-cultural settings; iii) to elaborate on how new media technologies play a key role in urban transition, "making" sense of city life, and infusing alternatives perspectives, as well as the emergence of new forms, structure, contents, and tensions in the city. The conceptual approach of the paper includes both critical geography and interdisciplinary framework – political economy of the city and telecommunication relations. Study provides a general perspective focusing on both developed countries and the emerging economies of the world such as in Asia.

Global Urban Transformation

The world combines of the *core* and the *periphery*. The core is understood as geographical area which includes modern world powers. Most of the wealth of the earth is concentrated in such countries (including Europe, the United States, Canada, Australia, New Zealand, Japan, South Korea and Israel). They have been forerunners in industrialization, urbanization, technological advancements and latest in the series is globalization. The periphery comprises of such countries that have not fully experienced the positive lures of development and now of the globalization. Periphery exhibits a higher population growth, limited ability to move and they also experience lower level of development coupled with lack of housing and increase in urban slums. The countries include in Africa, South America, Asia, Russia and many of its neighbours. The disparity of wealth between core and periphery countries is really unimaginable as about 75% of the world's annual income is confined to a 15% of the global population mostly belonging of the core. The top twenty countries, as ranked by the UN Human Development Index, 2019 most of them are in the core. However, with the wider changes taking place in the development process – a consequence of new economic patterns – most of the periphery of the world is exhibiting a new transition. Conventional peripheral areas which included first industrialized areas, colonised areas, and areas of underdeveloped world etc., are catching up with advanced regions of the world. Clark in his volume on *Urban World/Global City*, noted that, "[S]ince the mid-twentieth century, and especially over the past 20 years, the global economy has subsumed local and regional economies and territories have been drawn into the world economic system" (1996: 100). This led to newer form of development and entry of globalization through transnational and global connectivity caused by the technological and economic shifts.

This process seems to be happening due to the opening of economies, the expansion of telecommunications and their wider uses by society and economy. Each such region has gone far to revamp economy by incorporating a range of structural components, and enriched a good number of well developed networks. In the whole process to be operationally successful, important hubs are the great the cities. In recent times, process of industrialization and introduction of globalization has been playing a key role in rapid economic growth in many of the emerging economies like India, China, Brazil, Nigeria, etc. Rapid urban growth tends to contribute to higher rate of urbanization and an increase in the number of cities. Present urban scenario of the world shows that most urban growth is now taking place in the developing countries. However, the levels of urbanization in developing countries still remain much lower than in the developed countries. The gap of disparity may shorten in the time to come. According to the UN report on *The Components of Urban Growth in Developing Countries,* "in 1975 there was a 43 percentage point difference in levels of urbanization between developed and developing regions, by 1995 this had been reduced to a 37 point difference, a difference that is projected to decline even further to 32 percentage points by 2015". This change does not mean that only urban areas are growing more quickly than their counterpart rural, the absolute numbers of persons living in the urban areas are increasing unprecedentedly. A recent UN report (2014) stated that just three countries – India, China and Nigeria –are expected to account for 37% of the projected growth of the world's urban population between 2014 and 2050. The majority of rapidly growing cities known as *megacities* (each having population more than 10 million) are located in the peripheral areas of the world – so-called the developing countries. Such megacities are conceived as major hotspots of industry, manufacturing and export activities (e.g. Shenzhen, and Delhi). They have great importance since there goods are produced efficiently and at much lower costs to fill the major world markets. These cities are also key markets for basic raw materials, components, and energy resources. Most of these cities remain well connected through information and telecommunications with those global cities found in the core. At the same time, the important cities in peripheral areas do exhibit their own patterns of development process and socio-economic dichotomies. The changing pattern of urbanization has been extensively studied in the past which provided clues on how world changes. Brenner and Keil noted that, "[S]ince the early 1980s, critical urban researchers have devoted intense energies to precisely these questions – on the one hand, by analyzing emergent forms of globalized urbanization and their impacts upon social, political and economic dynamics within and beyond major cities; on the other hand, by introducing a host of new methods and conceptualizations intended to grasp the changing realities of planetary urbanization under late 20th- and early 21st-century capitalism" (2014: 2). This could offer a deeper understanding nature of development and urbanization in the world particularly in the core and the periphery.

Thus, the growing cities of third world experience an unimaginable challenge and crisis and create a distinctive from of geographies. Brenner and Keil's study claimed that the linkages lie in contemporary telecommunications and urbanization: "the combined demographic, economic, socio-technological, material-metabolic and socio-cultural processes of urbanization have resulted in the formation of a globalised network of spatially concentrated human settlements and infrastructural configurations in which major dimensions of modern capitalism are at once concentrated, reproduced and contested" (ibid.:1). This process is termed as a global urban reality as the pace of modern capitalist methods of development has already penetrated into developing countries and advanced the technological sector. The dark side of this approach hides everything that is *unjust* and *uneven*. Brenner and Keil elaborated upon that "this is not to suggest that the entire world has become a single, densely concentrated city; on the contrary, uneven spatial development, polarization and territorial inequality remain pervasive, endemic features of modern capitalism" (Ibid.:2). The basic point is that present forces of urban transformation have resulted in not only higher growth in urbanization and an increase in number of cities in the Global South, but also brought into being new *core* in the peripheral regions, further exaggerating *actually existing* spatial inequalities and uneven development. Accessibility to and the use of new media technologies, largely by urban society, have produced not just geographies of digital divide, but this also affects the social and public sphere. Similarly, the role of urbanization in the accumulation and reproduction of capital, innovation, and advances in new media technologies and the manoeuvring of the public could be a best possible understanding of changing urban condition.

New Media and Social Production of Urban Space

The very idea of the city has undergone a change tremendously over recent decades with the advancements in ICTs. The inevitable impacts of this change are evident in urban areas and in changing the content and meanings of urban *space*. To understand better the role of space and its production, and its influence on society and people, Lefebvre offered an interesting and critical perspective. Lefebvre, a French thinker, is widely acclaimed for his contribution towards a critique of everyday life and studies of urbanization, space, and state. Critique of state is not just of the *bourgeois* state, but of any state as form of power. For Lefebvre, the *production of space* has a three-dimensional (3D) aspect: perceived (material); conceived (ideological-institutional); and experienced space (lived-symbolic) (see Kipfer et al., 2008:8). The third category, or "lived-symbolic," consists of social practices and real space, the material world, and the experiences of their realization. This trialectic of spatiality (firstspace – secondspace – thirdspace) enables one to understand the process of the creation of space. Here, within the trialectics of spatiality, the "lived"occurs as a result of firstspace and secondspace duality. The thirdspace is a space that is reimagined from the absolute space to a third element. This is the space where social relations take place and where we actively experience it in everyday life. Salerno suggests that, "[F]or Lefebvre lived space was both physically and mentally distinct from space: instead, it embodies the real and imagined world of life experiences, emotions, events and policy choices" (2015:186). So, to understand the practices in urban space, with the dominance of a specific "space" over the other, Lefebvre offered this approach to examine the conflicting nature of urban space and the role of various processes in urban making: "[A]s a social product, space is a potential object of controversy among actors competing to establish a specific "space" as dominant. This is especially true for urban space, where governance models are plural and fragmented and transformation processes are constant" (Tarantino and Tosoni, 2013:3). This points to the fact that actually existing socio-spatial process remain powerful in affecting cities and emergence of new geographies of exclusion, poverty, and modern spaces of consumption.

The role of digital media or new media is now substantially important in shaping urban imaginations and everyday life. Salerno further notes that, "there is no doubt that the urban imaginary in contemporary society is conveyed also through digital media; by means of them in fact, true mental constructs of the city can also be manifested through visual effects" (Op.Cit.,:187). Furthermore, the physical space is being overtaken by the virtual space with the rapid use of new media technologies and the increasing role of information and communication systems. It may be assessed at various scales. The new media technologies have their own impacts over the social interaction within houses and families in different ways. The outcome of this impact is twofold: one, new media technologies enable a bond among the families by bringing them closer and together; and two, new media technologies also work towards causing a growing privatization within the family, as individuals use technology and technology enabled services more independently.

Changing Patterns of Communication

The world is changing more rapidly than ever before in terms of the expanding use of telecommunication and the flow of information. The assessment of such a change provides insights on how the changed-world is expressed. Kamp writes that, "[I]n what we refer to as the "information age" or "digital age" our technological advancements in the area of ICT have helped overcome limitations of time and space in communication, information sharing and networking" (2016: 1). The change has had a huge effect on how we all interact and communicate in the world and also in the public sphere. A new aspect of this new-media technology-driven society is that people have easy access to the state via virtual communication. There are various examples of positive-adverse impacts (i.e. uprisings against the state) of the new media environment. Brown, Guskin and Mitchell contextualize the Arab uprisings and noted that, "[S]ocial media indeed played a part in the Arab uprisings. Networks formed online were crucial in organizing a core group of activists, specifically in Egypt. Civil society leaders in Arab countries emphasized the role of "the internet, mobile phones, and social media" in the protests. Additionally, digital media has been used by Arabs to exercise freedom of speech and as a space for civic engagement"(2012). Although individual access to the internet would have not been in large proportion, the dissemination and passing of information to the public played an important role. The India Against Corruption (IAC) campaign in 2011 in India was all a new media driven movement to mobilise people and brought masses together from different walks of life for the noble cause.

Khan offers an interesting insight on the Arab event: "Despite the risk of overestimating its potential, the so-called "new media", such as the internet or mobile Cell phones and print media have certainly played important roles in modern political revolutions and how the democratization of the process takes place, and where these events support the way and are supported by external actors" (2012:57). The premises of such uprisings are embedded in socio-political circumstances and unrest among the masses against the state. The point to be highlighted here is that use of new media by the citizens is, in a way, facilitated by the state through its public policy toward ICTs, and the use of this platform as a public response is strengthened with an evolution of the sense of state affairs and its wider consequences. The state is connected to its citizens through the media. The state has a major role in the control, organization, and the dissemination of information through the following methods: the legislation regulating rights and responsibilities in various fields of communications; the regulation of conditions governing media ownership and communication activities; the control of communication channels and carriers; the direct involvement in various communication activities by creating national, regional, and local public bodies; the measures aiming to prevent the spread of distorted views and the abuse of communication practices; and the limitation of important content and messages, etc. (see, Bibu, V. N., 2016:65). Thus, it is never a one-way process, and the citizens' response is collective against the state revolving around certain manufactured circumstances.

Kamp noted that "unlike traditional media, social media are an open space, potentially giving every individual a means to directly reach out to the public. The advancement of online content and social media has greatly expanded the variety of sources of information" (Op. Cit., 1). A similar though not equal change is seen in so-called "intelligent cities" or "digital cities" as they are a space of media driven society. This change holds potential to challenge our common conception and imagination of the city. In such cities, one experiences and navigates the city in intertwined/virtual worlds and physical space. Handlykken argued that "[T]he city and things become sentient, mobile devices, non-human actors and places are embedded with sensors, tracking and location-based applications such as geo-tags" (2011:23). This shift is rapid in the cities of the highly developed economies of the world known as global cities, although major cities in developing countries do exhibit similar characteristics such as Hong Kong, Shanghai, Mumbai, Bengaluru etc. However, this shift comes with socio-media exclusion in the developing countries, as those who are better educated and have knowledge about the system and can afford high prices of communication devices can, thus, have a larger say in the public sphere created via social media. Therefore, access to new media technologies is one of the aspects, the better use of such ultra-modern facilities in an effective manner is very much determined by the individual exposure to everyday affairs. The fact is that people's dependency on the traditional media has a great significance for being informed about news and views in cities of developing countries, but now new urban middle class also have option to switch to online for quick and divers information. With advancements in the information and communication technology people have knowledge of diverse views and are also exposed to "new" ways of thinking, methods of speaking, and modes of interacting. With the internet availability and accessibility at their fingertips, individuals can dare to express their concern and indulge in interpreting the events according to their understanding.

There are three types of general practices that use new media in the urban environment. These types are commercial, military, and artivism. Ampatzidou and Molenda argue that, "[E]ach of the three practices explores a different political dimension of influence on social matters and consequently on space, through a substantially different approach towards notions of democracy and the commons" (Op. Cit., 109). The first practice combines the production, collection, and analysis of crowdsourced data; for the second, securitization and surveillance imperatives are strong drivers in the digitalization of urban space; for the third, "artivism is connected to subversive actions directed against the commercialization and militarization of space, and it foregrounds the social needs connected to democracy and commonality" (Ibid., 111). A new trend in urban planning focusing more attention toward "smart cities" is very much associated with using strategies of the first (commercial) and second (military) types rather than the third (artivism). Masdar (The UAE) and Songdo (South Korea) are only two examples of many new cities that aspire to construct a smart and sustainable urban future by using the technology. However, different versions of smart cities are adopted by the nations such as *smart cities mission* (SCM) in India. Here, a smart city is imagined one which is ICT driven and uses smart solutions to fix the problems and in the delivery of services to the citizens leading to make it sustainable.

Urban Life and New Media

The present-day advances in technologies are extensions of various developments taking place in the modern way of life. From the Industrial Revolution onwards, there have been important technologies and innovations as the crusader in changing human living from the rural to urban. Even the concept of *time* has been transformed from being "sacred time" to clock time during the modernization and urbanization of society. Hubbard notes that, "[N]ew media-the photograph, the telegraph, film, newspapers – were also representative of [this] timed modernity. Embedded in the city, these media offered novel ways of recording and circulating modern time, simultaneously helping citizens adjust to the new rhythms of modern urban life"(2006: 135). This change was associated with the dynamic environment of urban spaces in comparison with languishing rural spaces. The organization of modern metropolis life revolved around *time* and its determinantal influence in shaping the social and economic milieu. The infrastructural establishments and transportation facilities provided a new outlook on the city, and the industrial urban space was automobile-oriented. Technologies' spatial effects can be sensed from the urban planning of major metropolises, such as Haussmann's Paris and Robert Moses's New York. Hubbard documents that, [L]atterly, physical channels of movement in the city – along which people, goods and traffic can flow – have been increasingly supplemented by *virtual* connections.

Basically, each city is differently governed and managed, as well as having a distinct level of all such urban facilities for citizens, which culminates into *urban advantage*. Therefore, the role of technologies should not be understood as determinantal, but the way urban citizens use and consume them also plays an important part in the vibrancy of the metropolis. Brugmann noted that, "[M]ost cities, unless they are entirely new, have accumulated a unique legacy of urban advantage, bequeathed by the strategies of earlier urban pioneers who designed and built their cities in specific ways to secure their own advantage" (2009: 25). Such advantages range from strategic location and setting to a mix of activities – production, commerce, culture, and residential life – known as "agglomeration economies," and a *city syste*m if social and ecological elements are embraced in it. Brugmann cited the example of Bengaluru, stating that "in the 1990s, it became a world-changing city, seemingly from nowhere. But its growth into a leading center of high-tech industry was built on a centuries-old foundation of developed urban advantage" (Ibid: 25). In fact, reorienting historical growth and evolution of the city offers a significant understanding to make sense of media or new media in its making, connectivity, and emergence of a distinct urban place. However, Banerjee-Guha suggests that, "uses of space and time with transition from Fordism to post Fordist flexible accumulation has led to an intense phase of time-space compression having a disorienting impact on the entire gamut of political and economic practices and socio-cultural lifestyles" (2004:66). This factor has given a new meaning to *urban*. Of course, the internet and new communication technologies have made the "urban" centreless and highly decentralized. At the same time, "technologies are not drivers of urban change in and of themselves, and co-evolve with the urban fabric as they become woven into social, economic and political life cities" (Hubbard, Op.Cit.: 142). Quite often, contents, news and information delivered to the mass is politically superseded and influences the thinking and imagination of people for long before a sudden change occurs.

The Networked Nature of Urban Technology

Sassen opined that, "Over the centuries cities have been at the intersection of processes with supra-urban and even intercontinental scaling. What is different today is the intensity, complexity and global span of networks, and the extent to which significant portions of economies are now dematerialized and digitized and hence can travel at great speeds through networks" (2001: 411). Of course, this change in urban systems has offered important cities a new competitive advantage. Simultaneously, the city can be perceived as "hybrid" space. The conventional public space no more exist in the same way but it has become layered with wireless networks. The mobile devices allow people to create their own private spaces and be connected within in the urban space. Moving away from technological determinism, Graham and Marvin, in their volume on *Splintered Urbanism* described that they way capitalist societies largely depend on the *web of infrastructure networks,* have caused a more dense and expansive city infrastructures (cited by Hubbard, Op.cit: 143). The point to be made here is that this is not simply about the *impacts* of technologies on human society, but rather that the relations between both are reciprocal, mutual, and interrelated. Many such developments are often found in large cities or metropolises of the world. These types of urban places are globally connected and have a presence of a higher level of urban functions. Such cities emerge world cities which have their role to play terms of sites of accumulation and concentration of capital (see,Clark Op.Cit.: 151). It's noteworthy that much of technological advancements and their wider applications and social consumption is more urban centred and middles class oriented.

The Digital World, Socio Exclusion, and New Media

The world is urbanizing at a rapid pace and the majority of large urban centers control and regulate economic functions and technological innovations in the regions in which they are located, as well as beyond their spatial limits. Today's world is expressed in terms of extended phenomenon of being urban and living lifestyles of urbanites as accentuated by urban growth and urbanisation. The question arises is whether cities with digital networks and increasing consumer culture and penetration of new media technologies in social life become more inclusive spaces. This question demands a closer look at how a variety of groups – the poor, women, those racially discriminated against, and the excluded – and people live in and accommodate themselves in the changing urban conditions. There are many restrictions on the use of the internet and new media for females compared to males in a patriarchal system such as that in India. Within this wider communication and information transformation of the world, there lies a form of *digital exclusion* juxtaposition to social exclusion. The exclusion involves unequal access and capacity to use ICTs, meaning the new media technologies that are seen as essential ways through which individuals and group of people participate in the networked society affairs and claim a space. This is to be seen in the way that there is kind of relationship between social inequalities and unequal access to digital technologies (see, Van Dijk, 2005). There seems a combined effect of both the material factors that drive digital exclusion as well as the attitude, skills and cultures of internet use. At present, "[A]ccess to technology is therefore valued highly and is directly related to the quality of everyday life, but there remain people with no access to the online world" (Crnic, 2013:928). This is true in the sense that a number of socio-cultural and economic factors underlie such exclusion and in access to the present ICTs. This exclusion has been conceptualized as a division between the "information poor" and the "information rich." Crnic's study states that, "inequalities in access to technology result from an asymmetrical distribution of economic (money, ownership), social (social relations, power) and cultural (skills, cultural practices) capital, and should not be understood as the factors of social stratification as such" (Ibid: 928). For a long time marginalised communities so as in India known as *Dalits* have remained away from the mainstream media and participating and presenting themselves public sphere. Access to internet is now selectively used by the people living on the margin of the society as an alternative to the mainstream media. They have started using smart phones, communicating with fellow peoples and also sharing their common ideology and thoughts of change and raising voice for social reforms in the society. In this context, new media technologies do offers hope and space for people living on the margins. However, it is not to say that this happening at the same pace across the regions of the country.

Inequalities in access to new technologies are a multidimensional phenomenon and demand a deeper understanding of distinct elements of the social-cultural system and media preferences. Based on a study of two Slovenian cities – Ljubljana and

Maribor – Crnic identified three types of digital: digitally unmotivated with high cultural capital; overall excluded with weak cultural capital; and digitally self-excluded with moderate cultural capital. Further this study suggests that these three digital exclusion groups are divided by cultural engagement and media taste. Since new media technologies are being implemented by the both public and private institutions, it is sometimes mandatory to follow them, and at other times voluntary. Some important studies reveal that, "ongoing digital developments are regarded as an important contributor to social stratification. In this sense, one has to follow the digital default or face social exclusion" (Marien, et al., 2016:167). What is not widely and clearly researched yet is how socio-economically disempowered and marginalized people see themselves in the changing circumstances around them when being *online* is a luxury in present affairs of the state. In urban India, the youth (18-22 years of age) hailing from marginalized communities use new media technologies such as Facebook out of their leisure-driven tendency (see Kumar, 2014). Even if they are fluent in English, a language of the state, elite and rich, entertainment and expanding social capital remains the main purpose of these youths. However, the majority of these youths are unemployed or underemployed. Kumar's study claims that, "these youths create avenues for fulfilling their aspirations. They are immersed in the culture of *jugaad*, a colloquial Hindi term that is used variously to refer to innovative and improvised solutions that arise as workarounds or shortcuts in response to the scarcity of resources such as time or money" (2014:4). What happens via use of internet platforms such as Facebook is that youths connect themselves with the outside world and through their self-expression. This approach in a way does not restrain them because of one's caste, education, status, and economic background. But once their thoughts gain wider acceptance by their fellow peers and challenge the state, there are instance that their views are misinterpreted and their new-media driven voices have been curtailed. However, the digital participation can play vital part in mitigation of social exclusion by allowing marginalised groups access to the world of internet and benefits of the internet use. One should not deny the fact that as along as social and economic inequalities exists and perpetuated offline, the same gets a going on the online media. Most of those who are historically, socially marginalized remain on the margins of computer knowledge and less likely use internet.

The increasing reliance on use of the internet by young people is only the beginning in developing countries such as urban India, where the effective use of technology is also lacking among most people. The social, economic, and political circumstances and hardships mean people do not engage effectively in the public sphere and think and comment about state affairs. A number of people come from the lower levels of society, living in poor pockets and having an adverse feeling about their relations with the state. This situation leads to socio-spatial exclusion in cities. The digitally spatially excluded groups amid the growing use of new media technologies and their increasing role in public sphere have pushed such people to the periphery, where they lag behind in the city-making strategies. For Byrne, there are two interesting aspects of socio-spatial division. The first is that, in contrast to division as expressed through household income, there is a rather sharp break located in the bottom half of the social order. With income, the rich are separate from the rest of us. With space, it is the poor who are separated off. Spatial exclusion is the most visible and evident form of exclusion in urban space. Regarding this aspect, Byrne cites the example of the "ghetto" estates of the cities. The second aspect is that there is a double dynamic of space: the first includes the actual movement of households around social space, and the second the character of social spaces themselves.

New media is not a universalization process. The traditional gadgets like radios are still used by the folks in the country like India to get update on the ongoing-affairs of the nation, while new generation and young-exposed-to-urban holds phones and sometimes smart phones, which, for them, is meant more for entrainment than for other purposes. The poor and marginalised groups remain out of the coverage of national news reporters and broadcasting channels. The COVID-19 pandemic has exposed the real side of so-called development and progress. Though many things have gone online like education and delivering lectures and conducting a class during pandemic, the access to internet and gadgets has come out a fundamental gap in country like India. Two years back, a report entitled "Key Indicators of Household and Social Consumption on Education in India (2017-18)" by the Ministry of Statistics highlighted that internet access is disproportional across states. According to the Internet and Mobile Association of India report, on the national level, identified that fewer women (33 per cent) have access to internet compared to men (67 per cent), with rural areas experiencing more disparities (28-72 percent) compared to urban areas (38-62 percent). The poorest students do not have access to smartphones, and even if they do, net connectivity is poor, and content is often not available in vernacular languages. This gives rise to discrimination in access to education. Mobile phones are the most popular medium of accessing internet in both urban and rural areas as per the report.

Convergence of Technologies and the Urban Society

Talk of *convergence* was a major trend and a buzzword in media circles during the 1990s. Policymakers began to pay attention to the concept in terms of how to approach it. With digitization and further technological advancements, convergence is visualized as an important channel to offer access to information and services, to deliberation, and to participation of the people. Of course, convergence has already resulted in "time-space compression"(i.e. eliminating the effects of distance). Today, every activity is possible in "realtime". Convergence is conceptualized as carrying "a vision that digital technology leads to a more integrated media and communications landscape in which earlier boundaries between telecommunications, broadcasting and computing vanish"(Storsul and Stuedahl: 2007:12). There was a rapid convergence of Information Technology (IT) and Communication Technology at three layers of technology innovation – cloud, pipe, and device. Huang et.al state that, "internet services, telecommunications value-added services, and even media services are converging for both consumer and industry. Services carried by optical networks and other modern wireless "pipes" are moving to the cloud, and both industries and consumers are utilizing those services through a variety of integrated smart devices" (2012:35). However, the repercussions of this change are twofold. First, the rapid growth and advancements in IT will create an even more spatially dispersed and footloose economy, signaling toward metropolitan areas becoming larger and more dispersed. Second, this change posits that technological change will reinforce the position of cities as "nodes" on the information superhighway, which will lead to agglomeration economies (see, Atkinson, Robert D. "Technological Change and Cities," 1998).

The hyper connectivity of the present world is unprecedented and it has enabled urban people to use ICT-enabled facilities and services more than their counterparts in rural areas in the world and so in India. With economic reforms in the 1990s, liberalization, privatization, and globalization policies have led to immense developments and advancements in ICTs in India. Global manufacturing brands have their production or manufacturing systems in high-tech cities of India, such as Bengaluru, Chennai, Greater Noida, Hyderabad, Gurugram, New Delhi. The social implications of this change include the rise in the "new" Indian middle class, which is global, highly employed in the IT sector, and living a super-rich lifestyle in "gated communities." This rise indicates a move toward spatial segregation in metropolitan areas. A study on the social wellbeing of urban communities in Bengaluru presented interesting findings, noting that the divorce rate in the city has increased, particularly among IT professionals, for whom extra-marital cases have increased also, and there is widespread use of "hacking techniques to collect evidence against each other, "as well as the number of social-networking-sites-based marriages that generally have shorter lifespans (see, Vonodh Kumar G.C., 2013). These are varied experiences of urban space with advancements in technological sector and its social applications.

CONCLUSION

This paper discussed how the mode of urban life is changing due to developments and advancements in the technological sector. The world is urbanizing more quickly than ever before, and a new type of consumer culture is spreading within urban space, not only in the developed West, but also in cities in emerging economies. The use and consumption of ICT form a new mantra of urban life and govern everything in the urban system. Similarly, the new media technologies are all pervasive and play a key role in the way people connect themselves with others. The use and acceptance of these new technologies depend on status, education, and participation in the public sphere, but also very much on the socio-cultural system. However, the effective use of new media is constrained by socio-spatial factors that lead to socio-spatial exclusion that is further supplemented by digital exclusion.

REFERENCES

Ampatzidou, C. and Ania, M.(2015). New Media in Old Cities: The Emergence of the New Collective.*FOOTPRINT – Commoning as Differentiated Publicness*, Spring: pp. 109-122.

Atkinson, R.D. (1998). Technological Change and Cities.*Cityscape: A Journal of Policy Development and Research*, Vol.3. No.3: pp. 129-170

Banerjee-Guha, S. (2004). Space, Society and Geography – Investigating the Crisis of Postmodern Urban Space.In Swapna Banerjee-Guha, ed., *Space, Society and Geography*, Jaipur: Rawat Publications: pp. 3-82.

Brenner, N. and Roger, K. (2014).From Global to Globalized Urbanization.*Glocalism: Journal of Culture, Politics and Innovation*, Vol. 3: pp. 1-17

Brown, H., Guskin, E. and Micthell, A.The Role of Social Media in the Arab UprisingsRetrieved from http://www.journalism.org/2012/11/28/role-social-media-arab-uprisings

Brugmann, J. (2009). *Welcome to the Urban Revolution: How Cities Are Changing the World*, Noida: HarperCollins Publisher

Byrne, D. (2005). *Social Exclusion*, Jaipur: Rawat Publications

Carr, Michael (1987). *Patterns: Process and Change in Human Geography*, London: Macmillan

Clark, D. (1996). *Urban World/Global City*. London: Routledge

Crnic, T.O. (2013). Slovenians Offline: Class and Cultural Aspects of Digital Exclusion. *Czech Sociological Review*, Vol. 49, No. 6: pp. 927-949

Gharbawi, A. *Revolution of the Internet*, Retrieved fromhttp://www.cs.ucsb.edu/~almeroth/classes/F04.176A/homework1_good_papers/Alaa-Gharbawi.html

Graham, S. (1997). Cities in the Real-Time age: The Paradigm Challenge of Telecommunications to the Conception and Planning of Urban Space.*Environment and Planning A*, Vol. 29: pp. 105-127.

G.C., Vinodh Kumar. (2013). Information Technology and its Effects on Urban Communities with Special Reference to Bangalore City.*IOSR Journal of Humanities and Social Sciences*, Vol. 17. No.6: pp. 84-89

Handlykken, A.K. (2011). Digital Cities in the Making: Exploring Perceptions of Space, Agency of Actors and Heterotopia.*Ciberlegenda*, pp. 22-37

Hinshaw, J. and Petern N.S. (2013).*Industrialization in the Modern World: From the Industrial Revolution to the Internet*, Vol 1. Santa Barbara: ABC-CLIO

Huang, I.RG., Harry Xie and Zhengxiang Wu. (2012). The Convergence of Information and Communication Technologies Gains Momentum.In Soumitra Dutta and Benat Bilbao-Osorio, eds. *The Global Information Technology Report 2012 – Living in a Hyperconnected World*, Geneva: World Economic Forum: pp. 35-46

Hubbard, P. (2006). *City*, Oxon: Routledge.

Kamp, M. (2016).*Assessing the Impact of Social Media on Political Communication and Civic Engagement in Uganda*. Kololo: Konrad-Adenauer-Stiftung

Khan, A.A. (2012). The Role of Social Media and Modern Technology in Arab Spring.*Far East Journal of Psychology and Business*, Vol.7, No. 1: pp. 56-63

Kipfer, Stefan et al. (2008). On the Production of Henri Lefebvre.In Kanishka Goonewardena, Stefan Kipfer, Richard Milgrom and Christian Schmind, eds., *Space, Difference, Everyday Life: Reading Henri Lefebvre*, New York: Routledge: pp. 1-23

Kumar, N. (2014). Facebook for self-empowerment? A Study of Facebook Adoption in Urban India.*New Media Society*: pp. 1-16.

15

Maried, I., Heyman, R., Salemink, K. and Van Audenhove, L.(2016). Digital by Default: Consequences, Casualties and Coping Strategies.In Rowman and Littlefield, *Social Inequalities, Media and Communication: Theory and Roots*: pp. 167-188.

Ministry of Statistics and Programme Implementation (2019): *Key Indicators of Household Social Consumption on Education in India*, Government of India.

N, Bibu V. (2016). New Media and Governance: Issues in Democracy and the Transiting Public Sphere in India.*Amity Journal of Media & Communication Studies*, Vol. 6, No.2: pp. 64-72

Sareno, R. (2015). City Ideologies in Techno-Urban Imaginaries.*Urban*: pp. 185-192

Sassen, S. (2001). Impacts of Information Technologies on Urban Economies and Politics.*International Journal of Urban and Regional Research*, Vol 25, No. 2: pp. 411-418

Storsul, T. and Stuedahl, D.(2007). Ambivalence Towards Convergence.In Tanja Storsul and Dagny Stuedahl eds., *Towards Convergence – Digitalization and Media Change*, Goteborg: Nordicom: pp. 9-16

Tarantino, M. and Tsosoni, S.(2013). Media and the Social Production of Urban Space: Towards an Integrated Approach to Controversial Nature of Urban Space.In Simone Tosoni, Matteo Tarantino and Chiara Giaccardi, eds., *Media and The City: Urbanism, Technology and Communication*, Tyne: Cambridge Scholars Publishing: pp. 2-31.

United Nations (2001). The Components of Urban Growth in Developing Countries. Population Division, Department of Economic and Social Affairs.Retrieved fromhttps://esa.un.org/unpd/wup/Archive/Files/studies/United%20Nations%20(2001)%20-%20The%20Components%20of%20Urban%20Growth%20in%20Developing%20Countries.pdf

———— (2014). World Urbanization Prospects.Retrieved from https://esa.un.org/unpd/wup/publications/files/wup2014-highlights.pdf

Van Dijk, J.A. (2005): The Deepening Divide: Inequality in the Information Society, London: Sage Publications

CHAPTER 2

Making or Destroying the City?:
American Corporate Culture in Network Neutrality

Marcus Breen
Communication Department
Boston College, USA

ABSTRACT

Urban life in the US was defined by the Open Internet, offering citizens networked communications regulated by the Federal Communication Commission (FCC). A political struggle ensued over how the internet would be regulated, which was only heightened following the 1996 Telecommunication Act. Several years of intense public policy debate about regulating the internet ensued, focusing on evidence that the private firms that provided services would "throttle" the flow of information and unfairly manipulate prices of the Open Internet. In December 2017, this openness, known as Network Neutrality, was removed by the FCC in favor of competitive innovation by private telecommunication providers. Aspects of this debate are explored by deploying an assemblage methodology to draw attention to the ways the interests and forces of private concerns have directed resources to profit centers and away from regulated public universal openness. The assemblage addresses the complexity of actors engaged in the struggle over information resources for US citizens. Consequently, the decision to end Network Neutrality provoked a struggle by advocates arguing for a system of public regulation. The battle for a solution to universal openness has recently been extended by public information advocates such as media and community groups that have operationalized state and local government regulation. Various assemblages have emerged, evolved, faded and been revivified in the struggle over Network Neutrality. Given the dependence on networked internet technologies in US cities, the removal of Network Neutrality leaves large sections of the population without connection to high-speed broadband and information resources for living.

An Unequal Assemblage: The Public City Versus the Private Telecommunication Firm

There are usually many sides to every story about a city, the countryside and their relationship with the sovereign state of which they are a part. In some stories, one side gains prominence, as the participants argue; some actors in the story win while others lose or are neutralized, only to fade from public view. In some cases, those actors may never have appeared in the story, even though they played a part in it. Nowhere is this curious present-yet-absent arrangement more evident than in recent public policy debates in the US about the national public networked communication system.

In the Network Neutrality or 'The Open Internet' case, the FCC had a key role in regulating such openness for communication, even though members of the American public, of civil society, rarely, if ever, participated in the debates. First proposed by Tim Wu in a 2003 article entitled "Network Neutrality, Broadband Discrimination," Network Neutrality followed the public policy principle that vertical integration negatively impacts internet service providers (ISPs) and cable companies, which should treat all data on the internet equally, and not discriminate or charge fees depending on the user, the content, the website, the platform, the application, the type of equipment used, or the method of communication deployed to transport the data. This complex story illustrates the struggle over the internet by exploring the way US telecommunication regulation has been structured to evolve in line with what Wu suggests was "Darwinian competition," in which "only the best survive" (Wu, 2003: 142). In fact, the situation is more extreme than that. In the hyper-competitive dog-eat-dog world described by Wu, many Americans are absent, with their voices left unconsidered, their material interests dismissed and, given contemporary reliance on networked technologies, their psychic welfare abused because of such absence from the regulatory process (Langlois, 2013).

In the US, the Network Neutrality story reveals how regulation has been actively reconfigured, remaking cities in line with Wu's Darwinian approach to regulation, highlighting a struggle over access to public communication resources. In such an evolutionary approach, there are the missing millions: Americans in urban centers who suffer from the blights of poverty and racial, ethnic and age discrimination, and those who cannot participate in contemporary city life as advertised, where gentrifying neighborhoods are studies in human displacement and class polarization (Newman and Wyly, 2006).

Given these broad brush strokes, the Network Neutrality story has been characterized by cheers of celebration announcing equal access to the internet for all (regulated neutrality), followed by tears of anguish as the idea of universal access to the internet evaporated under the pressure of private, for-profit telecommunication firms. The question is how best to reconstruct a model of regulation that suits the transformations of "network society" (Castells, 2015) in a context that increasingly makes communication the central feature of contemporary social life. Indeed, Network Neutrality has provoked debates about telecommunication regulation, raising the prospect for "new frontiers" of regulation pressing in on established approaches (Wu, 2006). All these issues could be dismissed as a somewhat esoteric set of specialist concerns given the prevailing "strong will survive" Darwinism that dominates telecommunication and public policymaking in contemporary capitalism.

Meanwhile, the idea of the poor is being redefined in relation to networked technology, as noted in the December 15, 2017 "Statement on Visit to the USA, by Professor Philip Alston, United Nations Special Rapporteur on extreme poverty and human rights in the US." Alston argued that, "neither its [the US] wealth nor its power nor its technology is being harnessed to address the situation in which 40 million (12.7 per cent of the population) people continue to live in poverty," to become informationally disenfranchised, confronted *not* with neutral approaches to the flow of information across the network, but increasing evidence of a bias in favor of major corporations, which exclude or "redline" uneconomic internet users. As "What Unites and Divides Urban, Suburban and Rural Communities," a May 2018 Pew Report notes, "Urban areas are at the leading edge of racial and ethnic change, with nonwhites now a clear majority of the population in urban counties while solid majorities in suburban and rural areas are white" (Parker et al., 2018: 1). For regulators, this factor is a part of an environment in which communication innovations and increasing digital consumption can be set against a 31% rise in poverty in US cities and a 51% rise in US suburbs between 2000 and 2016 (Parker et al., 2018, np).

Across this terrain, visible and invisible forces intersect in the ongoing unfolding of American liberal democracy. In cities and towns, the forces are pulling and fracturing in different ideological directions. The fields of intersecting research in which these forces operate include the following:

- government regulation
- private capital
- public communication
- social movement activism.

In exploring the US experience of Network Neutrality, these intersections happen in the context of a rapid growth in "denser urban locations" starting in 2000 (Lloyd, 2018: np). More recently, between 2010 and 2017, rental apartment inventory in urban centers grew by 32%, while housing inventory in the suburbs grew by 16% (Lloyd, 2018: np). As US urban centers concentrate larger populations, the connections between the fields intensify and accelerate in keeping with "flexible capitalism" (Lessenich, 2015: 128). The effect of networked technology generates an unequal assemblage of power across diverse, increasingly populated demographic terrains.

Assemblage theory is described by French researchers Gilles Deleuze and Félix Guattari in *A Thousand Plateaus: Capitalism and Schizophrenia* (1987). Assemblage is a machine-like multiplicity of forces operating across intersecting axes with multiple flows of meaning, grounded in material and social foundations:

> On a first, horizontal, axis, an assemblage comprises two segments, one of content, the other of expression. On the one hand it is a machinic assemblage of bodies, of actions and passions, an intermingling of bodies reacting to one another; on the other hand it is a collective assemblage of enunciation, of acts and statements, of incorporeal transformations attributed to bodies. Then on a vertical axis, the assemblage has both territorial sides, or reterritorialized sides, which stabilize it, and cutting edges of deterritorialization, which carry it away. (1987: 88)

In Deleuze and Guattari's "complex configuration of machinic and enunciative elements," the role of networking technology within the assemblage of the city becomes less humanized. Machines announce their domination while expanding the complexity of the interactions between urban life and the communicative infrastructures that make life possible (Bogard, 2009: 15-16). A fluidity of assemblage result, as large-scale or macro-alliances form, disband and reform with and against micro-level participants (Kivikuru, 2018). Within this complexity, some machines claim power, not by anthropomorphizing, but through the agency their owners and advocates generate by being associated with them, orchestrating an assemblage mostly according to the institutions with power; what the American sociologist Thorstein Veblen calls "vested interests" (Veblen, 1919/2005).

This claim to power oscillated unevenly in the Network Neutrality case in the US; sometimes at the expense of agents with little or no capacity to claim it (poor, black and Hispanic urban citizens), and at other times reflecting that interests of ISPs that were already powerful, especially those with access to capital and pre-existing control of the digital network. Inevitably, the Network Neutrality assemblage moved unevenly, from success for the public before switching to success for private capital. This fluidity illustrates how the structures of public administration within the US Government had become incapable of meeting its statutory obligations to regulate the national public communication apparatus. As well as identifying the limitations of US regulation in Network Neutrality's impact on cities, a further theme can be identified within the story: that is, the inability of liberal democracies to respond to and meet the communication needs of a nation's citizens in the era of market fundamentalism, or neoliberalism. In effect, US Network Neutrality highlights the impending failure of regulation as populations concentrate in urban centers in an assemblage that grows more complex.

Moments of Exclusion and Confusion

Telecommunication technologies have evolved from colonial times, when horse-riding mail-delivery persons delivered letters, to the telegraph, to the Plain Old

Telephone System (POTS), to the internet's global networked system characterized by converged digital data flows. In effect, the rise of the contemporary multipoint communication network describes a chaotic assemblage of data. Importantly, Network Neutrality illustrates several limitations in US public policy, especially the exclusion of those already without a voice who historically relied on public interest regulation to provide them access to information resources. In making these assertions, assemblage avoids, as far as possible, "simplistic explanations" that have characterized a teleology or Whig history of networked technology, recognizing the complexity and aided by analysis drawn from critical Marxian political economy (Campbell-Kelly & Garcia-Swartz, 2013).

Without identifying every step along the way to illustrate how US regulation has been constructed as an assemblage that excludes members of US society, it is fair to say that the 1996 Telecommunication Act was launched with the hope that an unregulated Open Internet would facilitate unrestricted data flow from creators to users and back in an interactive nirvana. Nevertheless, it was always a provisional openness dominated by competition and private interests, as noted in President Bill Clinton's statement when the 1996 Act was signed:

> This landmark legislation fulfills my Administration's promise to reform our telecommunications laws in a manner that leads to competition and private investment, promotes universal service and open access to information networks, and provides for flexible government regulation. (Clinton, 1996)

Private interests gave rise to the internet bubble of the late 1990s, when ISPs became for-profit points of access to data. These ISPs tended to be startup firms that were steadily purchased by legacy cable and telephone companies in a rush to digital riches. Within the assemblage that led to Network Neutrality, private competition collapsed as the focus shifted to profit maximization, steadily reducing the legitimacy of the regulator – the FCC. In this model of regulation, the idea that the public interest would be given an equal place in the regulation processes hardly mattered, given the privileging of for-profit firms in the 1996 Act.

The first significant instance of Network Neutrality was proposed in 2005 by the FCC in a ruling "to preserve and promote the vibrant and open character of the internet as the telecommunications marketplace enters the broadband age" (FCC05-151A1, 2005). Putting itself at the center of the internet assemblage in which it regulated data to flow "neutrally," the FCC believed it had been given such a responsibility within its jurisdiction by the US Congress (FCC05-151A1, 2005). Contextually, this ruling and the emergence of Network Neutrality can be set as the historical point at which ISPs and internet firms began to apply statistical models directed at maximizing profit by excluding some internet users and sections of cities that did not meet their business priorities (O'Neil, 2016). At this conjuncture, computer "quants" calculated "predictable patterns" using "computer-driven mathematical models" to encode decisions about the costs and benefits of services. As

I discuss later, the quants approach made no reference to the universality of national telecommunication as a public good. Instead, mathematical models that identified high-profit customer segments accompanied the emergence of a new semiotics of regulation, replacing citizenship with customers, who were, in turn, known not as people but profit centers. Rather than internet users engaged in human communication, communication was valued as a trading opportunity for Wall Street valuations, massaged for personal enrichment instead of public services (Patterson, 2010: 4-5). From the ISPs' perspective, the assemblage was open to manipulation. Internet users could become targets of action based on quant calculations; whereas, from the FCC's perspective as regulator, the assemblage was legitimated by law, precedent and institutional jurisdiction, with implications for urban communities. In this 2005 iteration of neutrality, the FCC insisted on its regulatory role while giving way to the computer smarts of private companies.

Then, between 2005 and 2012, the US Congress attempted to introduce limitations on Network Neutrality to benefit ISPs. This action can be viewed as a move to undermine the independence of the FCC, whose authority was called into question by actions taken in Congress as well as the US courts to subvert its regulatory legitimacy. In these moves, the rationale for public regulation was unraveled as ISPs challenged the FCC's claim to regulate. It became a steady drum-beat of specialist legal arguments about regulating the internet as a neutral transport system. For example, in an April 6, 2010 decision by the US Court of Appeals, District of Columbia Circuit, Comcast challenged the FFC's "authority to regulate an Internet service provider's network management practices," even though Comcast was found to be "interfering with their use of peer-to-peer networking applications" (Compact, 2010: 1). Comcast argued that the FCC had no jurisdiction for regulatory authority over what it did with the internet, either through its role as a regulator or due to an FCC claim for "ancillary authority" to regulate. In fact, Network Neutrality was presented by ISPs as an anti-competitive concept, as was the regulatory regime itself, as the forces of private and vested interests created a telecommunication assemblage unfettered by regulation that aimed to meet citizen interests.

Lest it be thought that Congressional and Court proceedings against Network Neutrality were outliers in regulatory public policymaking in the US, it is helpful to note how comprehensively the pieces to reduce regulation of the internet were put together to shift the logic of neutrality away from public regulation. For example, indicators of this ideological shift can be seen more broadly at the international level, when the US State Department told the World Conference on International Telecommunications that it would "not support proposals that would increase the exercise of control over internet governance or content" and "would oppose efforts to broaden the scope of the ITRs [international telecommunications regulations] …" (Stanton 2012). Pushing even further in internationalizing its priorities, the US wanted to update agreements to reflect a world in which "most traffic is exchanged under commercial arrangements between carriers in competitive environments where there are multiple competing services" (Stanton 2010). The opponents of Network

Neutrality were engaged in determined politics in the US and internationally to privilege a market-focus in which users were embedded in a network offered by commercial providers. As these anti-regulationist forces advanced, poor and underserviced urban dwellers were nowhere to be heard in the discussion. This focus on market-based solutions proceeded despite claims by the FCC Chairperson, Julius Genachowsi, in 2010 who conflated market-based economics with "the marketplace of ideas," an equivalence long devoid of salience, as if capitalism delivers information based on fairness or justice.

> First, consumers and innovators have a right to know the basic performance characteristics of their Internet access and how their network is being managed. We have adopted a transparency rule that will give consumers and innovators the clear and simple information they need to make informed choices in choosing networks or designing the next killer app.

> Second, consumers and innovators have a right to send and receive lawful traffic – to go where they want, say what they want, experiment with ideas – commercial and social, and use the devices of their choice. Our new rules thus prohibit the blocking of lawful content, apps, services, and the connection of devices to the network.

> Third, consumers and innovators have a right to a level playing field. No central authority, public or private, should have the power to pick winners and losers on the Internet; that's the role of the commercial market and the marketplace of ideas. (2010)

Of course, Genachowski did not really believe the fantasy that things worked this way; he told the World Conference on International Telecommunications in 2012 (referenced above), that he was "proud to support a vision for the future put forth by the US in its filing today, a vision which embraces competition, market-based policies, and the current multi-stakeholder model of internet governance" (Stanton, 2010). As the Open Internet assemblage continued moving away from a regulatory structure directed at the open flow of information, the quants built out smarter systems for those most likely to pay a premium for services.

To add to the diminished rationale for regulation, in 2014, the District of Columbia Court of Appeals ruled that the data flowing on the internet were classified as Title 1 and should not be regulated by the FCC for everyone's benefit, despite Genachowski's high-minded description of the Open Internet rules in 2010. Then, in 2015, following a major public campaign advocating for neutrality, the FCC ruled that data should be classified under common carriage rules of Title 2: "Today is a red-letter day for Internet freedom," announced Tom Wheeler, the FCC Chairperson, on February 26, 2015. With that statement, the FCC announced its decision to support Network Neutrality, shifting data and the transport of data to the utility category under the FCC's Title 2 rule of Common Carriage. In doing so, the FCC codified its meaning in an articulation with citizenship – that is, the network must be neutral for society to offer civilization, in the same way as a society should offer potable water, electricity and roadways.

This utility model of Network Neutrality meant that, "consumers can continue to enjoy unfettered access to the internet over their fixed and mobile broadband connections" (FCC 15-24, 2015: 3). However, the commitment to consumer freedom was confused and diluted by an equal commitment (made in the same sentence) in which "innovators can continue to enjoy the benefits of a platform that affords them unprecedented access to hundreds of millions of consumers across the country and around the world, and network operators can continue to reap the benefits of their investments" (FCC 15-24, 2015: 4). Given the ambiguity of the claim that co-joined consumers with innovators and investors, it became evident that the ruling was unsustainable because it was constrained by a privatizing market-orientation even while it was "open" to the concept of free speech and consumption. Consequently, what has become clear in recent years is that American free speech has become contingent speech, relying on assumptions about a regulated public communication infrastructure that no longer guarantees every citizen the right to see and hear and speak, segmenting cities into information haves and have-nots. It became, as Dawn Nunziato foresaw, a situation in which "Internet speech conduits – such as broadband service providers – are now responsible for facilitating a vast amount of expression," and as such interpret speech not through the openness of Network Neutrality but through the clouded corporate lenses of innovation and investment (2009, xiii).

The 2015 ruling and "victory" for Open Internet advocates was short-lived; in 2017, the FCC ruled against the Title 2 category for the internet and its traffic to be treated as a utility, returning it to the unregulated ("light touch") Title 1 space: "We reverse the Commission's abrupt shift two years ago to heavy-handed utility-style regulation of broadband Internet access service" (FCC 17-166, 2017: 1). Now, ISPs could once again manage the flow of information and prices, thereby establishing a foundation for discrimination through "throttling" or slowing down traffic and allowing competitive price discrimination on the network. The "Restoring Internet Freedom Order" from the FCC went into effect on June 11, 2018: Network Neutrality as a national telecommunication project was over.

Moving to Advocacy Amidst Virtual Private Networks

Despite the defeat of Network Neutrality, other efforts were made to bring back it back. For example, Massachusetts Senator Ed Markey:

> In 2018, access to the internet is a right, not a privilege. That's what net neutrality is all about. It is about the principle that the internet is for everyone, not just those with deep pockets. It is about the public, not a handful of powerful corporations, having control. All of that is under attack.

In December, President Trump's Federal Communications Commission (FCC), led by Ajit Pai, eliminated the rules that prevent your internet service provider – Comcast, ATT, Verizon, Spectrum – from indiscriminately charging more for internet fast lanes, slowing down websites, blocking websites, and making it harder and maybe even impossible for *inventors, social advocates, students, and entrepreneurs* to connect to the internet. If that sounds wrong to you, you're not alone. Approximately 86% of Americans oppose the FCC's decision to repeal net neutrality. (Emphasis added) (https://i.redd.it/v2ulhgs7row01.jpg)That's why today, I am officially filing the petition to force a vote on my Congressional Review Act resolution, which would put net neutrality back on the books... (https://www.facebook.com/EdJMarkey/) (February 27, 2018)

Critics correctly contended that Markey's effort would fail due to the absence of Network Neutrality supporters in the Congress and the US Senate (Coldewey, 2018: np). An evaluation of Markey's call notes the categories of internet users to whom Markey appealed: "inventors, social advocates, students, and entrepreneurs" were targeted by Markey's social media campaign. The senator's efforts reflected the postmodern fragmentation of the internet user base, away from "the public" into an assemblage that called out specific users and constituencies in social media. The attempt was a form of post-factum effort to bring back Network Neutrality for particular social groups, not the public. Such moves indicate the absence of regulatory coherence for US telecommunications, as national public interest regulation disintegrated under market-focused ideals in which the FCC's role had changed immeasurably.

Another actor attempted to sustain the case for Network Neutrality regulation, highlighting another aspect of the struggle. Public interest advocacy group Free Press appealed to the FCC on several occasions arguing for Network Neutrality. The organization noted the FCC's "need for a rulemaking," acting as an "Agency identification of a problem" by submitting a "petition for rulemaking." Such social movement activism serves as an example of a counter-assemblage to the one privileged by the free market, a point around which the city and the dispossessed might cohere:

This fight is so vital because, at its core, saving Title II Net Neutrality is about preserving civil rights online. The Open Internet is a place where movements are born, where communities often ignored or stereotyped by mainstream media can tell their own stories, and where families, friends and people who might have never before connected can build community. (Free Press, nd, np)

In its explicit claim to "civil rights" and "community," Free Press offered a window into how the loss of Network Neutrality would undo the assumptions of

American democracy, assumptions that relied on public open speech in US cities, even as evidence revealed that a "homework gap" existed in poor neighborhoods where children had no internet access with which to do their homework (Horrigan 2015: np). As it continued the campaign, Free Press noted that 81% of white people have home-internet access, compared with 70% of Latinx people and 68% of black people (Free Press, 2018: np). Given this gap, Free Press advocacy connected with Markey's to position Network Neutrality within "contentious politics," prompting a shift to social movement mobilization (Tarrow, 2011: 7, 34).

It is significant how Free Press and Senator Markey embodied advocacy roles for Network Neutrality. As they lobbied using mechanisms aimed at shared goals, their work showed how US telecommunication regulation had shifted from a field in which the FCC played the leading role, to one in which the ISPs as vested interests controlled the story. In a regulatory system that relied on advocacy, it was inevitable that those interests with the most to gain would receive support, thereby enlivening the contentiousness of the debate as a political struggle. Meanwhile, in the face of a process that relied on advocates acting outside the regulatory institution to apply pressure to renew Network Neutrality, the following question has to be asked:

Is an Open Internet as a concept even possible as structural changes to US cities reconfigure communication and the regulator backs away from regulating openness based on claims to competitive success?

Without Network Neutrality, What Becomes of US Cities?

To answer these questions is to identify more fragmentation in the US telecommunication sector characterized by private interests that are not regulated by the FCC. For example, virtual private networks (VPNs) were established to provide unimpeded end-to-end interactions. With VPNs, always-open high-speed broadband network connectivity is available to those with the ability to pay, shifting any idea of an Open Internet into a space in which the ability to pay for private dedicated access offered a model of a digital divide that can transmogrify into a digital chasm. As one advisory noted, describing the benefits of VPNs after the 2017 decision by the FCC: VPNs mean that a service provider cannot see user data and does not know which websites are being visited. Furthermore, internet traffic is routed through VPN servers and the ISP knows that there is a connection to a VPN server, meaning that an ISP will not block or slow a particular website (Fossbytes, 2017, np). In the US, in 2018, 5% of internet use was on VPNs. An expected surge in unregulated VPNs raised concerns about how ISPs treated user data, thereby creating a new assemblage that further removes information flows from public regulatory oversight while creating new tiers of users with access to power through information flows (Mason, 2018: np). An example of tiered communications applies to US universities in US cities that have purchased a dedicated VPN for faculty, student and staff use, while in neighborhoods alongside universities, residents do not receive broadband internet services. Elsewhere in US cities, VPNs are installed for corporations, banks and high-end accommodations, bypassing citizens to unmake urban areas that were previously defined as shared communicative spaces and places. This issue is a global debate that involves the intersection of private communication infrastructures with national regulators and public policy goals (Kreider, 2016). Indeed, the prospect of reduced communicative spaces in which US democracy could evolve through public deliberation was at the heart of the argument informing Free Press and Senator Markey's advocacy.

Generally, Network Neutrality followed the economic trend in US cities (and the Organization for Economic Co-operation and Development [OECD]), where, as capitalism accelerated, there has been an increase in poverty in the US that matches the rise of digital "superstar firms" whose "winner-takes-most" approach to business involves "capturing an overwhelming share of the market" using anti-competitive approaches (OECD, 2018: 64, 67). Included in such approaches are pricing strategies that negatively impact those Americans living in poverty. As an FCC commissioner supporting Network Neutrality noted in response to the FCC's 2018 *Broadband Deployment Report*:

> the report goes further by removing price as a factor in its analysis. Price is a well-known indicator for assessing broadband availability. A previous study found that 71% of those without broadband identified affordability as a major factor. What is painfully clear, is that a service cannot truly be available if you cannot afford it. But in the majority's rush to declare victory and rack up brownie points, they once again disregard the plight of low-income Americans. (Clyburn, 1)

The Unsustainable Assemblage of Network Neutrality in Liberal Democratic Regulation

Following the 1996 US Telecommunication Act, the firms that owned, controlled or managed the production of digital content and its transportation across the national infrastructure were given agency to act profitably. As private firms, their actions set off a rush to riches as the network opened to a host of cultural forces that entered public discourse and political life (Breen, 2011). The pro-corporatist assemblage is defined by Victor Pickard as corporate libertarianism, an ideological framework in which "press freedoms were understood primarily as protecting commercial media institutions" (2014: 5). As the reconfiguration of regulatory governance has evolved in favor of corporations, the political aspects of the contest between the interests participating in telecommunication regulation have sharpened. A new competitive environment has emerged, even while Network Neutrality can be viewed as an event that reached back to normative (what ought to happen?) FCC regulation concepts in US democracy in which "the public interest" or "justice and reasonableness" drove the historical regulatory assembly. However, the idea that truly informed the debate was "universal service," which offered a regulatory catch-all concept under which all human capital could engage in communicative action (McCarthy & Tétrault, 2000: 1-6; Melody 2002). The more telling point was that regulation had been based on processes of state intervention in favor of access to public communication to "prevent monopolistic abuse" (Bó, 2006: 204). This situation increasingly relied on specialists and experts in an intensified yet circumscribed environment characterized by regulatory capture by legacy and incumbent telephone operators and network owners of ISPs, such as AT&T, Comcast and Verizon. Furthermore, established experts contained, limited, then excluded universal service as an expression of the public interest. The consequence of this assemblage was that the daily communicative needs of people in urban centers were subject to erasure because they were uneconomic, meaning unprofitable.

Network Neutrality in the US is a case study in telecommunication regulation failure, illustrating how the historical universalist rulemaking system is ill-suited to the shifts in the assemblage of neoliberal interests. In keeping with an analysis such as the one used here, critical assemblage has, at its core, a commitment to evaluate those components within the assembly that claim agency and utilize their agency within the ostensibly open system to the detriment of other options operating on other planes of social and economic life. In a system of Darwinian liberalism, the strongest are encouraged to succeed, with inevitable consequences for winners and losers. It is a system of assemblage closed by strong corporations. Unfortunately, the originalist liberal conceits of the universalism of US telecommunication regulation ultimately default to those agents in the assemblage with the most power. In this context, Network Neutrality was, as Tim Wu anticipated, the archetypal set of events in which "conflicts between the private interests of broadband providers and the public's interest in a competitive innovation centered on the Internet" (2003: 141). Rapidly evolving against traditional regulatory concepts such as universal service, the success of the FCC case against Network Neutrality in the US is the moment of refusal for the principle of the universality of public communication. The result was an assemblage constructed against the hoped-for ambitions and assemblage of public telecommunications.

The impact of such an assemblage is undemocratic in the way it excludes and disempowers some citizens from participating in decisions about their cities. This shift away from democratic regulatory forums in US institutions such as the FCC in favor of corporations rather than the public has been caught up in the structural preferential corporate regulation in general. For example, the "Searching for and Cutting Regulations that are Unnecessarily Burdensome Act," SCRUB Act (H.R. 998, 2017-2018), entailed a review of the Federal Code of Regulations, which was a move by corporate interests to reduce the legitimacy of regulations in general, claiming they hindered business profitability.

Critical Communication in Urban Assemblage

The missing piece of the Network Neutrality story in the US is the urban digital divide, in which "underserved, low-income, and minority population[s]," without affordable "home access" were erased from the discussion (Schneider and Buckley, 2002: 451). This absent part of the narrative means that few, if any, opinions from the urban poor were heard in the debate because neoliberalism has sought to remake urban life as a space in which homelessness and hunger is managed, even normalized as an unseen and erased social condition (Cooper, 2017: 301). Meanwhile, access to information is restricted by an unregulated digital communication system that does little to address equality of information access as new "complex urban cosmopolitanism" takes shape in US cities (Raco, 2018). In Cleveland, for example, as the FCC handed power to corporations to compete for internet subscribers, a report by Connect Your Community (CYC) and the National Digital Inclusion Alliance (NDIA) identified "digital redlining" income-based discrimination against residents of lower-income urban neighborhoods in the types of broadband service AT&T offers, and in the company's investment in improved service, highlighted by "a glaring correlation between areas where AT&T has not invested in Fiber to the Node (FTTN) service and areas of high poverty" (CYC, 2017: np). As noted previously, arguments against urban informational deprivation rely on advocacy by organizations such as CYC, National Digital Inclusion Alliance (NDIA) and Free Press to assemble the public interest, and less on the FCC as it steps away from its public obligations in favor of private firms.

Adding to this problem is the absence of accurate data on broadband internet access in the US with which to regulate or advocate for a universalized urban life in a Network Neutrality context. "As of 2018," said Arizona State University researchers, "we do not have precise or accurate estimates of broadband adoption and use for the population"; instead, a "hazy picture" prevails (Malone & Nguyen, 2018: np). Private ISP firms such as Verizon confuse the topic by distinguishing "broadband availability and broadband adoption," thereby removing points for discussion about costs to users and access (FCC 2016: 44).

In its *2018 Broadband Deployment Report*, the FCC claimed that its 2017 move against Network Neutrality was a success:

> In the time since the last report, the Commission has acted aggressively "to accelerate deployment of [advanced telecommunications capability] by removing barriers to infrastructure investment and by promoting competition in the telecommunications market." As the above discussion details, we are hard at work facilitating deployment—for instance, by reducing regulatory barriers to the deployment of wireline and wireless infrastructure, reforming the universal service program to make it more efficient and accessible to new entrants, modernizing the business data service rules to facilitate facilities-based competition, freeing up additional spectrum for terrestrial and satellite

services, and ending the adverse impact on investment caused by the Title II Order. (FCC 2018: 49)

A critical response suggests a less positive outcome:

> The ending of net neutrality augurs a future in which the public will wield much less of a voice in determining access to social media, the internet, and other informational services on which both the major economies of the world and, increasingly, the smaller ones depend. (Sussman 2018)

Lost voices from US cities can be added to the impact of the ending of Network Neutrality. Although the evidence is inconclusive about who exactly has broadband internet in US cities, urban life is an uneven assemblage. Indeed, privileging telecommunication firms' interests risks missing the complexity of how cities are being unmade, then remade. For example, in 2016, Matthew Desmond documented the way urban life in the US is defined by "83 million eviction records," a situation in which people who are evicted fall further into poverty, losing information access (Page and Bui, 2018: np). As the headline of a report from the Center for Public Integrity said: "Rich people have access to high-speed internet; many poor people still don't. Left behind at school, at home and at work: 'The Civil Rights issue of our time'" (Holmes et al. 2016), with at least one black newspaper noting that the solution was either regulation or subsidies to cover the costs of unregulated ISPs (Jackson, 2017: np). Following Network Neutrality solutions such as these will be difficult to realize given that private firms operate according to the market in which "market failure" reinforces the case against regulation (Malone & Nguyen, 2017). Most pessimistically, the contemporary US assemblage has led to a "balkanized internet" with cities of the information rich and the poor (Alexander, 2017, np).

A Concluding Local Assemblage for Cities: Uncertain Resistance

One response to the FCC ruling was that US cities and some US states refused to give up Network Neutrality. This reaction was before public polling in 2019 showed that 80% of Americans support Network Neutrality (Birnbaum np). Previously, Mayors for Net Neutrality issued the following statement through Action Network:

> The FCC's massively unpopular decision has sparked a national movement to demand the return of real Net Neutrality. Millions of people across the political spectrum are taking action in the streets, at their statehouses, outside the FCC and before Congress. Mayors are taking action, too. Mayors Bill de Blasio of New York, Ted Wheeler of Portland and Steve Adler of Austin recently called on all other US mayors to join them in a Cities Open Internet Pledge, which requires all internet providers with whom

they do business to follow a strong set of Net Neutrality principles. Within a week, more than 20 mayors took the pledge. (Action Network undated, np)

As Network Neutrality became a historical artifact in the FCC's public regulatory narrative, advocates constructed this social movement as a conjunctural assemblage: forces organized locally in states across the country. California passed a bill on August 22, 2018 to "bar internet service providers from blocking, speeding up or slowing down websites and video streams, or charging websites fees for faster speeds" (Ulloa, 2018: np). As the politically contentious arguments continued, this resistive assemblage emerged aimed at connecting citizens in cities.

Such mayoral and state legislative advocacy shares the characteristics of a social movement that connects with "libertarian municipalism" (Bookchin, 1984), a theory that argues that social life flourishes when the full range of communicative capacities are owned, managed and shared within local communities. Further support for state and local openness came with the "Mozilla v FCC Ruling" by the US Court of Appeals for the District of Columbia on October 1, 2019 (USCA Case #18-1051). The Court judged the FCC to have acted correctly in putting an end to the FCC's 2015 public-utility-style ruling in favor of Network Neutrality, accepting the FCC's 2017 preference for a "market-based, "light touch" policy for governing the Internet" (2019: 10). Furthermore, the Court accepted that states could pursue their own Network Neutrality schemes. This ruling led one journalist to note that, "net neutrality at the federal level has turned into a legal quagmire with almost no relationship to the real issues regular people face in the market for internet access" (Patel, 2019, np). This comment signals how the intersection of assemblages in this ongoing struggle demands a framework for critically assessing the trajectories of corporate power against the public interest. Such a framework is necessary for a truthful analysis of social life and its relationship with informational capacity in dramatically changing urban landscapes. One plan is that cities and citizen data flows will be controlled through localized networked neutrality systems, adding another assemblage to the struggle of American cities for public regulation.

REFERENCES

Alexander, B. (2017). Higher Education, Digital Divides, and a Balkanized Internet. *Educause Review* (October 23). Retrieved from https://er.educause.edu/articles/2017/10/higher-education-digital-divides-and-a-balkanized-internet

Alston, P. (2017). Statement on Visit to the USA, by Professor Philip Alston, United Nations Special Rapporteur on extreme poverty and human rights. Retrieved from https://www.ohchr.org/EN/NewsEvents/Pages/DisplayNews.aspx?NewsID=22533

Birnbaum, E. (2019). 4 in 5 Americans say they support net neutrality: poll. *The Hill*, March 20. Retrieved from https://thehill.com/policy/technology/435009-4-in-5-americans-say-they-support-net-neutrality-poll

Bó, E.D. (2006). Regulatory Capture: A Review. *Oxford Review of Economic Policy*, Volume 22, Issue 2: pp. 203–225. Retrieved from https://doi-org.proxy.bc.edu/10.1093/oxrep/grj013

Bogard, W. (2009). Deleuze and Machines: A Politics of Technology? In M. Poster & D. Savat (eds.), *Deleuze and New Technology*. pp. 15-31. Edinburgh: Edinburgh University Press. Retrieved from http://www.jstor.org.proxy.bc.edu/stable/10.3366/j.ctt1r2cfn.5

Bookchin, M. (1984). Theses on libertarian municipalism. Retrieved from http://habitat.aq.upm.es/b/n40/amboo.en.html

Breen, Marcus. (2011) *Uprising: The Internet's Unintended Consequences*. Champaign, Illinois: Common Ground Publishing.

Brenner, N. & Theodore, N. (2002). Cities and the Geographies of "Actually Existing Neoliberalism." *Antipode*, Volume 34, Issue 3: pp. 349-379.

Campaign Action (undated). Sign to email your mayor: Save net neutrality in my city! Retrieved from https://actionnetwork.org/letters/sign-to-email-your-mayor-set-net-neutrality-protections-in-my-city?source=MayorsNNPledgeSWDP&referrer=group-demand-progress-3

Campbell-Kelly, M. & Garcia-Swartz, M. (2013). The History of the Internet: The missing narratives. *Journal of Information Technology*, Vol 20, No. 1: pp. 18-33.

Castells, M. (2015). *Networks of Outrage and Hope* (second edition). Cambridge: Polity.

Clinton Willian, J. (1996). Statement on Signing the Telecommunications Act of 1996 (February 8). Retrieved from http://www.presidency.ucsb.edu/ws/?pid=52289

Clyburn, M. (2018). Dissenting Statement of Commissioner Mignon L. Clyburn Re: Inquiry Concerning Deployment of Advanced Telecommunications Capability to All Americans in a Reasonable and Timely Fashion, GN Docket No. 17-199. Retrieved from https://www.fcc.gov/reports-research/reports/broadband-progress-reports/2018-broadband-deployment-report

Coldewey, D. (2018). Senator Markey officially introduces legislations to reestablish Network Neutrality. *TechCrunch* (February 27). Retrieved from https://techcrunch.com/2018/02/27/senator-markey-officially-introduces-legislation-to-reestablish-net-neutrality/

Comcast Corporation, Petitioner V. Federal Communications Commission and United States of America, Respondents NBC Universal, et al., Intervenors. United States Court of Appeals, District of Columbia Circuit. Comcast Corp. v FCC 600 F.3d 642 (2010) Retrieved from https://www.leagle.com/decision/infco20100406148

CYC. (2017). AT&T's digital redlining of Cleveland. Retrieved from http://connectyourcommunity.org/atts-digital-redlining-of-cleveland-report/

Federal Election Commission. (2005). Appropriate Framework for Broadband. Access to the Internet over Wireline Facilities etc., FC 05-151. (September 23). Retrieved from https://apps.fcc.gov/edocs_public/attachmatch/FCC-05-151A1.doc

———— (2010). Citizens United vs FEC. Retrieved on 3 September 2018 from https://www.fec.gov/updates/citizens-united-v-fecsupreme-court/

———— (2016). 2016 Broadband Progress Report, FCC16-6. Retrieved from https://www.documentcloud.org/documents/2801013-2016-Broadband-Progress-Report.html

———— (2017). DECLARATORY RULING, REPORT AND ORDER, AND ORDER. (December 14). Retrieved from https://transition.fcc.gov/Daily_Releases/Daily_Business/2018/db0104/FCC-17-166A1.pdf

———— (2018). Rulemaking Process. Retrieved from https://www.fcc.gov/about-fcc/rulemaking-process

———— (2018). Broadband Deployment Report. FCC 18-10 (February 2). Retrieved from https://www.fcc.gov/document/fcc-releases-2018-broadband-deployment-report

Fossbytes. (2017, December 15). Can A VPN Bypass Net Neutrality Rollback and Throttling? — Here Are 3 Top Services to Help You. Retrieved from https://fossbytes.com/vpn-and-net-neutrality-bypass-throttling/

Free Press. (2018). The fate of Net Neutrality hinges on the house. Retrieved from https://www.freepress.net/

Genachowski, J. (2010). New Rules for an Open Internet. *FCC blog*. Retrieved from https://www.fcc.gov/news-events/blog/2010/12/21/new-rules-open-internet

Holmes, A., Fox, E., Wieder, B., & Zubak-Skees, C. (2016). Rich people have access to high-speed Internet; many poor people still don't Left behind at school, at home and at work: 'The Civil Rights issue of our time.' *Broadband*. The Center for Public Integrity. Retrieved from https://www.publicintegrity.org/2016/05/12/19659/rich-people-have-access-high-speed-internet-many-poor-people-still-dont

Horrigan, J. (2015). The numbers behind the broadband 'homework gap.' Fact Tank, Pew Research Center. Retrieved from http://www.pewresearch.org/fact-tank/2015/04/20/the-numbers-behind-the-broadband-homework-gap/

Jackson, D.A. (2016). Digital Redlining: How Major American Communication Companies Are Controlling Who Gets Broadband Access or Not. *Atlanta Black Star* (April 6). Retrieved from https://atlantablackstar.com/2017/04/06/digital-redlining-major-american-communication-companies-controlling-gets-broadband-access-not/

Kim, Y. & Warner Mildred E. (2016). Pragmatic Municipalism: Local Government Service Delivery After the Great Recession. *Public Administration*, Vol 94 (3), September: pp. 789-805. Retrieved from https://doi.org/10.1111/padm.12267

Kivikuru, U. (2019). From community to assemblage? ICT provides a site for inclusion and exclusion in the global south. *The Journal of International Communication*, Volume 25 (1): pp. 49-68 Retrieved from DOI: 10.1080/13216597.2018.1544163

Kreide, R. (2016). Digital spaces, public places and communicative power: In defense of deliberative democracy. *Philosophy and Social Criticism*, Volume 42 (4-5): pp. 476-486.

Lessenich, S. (2015). Mobility and Control: On the dialectic of the 'active society'. In K. Dorre, S. Lessenich, & H. Rosa (eds.). *Sociology, Capitalism, Critique*, translated by J.-P. Herrmann and L. Balhorn. London: Verso. pp. 98-142.

Lloyd, A. (2018). American city growth rate catching up to suburbia. *Housingwire* (July 2). Retrieved from https://www.housingwire.com/articles/43846-american-city-growth-rate-catching-up-to-suburbia

Lloyd, J. (2015). Fighting Redlining and Gentrification in Washington, D.C. The Adams-Morgan Organization and Tenant Right to Purchase. *Journal of Urban History*, Volume: 42 Issue: 6: pp. 1091-1109.

Malone, C. and Nguyen, M. (2018). We Used Broadband Data We Shouldn't Have — Here's What Went Wrong. *Five Thirty-Eight* (January 9). Retrieved from https://fivethirtyeight.com/features/we-used-broadband-data-we-shouldnt-have-heres-what-went-wrong/

Mason, J. (2018). VPN Usage, Data Privacy & Internet Penetration Statistics. *Best VPN*. Retrieved from https://thebestvpn.com/vpn-usage-statistics/

Melody, W.H. (2002). *The Triumph and Tragedy of Human Capital: Foundation Resource for the Global Knowledge Economy*. Faculty of Technology, Policy and Management, Delft University of Technology.

Mosco, V. (2017). *Becoming Digital: Toward a Post-Internet Society*. Bingley, England: Emerald Publishing.

Mozilla V FCC Ruling. (2019). USCA Case #18-1051, 1 October. Retrieved from
https://www.scribd.com/document/428285019/Mozilla-v-FCC-
ruling#from_embed?campaign=SkimbitLtd&ad_group=66960X1514734X22d8056d672ec252a
a60b29adb98f754&keyword=660149026&source=hp_affiliate&medium=affiliate

Newman, K. and Ryly, E. (2006). The Right to Stay Put, Revisited: Gentrification and Resistance to
Displacement in New York City. *Urban Studies*, Volume 43 (1): pp. 23-57. Retrieved 2
September 2018 from http://journals.sagepub.com/doi/abs/10.1080/00420980500388710

Nunziato, D. (2009). *Virtual Freedom: Net Neutrality and Free Speech in the Internet Age*. Stanford:
Stanford University Press.

O'Neil, C. (2017). *Weapons of Math Destruction: How big data increases inequality and threatens
democracy*. New York: Broadway Books.

Page, E. & Bui, Q. (2018). In 83 million eviction records, a sweeping and intimate look at housing in
America. *New York Times*, April 7. Retrieved from
https://www.nytimes.com/interactive/2018/04/07/upshot/millions-of-eviction-records-a-
sweeping-new-look-at-housing-in-america.html

Parker, K., Horowitz, J. M., Brown, A., Fry, R., Cohn, D.Richard D'vera & Igielnik, R. (2018). What
Unites and Divides Urban, Suburban and Rural Communities. Pew Research Center, (22 May).
Retrieved from http://www.pewsocialtrends.org/2018/05/22/what-unites-and-divides-urban-
suburban-and-rural-communities/

Patel, N. (2019). The Court Allowed the FCC to Kill Net Neutrality Because Washing Machines Can't
Make Phone Calls. *The Verge*, October 4. Retrieved from
https://www.theverge.com/2019/10/4/20898779/fcc-net-neutrality-court-of-appeals-decision-
ruling

Patterson, S. (2010). *The Quants: how a new breed of math whizzes conquered wall street and nearly
destroyed it*. Crown Publishing: New York.

Pickard, V. (2014). *America's Battle for Media Democracy: The Triumph of Corporate Libertarianism and
the Future of Media Reform*. Cambridge: Cambridge University Press.

Raco, M. (2018). Critical Urban Cosmopolitanism and the Governance of Urban Diversity in European
Cities. *European Urban and Regional Studies*, 25 (1) pp. 8-23 Retrieved from
https://doi.org/10.1177/0969776416680393

Schneider M. & Buckley J. (2002). Creating choosers: information, the digital divide, and the propensity to
change schools. *Social Science Computer Review*, 20 (4): pp. 451-470.

SCRUB Act, 115th Congress. (2017-2018). Retrieved from https://www.congress.gov/bill/115th-
congress/house-bill/998

Stanton, L. (2012). In submission to the ITU, U.S. delegation opposes internet governance changes.
Cybersecurity Policy Report, (August 13). Retrieved from http://aspenpubl.com

Supreme Court of the United States. (2009). Citizens United V. Federal Election Commission Appeal from
The United States District Court For The District Of Columbia, No. 08–205. Retrieved from
https://transition.fec.gov/law/litigation/cu_sc08_opinion.pdf

Susman, G. (2018). Review of Becoming Digital: Toward a Post-Internet Society. *Journal of
Communication*, Volume 68, Issue 2: E8–E10. Retrieved from
https://doi.org/10.1093/joc/jqy012

Tarrow, S. (2011). *Power in Movement: Social Movements and Contentious Politics*. Cambridge:
Cambridge University Press.

Ulloa, J. (2018). California net neutrality bill passes out of committee that initially tried to water it down.
Los Angeles Times, (August 22). Retrieved from http://www.latimes.com/politics/essential/la-

pol-ca-essential-politics-may-2018-california-net-neutrality-bill-passes-1534985347-htmlstory.html

Veblen, T. (1919/2005). *Vested Interests and the Common Man.* New York: Cosimo.

Wu, T. (2003). Network Neutrality, Broadband Discrimination. *Journal on Telecom & High Technology Law,* Vol 2: pp. 141-176. Retrieved from
http://www.jthtl.org/content/articles/V2I1/JTHTLv2i1_Wu.PDF

———— (2006). Why have a telecommunications law? Anti-discrimination norms in communications. (The Digital Broadband Migration: Confronting the New Regulatory Frontiers). *Journal on Telecommunications & High Technology Law*, Fall, 2006, Vol. 5(1): pp. 15-47.

CHAPTER 3

The Multiple Layers of Information Communication Technologies and Their Use in Urban Public Space: A Case Study of New York City

Pierre Depaz
New York University, Berlin
and
Nicolas Grefenstette
Starr Whitehouse Landscape Architects and Planners
New York, USA

ABSTRACT

The pervasiveness of digital communication technology transpires in our everyday lives partly because of its multi-layered nature. From connected home devices to wireless hotspots in public spaces, to neighborhood-wide access points and international fiber-optic cables, new telecommunications operate on multiple, interconnected scales. Similarly, the planning of urban environments is also one of the different geographies, including the design of living in cities, which takes place at the level of the building, the street, the public square, the neighborhood, the municipality, and the region. The chapter provides a new understanding of urban planning practices by examining initiatives taken at different geographical and physical levels in New York City, as well as analyzing how different technological infrastructures operate and affect us.

The new real-estate development project at Hudson Yards has been hailed as the first *"quantified community"* by planners and researchers across the NYC area. The project focuses on data gathering and processing to build *"the most connected, measured and technologically advanced digital district in the nation."* As Hudson Yards also claims to have *"the smartest park in town"* (Hudson Yards NY, 2017), the connection established in the project between connected technologies and the sustainability of public space becomes apparent. The near ubiquity of ICTs at all levels of an urban setting, from individual charging stations to neighborhood scale mapping systems and connected power infrastructure, is now posited to impact urban living at a variety of scales.

A core body of work has identified the role of ICTs in impacting the parameters that compose social sustainability, as well as questioning its very definition. At the larger scale, studies consider the relationship between ICTs and access to education, governance, health, and economic development (Farrell, 2007; Etta et al., 2005). Townsend's (2013) review of the advent of smart cities from the rise of digital technologies reveals a variety of impacts on factors of human development, from health to education to governance. When spatially focused on the urban environment, these studies have consistently informed conversations about smart cities and smart planning (Caragliu et al., 2011), observing ways in which they have transpired into everyday life, from monitoring the quality and status of infrastructure and services (Eckoff et al., 2017) to engaging civic participation, but few initiatives have been developed specifically regarding how ICTs have systematically influenced the transformation of urban public spaces (Trindade et al., 2017).

INTRODUCTION

Public space can be defined as a spatial framework within which civic, social and economic life can happen at any time of the day, and without obstruction, for members of any community. The construction of public space as a realm depends primarily on the interaction between physical components (e.g. qualities of the space or types of space) and social components (e.g. relating to contacts, relations, and collective uses) (Rapoport, 2002). Concerns over the erosion of existing systems of traditional public spaces (the square, the park, the sidewalk), whose core purpose is to connect people from various social groups for political, civic, social or economic transactions, have led some researchers to consider that there is a "crisis" of public space (Graham and Aurigi, 1997). Another set of studies, drawn from academia in urban design and planning, have evaluated the different forms in which public space is manifested (Carmona, 2010a).

These studies both reflect the impact that geographical processes, such as globalization, has had on a variety of socio-cultural and political-economic factors, and the decisions that policy-makers, institutions and citizens make regarding what they expect from public space, and thus how they intend to design, manage and sustain it. A successful public space is, then, one that maintains its usability and inclusiveness through the design and implementation of specific physical and digital infrastructures. While there is a dearth of fine-grained definitions of the features of a such a space, we begin from the different transformations of public space as explicated in Carmona's (2010a, 2010b) overview and assess the extent to which ICTs are reinforcing or subverting them. Usership of ICTs and dependence on them for access to and broadcast of data is rapidly growing across the world. Across cities, ICTs have transpired in mostly invisible ways (Batty, 1990) regarding how we use and perceive public space. By considering a set of technologies that directly relates to the use of public space, and specifically those that are currently deployed in it, we study how certain features or characteristics of new implementations of ICTs affect New York City's public space. Thus, we learn that concerns such as access to facilities, quality of living space and health, the degree of social interaction, and the introduction of seamless and personal networked computing technologies can profoundly modify the amount of civic engagement.

The Advent of Digital Technologies in the Public Realm

The concept of smart and mediated cities is far from being new. Shannon Mattern (2017) argues that, throughout history, city dwellers have developed means of information and communication that have made use of the urban environment, shaped that very environment, and were some of the main drivers in social development and sustainability. Up until the development of our modern ICTs, however, most of those communicative events relied on the use of public space. The call to prayer from the muezzin, the gathering of Greek cities' citizens in the agora, the display of theater programs on Litfaßsäule all represent instances in which technical infrastructure was developed in public space to blend public and private use. Public space has been intrinsically linked to the development of a media ecosystem intended to better our living together. These ICTs as we understand them today are characterized by three main components: the ability to store, process and transmit information virtually anywhere on the planet at a near instantaneous speed (Dodge and Kitchin, 2001).

Originally exclusively used by private institutions, ICTs now manifest themselves, through miniaturization, in most aspects of our lives, through personal computing devices, embedded systems and the set of affordable, multi-purpose computers referred to as the Internet of Things (IoT). What we have seen since the 1980s is the progression of a set of technologies transitioning from more private to public uses, insofar as their locus of action is no longer restrained to specific domains, and from a logic of quality to quantity, as this is a requirement for digital data processing. The computer being restricted to exclusively processing discrete information, it is both the manifestation and the symptom of a societal shift in which data become the principal means to manage and control (Foucault, 1975; Deleuze, 1992). While the open-source movement has been hailed for some of its achievements (the Linux kernel, the Wikipedia encyclopedia), ICTs are now mainly privately developed and owned, and have, therefore, sparked a debate about the merits of closed versus open technologies (Lessig, 2006), mirroring the debates in openness and closedness in urban spaces.

Today, the organization of data becomes a new sort of space in which individuals can inhabit and strive, sometimes referred to as virtual spaces, or cyberspace, which are sometimes included in discussions of new types of public spaces (Barlowe, 1996; Carmona, 2010a, 2010b). Moving from private applications to public use, and exclusive processing to mass communications, ICTs, in and of themselves, have radically changed social life by virtue of their improving our ability to exchange information across time and space at unprecedented scales. The ICTs that are being designed specifically to improve the use of public spaces, therefore, come from a triple tradition: they are (1) data-focused, if not data-exclusive; (2) privately-owned, and therefore answer to logics of private property, competition and sustainability; and (3) they generate spaces.

With this shift of ICTs toward public space and their near-ubiquitous presence at the societal level, their introduction has impacted the way people interact with the built environment. Mobility has been influenced using real-time mapping capacities, as mobile technology has redefined the concept of the physical landmark as meeting point, instead allowing early adopting populations, such as youth, to "flock" using "loosely [coordinated] movements and meetings through constant communications via mobile phone" (Townsend, 2000 in Zook et al., 2004: 167). The constant, highly decentralized, and primarily invisible flow of information, as described by Dan Hill in his essay on "The Street as Platform" (2015), exemplifies streets immersed in clouds of data (open and closed, aggregate and isolated), some of which enable users of public space to micro-coordinate everyday activities and, as such, have greater agency on defining which spaces are most and better used.

A study in 2011 by Microsoft that examined a variety of developed countries (US, UK, Japan, Germany, Canada) found that "everyday place negotiation" was the key object of the majority of location-based services, which can be broken down into the following categories: "GPS (70 percent), weather alerts (46 percent), traffic updates (38 percent), restaurants information and reviews (38 percent), and locating the nearest convenience stores (36 percent)," while "social networking (18 percent), gaming (10 percent), geotagging photos (6 percent) lagged behind, alongside enhanced 911 (9 percent)" (Wilken et al. 2013: 204). A Pew Internet research survey conducted in 2010 estimated that 4% of adults used location-based services (e.g. Foursquare), with 1% of internet users using these platforms on any given day. While at the time of these studies social networking was still a growing trend, internet-based wayfinding abilities (today often integrated into social networking platforms with live location updates) constitute a large part of how we navigate public space in 2019. Newer applications in the realm of augmented-reality (AR) games, such as Pokemon Go (2016), Ingress (2013) or Minecraft AR (2019), provide additional ways for users to explore and interact with physical space.

However, while technology plays a key role in changing human behavior in urban settings, larger societal and political trends are also held responsible for the way urban public space has been managed, which also impacts usership. In his overview of critiques of trends in public space, Carmona (2010a) attributes excess and deficiency of management to patterns of use, exclusion, and homogeneity in public space. Using this framework to categorize public space, certain critiques emerge as particularly salient to the increasing influence of ICTs.

The Transformation of Public Spaces: Towards New Management Typologies

Independently of technology, there are parallel debates about ownership of space in society. First, Carmona speaks of exclusionary spaces as a type of undermanaged space that suffer from a decline in physical quality or in "opportunities and activities it offers," (Carmona 2010a) leading to cycles of underutilization. Of these types of spaces, some are designed to exclude certain populations such as the physically disabled or the elderly, when accessibility, for instance, isn't considered; they may also be parochial or prescriptive by nature, dictating who is welcome and who isn't based on categories such as class, ethnicity, race, age, type of occupation (Carmona 2010a). In distinguishing itself programmatically, urban public space can also lead to spatial segregation: skateparks built in the outskirts of town force the youth into liminal spaces, or smoking bans and anti-sleeping hand rests on benches may exclude undesirables from high visibility plazas and streets. The fear of crime being almost as impactful as crime itself, leads to increasingly segregated spaces, allowing certain users to retreat from public space altogether, where the perceived threat of lawlessness and crime prevails. More traditional urbanists such as Whyte (1980) and Jacobs (1961) cite anonymity as a key component to the feeling of safety in public space, which is directly challenged by the increasing presence of centralized surveillance systems.

Second, the term third spaces, coined by geographers and urban designers such as Banerjee (2001), define those spaces such as cafes and bars which are neither fully public, nor fully private, in which an increasing number of everyday interactions and exchanges (from interviews, to purchases, to creative production, for instance) take place, where they would have previously taken place in the public realm. Users no longer need to agree on predetermined landmarks or specific places at which to meet but can instead rely on live updating abilities provided by applications such as Google Maps or Facebook to locate one another in a dynamic manner, which leads to "massively hypercoordinated urban civilization in the world's cities" (Zook et al., 2004). Here, data is accessible at rates higher than ever before (increased synchronicities), with increasing access to "the potential number of places where interaction could occur", with information on "traffic, weather, and economic conditions" demanding to adapt in terms of their everyday decision-making in cities. (Zook et al, 2004: 167). Furthermore, applications such as Yelp or Foursquare transform the experience one has of the city, providing further 'pull' factors towards certain venues or neighborhoods based on popularity ratings, creating new geographies based on consumption patterns, providing live forecasting of local economic trends (Glaeser et al., 2017): ICTs enable ways in which software can alter the "spatialities of consumption" (Kitchin et al., 2011), while different intensities of management can in parallel produce exclusionary or inclusionary public spaces, resulting in a dichotomy of open versus closed spaces, determined by the strength and fluidity of their boundaries.

Finally, overmanaged spaces are typically higher profile spaces that are subjected to a wide variety of policy and development practices which lead to privatization, commodification and homogenization, and are more or less exclusionary. What some refer to as privatized spaces are types of over managed public spaces (Carmona 2010a), products of new patterns in economic and political globalization: the experience of public space has changed, as people can now carry many formerly public functions in these semi-private environments using the internet (Boyer, 1996). The increased availability of internet both in private venues such as cafes and bars, as well as urban infrastructure increasing WiFi connections increases the potential number of work environments for people who would traditionally work at home. These increasingly homogenized spaces lead to depoliticization of public space, where the public realm is increasingly transformed into an area dedicated to personal experiences (Arendt 1994). Sennett concurs, adding that as spaces are increasingly not only areas for passive observation, they are also decidedly personal, a consequence of commodification and commercialization initiated in the 19th century (Sennett, 1992).

Closed Versus Open: The Role of Digital Geographies

The belief that "information wants to be free" (Denning, 1996) influenced much of the development of early public internet infrastructure and standards, from the Hypertext Markup Language (HTML) specification by Tim Berners-Lee in 1993, by allowing freedom of access, retrieval, and exploration of information. The bulletin board system (BBS) was a means for all with internet connectivity to have conversations, to ask questions and to collaborate on bottom-up projects in an outwardly public fashion. One of the most successful of these projects is the Linux kernel, today the most popular operating system for mobile, IoT and embedded electronics. The point of Linux is to provide an extensive and robust API (Application Programming Interface)—a way to interact with underlying hardware. In parallel, Hill (2015) argues that an open street can be "thought of as having an API, conveying its overall behavior to the world, each aspect of it increasingly beginning to generate and recombine data"; that is, there are things you can and cannot do in the streets that are directly correlated to how open or closed this interface is. One example, as described by Whyte (1980), is the mobility of the urban furniture of those spaces. A movable piece of furniture is a flexible API, while a fixed one is a closed API.

While traditionally ICTs were focused on enabling openness in public space, new trends of privatization and the public's removal from public space has reversed the trend as ICTs are now seen as reinforcing the closedness of those same public spaces. Carmona (2010b) recognizes the limitations of the different critiques of public space, arguing that they may just be "two sides of a same coin." To draw an analogy with Dan Hill's overview of technology in the main street (Hill, 2015), whether a space is over- or under-managed would likely lead to a "closed" street, where each parameter is on lockdown by a position of authority. He concludes that the "public" in public space is not a coherent group, but instead a fragmented society of different socio-economic groups further divided by age and gender (a process exacerbated by external environmental pressures), subject to constant change. Hill (2015) extends Castells' (1996) argument that urban technologies such as ICTs can reinforce (rather than break down) processes of socio-spatial polarization in cities, including in public space.

While New York City does not have formal gated communities in its urban center, there is an increasing reliance on public-private apparatuses to control usership. When discussing the political-economic perspectives on control in the public realm, Carmona deconstructs controls as "power relationships of access and exclusion," leading to a subtle array of hard (e.g. CCTV monitoring) or soft (or passive) restrictions to the use of public space. The increasing presence of an industry of private security is also an indicator of this type of perception. One example is Business Improvement Districts (or BIDs), which use increased tax revenue from businesses and property owners in exchange for private security, cleaning services and branding to create distinctive geographical areas. Similarly, spaces that straddle public and private space (such as third spaces) or privately-operated public spaces (or POPS) give building management companies better control on the rules of use of public spaces directly adjacent to or within buildings, providing control of aspects such as photography, times of operation, or the right to convene. Low and Smith (2006) argue that the rate of privatization has accelerated, and that there has been reciprocity between the increase of privatization in everyday life and of the nature of public space itself. Ironically, while POPS seem to be historically aligned with the incentive plaza program (Schmidt et al., 2011) developed in the 1980s, which was clearly giving agency to the city regarding the development of its public space in exchange for fewer regulations for developers, the trend is reversed today as POPS and BIDs give the advantage to the private sector regarding which types of user they would like to see in their public space. In cities such as Tel Aviv, the core values of its Smart City vision plan (2014) are built upon three-tiered models that overlay physical infrastructure, applications infrastructure and applications under the guise of providing "safer" public environments through a variety of customized services, justifying additional controls and the monitoring of urban public space, while at the same time conflating the roles of customers and residents through platforms such as DigiTel (Shechter, Sharon & Shmerling, 2015).

This process of design is based on the aggregated, stereotypical profile of users through sociological and quantified analysis, using the aforementioned categories. While the said process is implemented as a top-down approach, a similar dynamic is evident in the development of digital social networks. Through ICTs, social networks are both more strongly tied and more loosely bound, which reinforces social and behavioral distinction from one group to another (Lerman, 2016). When such a distinction impacts the use of public space, and when public use is no longer available to every city dweller but to a particular group, it reinforces a closed public space in which the user lacks agency.

This confluence between city planning and ICTs is highlighted by Hill (2015) when he argues that, "a new kind of city is emerging, an algorithmic city. It promises gleaming efficiency, citizen-centered services on demand. Yet the algorithms that produce these conditions—political, economic, cultural—are similarly challenging to parse, and are quite different to those that shaped cities previously." What is essential to recognize here is that most analyses view technology as an accessory to changing behaviors toward public space, when it should be a fundamental parameter. As Bijker (1997) has shown in his work on sociotechnical assemblages, technologies are, to a certain extent, developed within the scope of specific agendas of specific stakeholders —one agenda drives the features of a technology software, which impacts the environment within which it is deployed.

Case Studies of ICTs in New York City

Wireless Communications Networks Between Open and Closed

In 2014, New York approved the transformation of existing payphones into WiFi hotspots (deployed in 2015 onwards) as a means of bridging the "digital divide"—the uneven access to modern communications across geographical locations (Warschauer, 2004). The deployment of LinkNYC happened first as the replacement of payphones across five boroughs, for a total expected count of 7,500 kiosks at project completion. The LinkNYC infrastructure (made up of kiosks called Links), is developed by Intersection, a company financed by Google's parent company, Alphabet. The program is a step toward providing free city-wide WiFi and access to common city services and is considered by Intersection as a potential replacement to individual internet subscriptions, in addition to helping bridge the "digital divide," which particularly affects lower socio-economic classes.

This project extends the possibilities for people who already have good access to the internet at home, reinforcing openness in public space, but does not necessarily apply to those who lack a stable internet connection. One could argue that the use of internet at curbside, using a mobile phone, for instance, does not replace the need for more secure physical environments in which certain activities can take place (e.g. applying to jobs, filing taxes): not all uses of the internet are appropriate for a completely open public space such as the street, but networked digital technologies have been proven a driving force for the sustainability of third spaces, such as public libraries (Mattern, 2014). The New York Civil Liberties Union criticized the project for being unclear about the number and types of user data that would be retained (Heilweil, 2018), which could eventually be used in cases of digital, and potentially physical, segregation, something that has raised concerns from local civic organizations such as Rethink LinkNYC. The presence of two built-in cameras, in addition, could also raise concerns about increased control of public space from city agencies – although the company claims not to store video information for more than a week (Woyke, 2017). Financed by advertisement revenue, Links are also typically concentrated in denser, higher-income neighborhoods (Sinky et al., 2018), which erodes the argument of bridging the digital divide. The LinkNYC project was involved also in lawsuits from the National Federation of the Blind, arguing that accessibility for the disabled and hard of sight was limited (Heilweil, 2018), reinforcing the exclusionary and parochial character of a given public space.

Following an initial rolling-out phase and the development of the advertising and WiFi network capabilities, LinkNYC aims to integrate with other IoT technologies, such as augmented reality and autonomous vehicles (Woyke, 2017). Links would also provide platforms for the city to be more legible and responsive. Legible, in that it can reveal "flows of people, commercial activity, garbage services" (Fung, 2016), and responsive in providing access to services such as 311, leading to increased public sector efficiency and "one-stop shopping" for government information, applications designed to limit environmental degradation, citizen and emergency support services, and services to support inter-community meetings, contributing to the openness of public space. Financed by advertising revenue, the presence of Links also solidifies the privatized nature of public space.

Smart Urban Fixtures as an Internet of (Optimized) Things

Smart trash receptacles, called Big Bellies, another example of ICTs, can monitor the amount of waste or "fill level" at any given point, as well as rates of filling (measured by the "spike level"), frequency of collection and general data on the sensors (e.g. battery level) present in each receptacle. The data collected can then be relayed via cloud-based web services to the NYC Department of Sanitation: when 85% full, Big Bellies send texts to refuse collectors (Parkinson, 2015). In New York, these Big Belly receptacles have been deployed around the city since 2014, and as of 2015, 170 of these smart trashcans incorporated WiFi capabilities, providing access points for pedestrians. In addition to increasing internet connectivity and data collection, the bins also act as platforms for public service announcements or provide billboards for advertisements. Design flaws notwithstanding, the potential for smart litter receptacles to cull illegal dumping, and thus improve the aesthetic attraction of public space is high. In addition, inscribing itself in the ethos of smart cities, this development would improve efficiency in pickups, further reducing the amount of vehicular traffic in and around public space. In terms of experience, this benefit would also mean reduced traffic, noise and congestion, directly improving the quality of health and the living environment in public space.

The development of "smart" benches (such as those developed by Soofa, a spinoff of the MIT Media Lab), with WiFi, USB and phone-charging stations and solar panels, further cements the move away from benches for all, not only by fragmenting the continuity of the bench itself, but also by indicating that the desired users of public space should be able to benefit from such infrastructure in the first place (inscribing itself within the greater scope of what some refer to as "hostile architecture") (Petty, 2016). This is a move toward a more exclusionary city, as benches and seating arrangements are traditional ways for cities to indicate where public space begins by providing a place of respite. The Soofa bench was installed in 2018 by New York City Parks during a two-year pilot program: in addition to providing charging and WiFi hotspot features, the bench also counts unique users nearby within a 75-meter (240 feet) radius, provided WiFi is enabled on their mobile devices.

The Soofa bench, according to its founder, "embeds" in the community via its IoT features, allowing seamless and constant connectivity, with data collection being an asset to quantifying usership; thus, informing development or design decisions. The data collected are only available to the buyer (e.g. the city) and accessed via a custom Atlas dashboard developed by the company (NYCParks, 2018), and the information is gathered first before NYC Parks decides how to analyze it (Stone, 2016). By focusing WiFi access to specific nodes instead of trying to provide it city-wide, as LinkNYC's booths do, costs for cities would be limited, allowing for more flexibility of deployment since the benches are not deployed as permanent infrastructure. Here, we see existing views of public space and private technology at work together—both through the paradigm of exclusionary planning practices via physical infrastructure, and through the need to gather data without explicit intent on how to use it or clear ownership of it. When the Office of the Mayor of New York decided to deploy a bike-sharing system in New York City in 2013, it was designed to be the most ambitious on the East Coast of the US. With more than 730 stations and 10,000 bikes, the project is the largest in the country and has been undoubtedly successful. This success, however, has been measured essentially in terms of numbers (e.g. daily trips, numbers of stations, number of annual memberships).

The Exclusionary Connectivity of Bike-Sharing Systems

The presentation of Citibike as an ideal solution to short-distance, one-way trips would indeed be suited to support inter-neighborhood travel, but its relative absence in the most populated boroughs of the city, as well as the fact that only 18% of all docking stations are located in neighborhoods with an average yearly income of $50,000 or less makes the current Citibike system a means of reinforcing segregation in urban space, and furthers the under-management of some public spaces.

The positive impact of docked bike-sharing systems, then, comes not only from economic incentives of facilitating the journey to work, but also from the positive environmental impact that increased ridership has on a city. As the success of Citibikes has resulted in the Office of the Mayor developing more bike lanes, the consequences in reducing noise and air pollution would indeed situate bike-shares as a positive force in providing more livable spaces. However, such benefits would only be concretized if the mode shift of the users was away from the most polluting means of transportation – private cars – and not from the least polluting – walking. Preliminary qualitative studies indicate that the main mode shift to cycling is from bus ridership and walking (City of New York, 2014), effectively leaving the number of car riders unchanged and exposing one of the limitations of the current form of the system.

While Citibike at this scale relies on an incredible digital network of data transmission, to maintain the optimal number of bikes per docking station at all times, and storage, to provide memberships on the go, the project's main drawback is that it continues to segregate public space by operating in strictly defined spaces, often extending the commuting space of only one of the five boroughs of the city. As of 2019, however, several pilot programs have been launched throughout New York City to test the possibility of dockless bike-shares. Dockless bike-sharing, by not relying exclusively on specific docking stations, allows for a much more fluid deployment of bikes (e.g. Washington DC), but has also been strongly encouraged by inhabitants' comments on the official pilot platform of the city. By being present in neighborhoods currently not targeted by the existing system, dockless bike-shares address some of the previous limitations regarding spatial equity and freedom of purpose.

The increased role of ICTs in the rapid rise of dockless bike-shares (Alta Planning, 2017) still presents new challenges for the city of tomorrow. One of the main foreseeable issues of dockless bikes regarding public space is the congestion of parked vehicles. To make sure that their bikes do not litter streets or private properties, companies can introduce more subtle forms of coercion, specific to modern computing and communication. For dockless bikes to be unlocked, it is necessary to be logged in and identifiable through a mobile application. One of the pilot companies, Limebike, uses this identifiability to establish a points system to motivate users to park their bikes in designated locations (Alta Planning, 2017). Failure to comply will establish a track record of misbehavior affecting the user's ability to further use the bike-sharing system. While enabling an apparent greater freedom, such a system maintains an underlying control on riders and undermines civic responsibility (Ian Kerr in Geist, 2010).

For the past decade, urban planners and decision-makers alike have considered the possibilities offered by new technologies in terms of reaching out to specific communities and obtaining their input regarding specific community-related matters. These so-called "citizen apps" rely on the idea of citizen involvement and citizen governance – that citizens know what is best for them and their neighborhood and can pinpoint their own priorities. "Citizen apps" establish a feedback system between community members, planners and decision-makers in which each member of that system influences every other member in a cybernetic rather than hierarchical relationship.

The Customization of Public Space Engagement through Individualized Communications

This section studies the contrast in mobile applications (apps) as they are developed either from a public or a private initiative, and how they affect the inhabitants' conception of public space. On the one side, the NYC311 app is a government initiative using modern technologies to further the purpose of the 311 support telephone line. Citizens can request garbage removal, flag potholes and signal abandoned vehicles, among others, for public services to address – the aim being to improve public service and public infrastructure through active collaboration of both parties involved, with mobile technologies empowering both the users themselves and the broader community, within a certain geographical proximity. On the other side, the Citizen app, launched in 2017 in NYC, is focused on communicating police reports and distress calls to a wide audience and mapping those calls on a map of the user's device. The affirmed goal of the app is to make the community safer by providing more transparency toward ongoing crime acts in the neighborhood.

The first comparison can be made in terms of actionability and empowerment. While NYC311 relies on user activity by signaling and commenting on potential issues, Citizen aims first at delivering information and then offers multiple ways for users to react to it – avoiding the locus of the crime, forwarding it to their communities, or starting a video-stream of the incident. These aspects represent clearly the difference between the physical and the virtual world. While both apps are focused on physical incidents, NYC311 aims at solving these incidents by a feedback loop of signaling and repairing, an action that benefits all those engaged with that space in the future; whereas, Citizen relies on data broadcasting to affect the behaviors of individual members in that space. As such, NYC311 presents a vision of public space as something to be maintained, while Citizen presents a vision of public space as something to be avoided (e.g. scary spaces).

This differentiation continues on the surface level. User interfaces and user experiences have been thoroughly known to influence and direct a user's actions and agency to further an ideological belief of the organization (Laurel, 1993) developing the app. NYC311 focuses on the report and the follow-up of localized events and aspires to maintain public safety through active engagement by providing follow-up reports of any action. While citizen science actively uses the citizen as a sensor, and the government as an actuator, the Citizen app is both the sensor (by broadcasting information) and asks the citizen to be the actuator (e.g. avoiding the scene of the crime) without providing any follow-up on the incident. This reversal of agency leads to a lack of choice (Friedman et al., 2013), and therefore a lack of ownership of the space in which these events are happening.

Finally, the question of social networks, now ubiquitous in ICTs and urban planning alike, is answered in very different ways by NYC311 and Citizen. NYC311 does not offer any ability to communicate with another user through the application. On the other side, Citizen relies heavily on "social features" such as live media broadcasting, live discussion and the possibility to set up "friends" – individuals whose safety you can monitor – and communities – a geographical location you can monitor even though you might not be present there. David Harvey talks of time-space compression (Harvey, 1990) – ICTs simultaneously expand our connection to the world and "shrink" uses of space, insofar as we no longer need to exploit its full extents, only those that we deem important to us. What we are seeing in these differences – an active 311NYC and a passive Citizen – is reminiscent of the difference between civic engagement and involvement (Amna et al., 2012), in so far as NYC311 asks citizens to be engaged while Citizen merely offers the opportunity to be loosely involved, remediating the public space as a virtual one (Bolter et al., 2000).

Conclusion

The cybernetic metaphor for the smart cities, that of input/output systems that can be regulated and optimized, is one that rose to popularity alongside the development and expansion of computational and digital technologies during the second part of the 21st century. As a holistic approach, this has been extensively studied and documented. We have pointed out how the different aspects of ICTs have been deployed throughout New York City, and how the technical and social context for these implementations have both used ICTs to either reinforce existing notions of the transformations of public space or challenge them. The main pattern found in the technologies surveyed points to two dynamics: the public/open versus closed/private debate does not disappear because digital technologies are used, and there can exist a superimposition of physical and virtual spaces as translated by these technologies. The danger is to provide too much connectivity, too much information, such that the most meaningful potential for action lies not in the physicality of a public space, but in a non-physical community through access to virtual private communities online – such as through LinkNYC and Citizen – rather than involvement and initiative through systems such as NYC311 and dockless bike-shares.

Despite the relative newness of the technological apparatuses investigated here, it is still possible to draw the conclusion that ICTs tend to favor the quality of life in public spaces when it encourages mode-switching in transportation technologies (such as dockless bike-sharing), and when it considers the affordances of fast, affordable wireless data transmission to move away from specific physical landmarks. By allowing bikes and wireless connections to be had virtually anywhere, the smart city is offering agency to its citizens by letting them decide where the use of this technology is most needed.

As such, the success of a city as a cybernetic system seems to depend on improving inhabitants' behavior within the built environment. The highlight on the user as a proactive initiator appears to be a richer solution to maintaining public spaces as places of social encounter, reducing segregated or exclusionary spaces altogether, rather than one that exacerbates economic functionalism and top-down management practices.

REFERENCES

Alta Planning + Design (2017). Not just Mobility: How E-bike Share Can Spark a Design Revolution. Blog. Retrieved from URL: https://blog.altaplanning.com/not-just-mobility-how-e-bike-share-can-spark-a-design-revolution-a90b87473dd9

Amnå, E., & Ekman, J. (2014). Standby citizens: diverse faces of political passivity. *European Political Science Review*, 6(2), pp. 261-281.

Arendt, H. (1958). *The human condition.* University of Chicago Press.

Banerjee, T. (2001). The future of public space: beyond invented streets and reinvented places. *Journal of the American Planning Association,* 67(1), pp. 9-24.

Barlow, J.P. (1996). *A cyberspace independence declaration.* Retrieved from URL: https://www.eff.org/cyberspace-independence

Batty, M. (1990). Editorial: Invisible Cities. *Environment and Planning B: Planning and Design,* Vol. 17, pp. 127-130.

Bijker, W.E. (1997). *Of bicycles, bakelites, and bulbs: Toward a theory of sociotechnical change.* MIT Press.

Bolter, J.D., Grusin, R., & Grusin, R.A. (2000). *Remediation: Understanding new media.* MIT Press.

Boyer, M.C. (1996). *CyberCities: visual perception in the age of electronic communication.* Princeton, NJ, Princeton Architectural Press.

Caragliu, A., Del Bo, C. & Nijkamp, P. (2011). Smart Cities in Europe. *Journal of Urban Technology,* vol. 18, no. 2, pp. 65-82, Aug. 2011.

Carmona, M. (2010a). Contemporary Public Space: Critique and Classification, Part One: Critique. *Journal of Urban Design,* 15:1, pp. 123-148, DOI:10.1080/13574800903435651

———. (2010b). Contemporary Public Space, Part Two: Classification. *Journal of Urban Design,* 15:2, pp. 157-173, DOI: 10.1080/13574801003638111

Castells, M. (1996). *The Rise of the Network Society.* Oxford, Blackwell.

Citibike (2018). Website. Retrieved from URL: https://www.citibikenyc.com/about

City of New York (2014). Vision Zero Action Plan, 2014. Retrieved from URL: http://www.nyc.gov/html/visionzero/pdf/nyc-vision-zero-action-plan.pdf

Deleuze G. (1992). Postscript on the Societies of Control. *October,* Vol. 59, pp.3-7, MIT Press.

Denning, D.E. (1996). Concerning hackers who break into computer systems. High noon on the electronic frontier. *Conceptual issues in cyberspace,* pp. 137-164.

Dodge, M. and Kitchin, R. (2001). *Mapping Cyberspace.* London: Routledge.

Eckhoff, D., Zehe, D., Ivanchev, J. & Knoll, A. (2017). Smart City-to-Vehicle—Measuring, Prediction, Influencing. *ATZelektronik worldwide,* 12(2), pp. 60-63.

Ellin, N. (1999). *Postmodern Urbanism,* rev. edn. Oxford: Blackwell.

Etta, F.E. & Elder, L. (2005). *At the crossroads: ICT policy making in East Africa.* East African Educational Publishers, IDRC.

Farrell, G. and Isaacs, S. (2007). *Survey of ICT and Education in Africa: A Summary Report, Based on 53 Country Surveys.* Washington, DC: infoDev / World Bank. Retrieved from URL: http://www.infodev.org/en/Publication.353.html

Foucault, M. (1975). *Discipline and Punish: The Birth of the Prison.* New York: Random House.

Friedman, B., Kahn, P.H., Borning, A., & Huldtgren, A. (2013). Value sensitive design and information systems. In *Early engagement and new technologies: Opening up the laboratory* (pp. 55-95). Springer, Dordrecht.

Fung, B. (2016). The Tremendous Ambitions Behind New York City's Free WiFi. 8 April 2016. *The Washington Post.*

Glaeser, E.L., Kim, H. & Luca, M. (2017). *Nowcasting the Local Economy: Using Yelp Data to Measure Economic Activity* (No. w24010). National Bureau of Economic Research.

Geist, M.A. (Ed.). (2010). *From "Radical Extremism" to" Balanced Copyright": Canadian Copyright and the Digital Agenda.* Irwin Law.

Graham, S. & Aurigi, A. (1997). Virtual cities, social polarization, and the crisis in urban public space. *Journal of Urban Technology,* 4(1), pp. 19-52.

Habermas, Jürgen (1989). *The Structural Transformation of the Public Sphere: An Inquiry into a Category of Bourgeois Society*. Thomas Burger, Cambridge Massachusetts: MIT Press

Harvey, D. (1990). *The Condition of Postmodernity*. Cambridge, MA: Blackwell.

Heilweil, R. (2018). Free WiFi kiosks in NYC coming to Philly with cameras, critics and lessons learned. The Inquirer, March 28th, 2018, Philadelphia.

Hill, D. (2015). The Street as Platform: How Digital Dynamics Shape the Physical City. *Architectural Design*, 85(4), 62-67.

Hudson Yards New York (2017). *The Smartest Park in Town*. Retrieved from URL: http://www.hudsonyardsnewyork.com/content/uploads/2017/03/Smartest-Park-20160824-Horizontal.pdf

Jacobs, J. (1961). *The Death and Life of Great American Cities*. New York: Modern Library.

Kilian, T. (1998). Public and private, power and space. In A. Light & J. M. Smith (Eds) *Philosophy and Geography II: The Production of Public Space*, pp. 115–134 (Lanham, Md: Rowman & Littlefield).

Kitchin R. and Dodge M., 2011, *Code/Space: Software and Everyday Life* (MIT Press, Cambridge MA).

Laurel, B. (1993). *Computers as Theatre*. Reading, MA: Addison-Wesley.

Lerman, K., Yan, X. & Wu, X-Z. (2016). The "Majority Illusion." In Social Networks, *PLOS One*, vol 11. Issue 2.

Lessig, L. (2006). *Code v2, New York, NY, Basic Books, retrieved from http://www.codev2.cc/download+remix/Lessig-Codev2.pdf*.

Low, S. & Smith, N. (Eds) (2006). *The Politics of Public Space*. New York, Routledge.

Mattern, S. (2014). Library as infrastructure. *Places Journal, retrieved from https://placesjournal.org/article/library-as-infrastructure/*.

———. (2017). *Code and Clay, Data and Dirt: Five Thousand Years of Urban Media*. University of Minnesota Press.

New York City Parks Department (2018). *Solar Benches*. Website. Retrieved from URL: https://www.nycgovparks.org/facilities/benches/solar

Parkinson, H. (2015). Internet of Bins: Wi-Fi to come to New York trash cans. The Guardian, 16 July 2015.

Petty, J. (2016). The London spikes controversy: Homelessness, urban securitisation and the question of 'hostile architecture'. *International Journal for Crime, Justice and Social Democracy*, 5(1), pp. 67-81.

Rapoport, A. (2002). The role of neighborhoods in the success of cities. *Ekistics*, 69(412/413/414), pp. 145-151.

Schmidt, S., Nemeth, J. & Botsford, E. (2011). The evolution of privately owned public spaces in New York City. *Urban Design International*, 16(4), pp. 270-284.

Sennett, R. (1992). *The Fall of Public Man*. New York, W.W. Norton.

Shechter L., Sharon Z. & Shmerling G. (2017), *Tel Aviv Smart City*. Retrieved from URL: https://www.tel-aviv.gov.il/en/WorkAndStudy/Documents/Tel-Aviv%20Smart%20City%20%28pdf%20booklet%29.pdf.

Stone, A. (2016). NYC's Smart Bench Pilot to Give Detailed Sense of Usage Trends in Highbridge Park. 5 August 2016, *Govtech*. Retrieved from URL: http://www.govtech.com/data/NYCs-Smart-Bench-Pilot-to-Give-Detailed-Sense-of-Usage-Trends-in-Highbridge-Park.html

Townsend, A.M. (2000). Life in the real-time city: Mobile telephones and urban metabolism. *Journal of Urban Technology*, 7(2), pp. 85-104.

———. (2013). *Smart cities: Big data, civic hackers, and the quest for a new utopia*. New York, W.W. Norton & Company.

Trindade, E.P., Hinnig, M.P.F., da Costa, E.M., Marques, J.S., Bastos, R.C. & Yigitcanlar, T. (2017). Sustainable development of smart cities: A systematic review of the literature. *Journal of Open Innovation: Technology, Market, and Complexity*, 3(1), p. 11-13.

Warschauer, M. (2004). *Technology and social inclusion: Rethinking the digital divide*. Boston, MA, MIT Press.

Whyte, W.H. (1980). *The Social Life of Small Urban Spaces*. Washington, DC. Conservation Foundation.

Wilken, R. & Goggin, G. (Eds.) (2013). *Mobile technology and place*. New York, NY, Routledge.

Woyke, E. (2017). The Startup Behind NYC's Plan to Replace Phone Booths with 7,500 Connected Kiosks. *MIT Technology Review, retrieved from* https://www.technologyreview.com/s/608281/the-startup-behind-nycs-plan-to-replace-phone-booths-with-7500-connected-kiosks/.

Zook, M., Dodge, M., Aoyama, Y. & Townsend, A. (2004). New digital geographies: Information, communication, and place. In *Geography and technology* (pp. 155-176). Springer, Dordrecht.

CHAPTER 4

Ghost Cities: Augmented Heritage

Rodrigo Cury Paraizo
Program in Urbanism
Federal University of Rio de Janeiro, Brazil
and
Marina Lima Medeiros
VRVis Zentrum für Virtual Reality und Visualisierung Forschungs
GmbH, Austria
Institute of Urbanism
Graz University of Technology, Austria

ABSTRACT

Based on examples of the authors' laboratory and from other researchers and artists' experiences, this chapter argues how the experience of urban cultural heritage through augmented reality transforms those models and images in digital spatialized ghosts. Within the theoretical framework of augmented space (Manovich, 2005) and hybrid space (Souza e Silva, 2006), the chapter focuses on augmented experiences of art and culture. The authors state that user engagement and its relation to urban augmented heritage changes our relationship with collective memory and the understanding of urban space itself, which is now understood as a medium.

Heritage practices can be defined as the management of values of heritage objects with the intention of transmission across generations. The idea of augmented heritage relates to the engagement created with the use of augmented technologies. For instance, 3D digital models of buildings or old photos can be geolocated and visualized in the context of contemporary cities through the screens of mobile devices, creating unique experiences that connect different ages in a hybrid space-time. We named "ghost architectures" buildings that persist in the memory of citizens even after they are gone – or even when they were never built in the first place but have strong influence as ideas. Augmented heritage is like those buildings, without physical space in the city but geolocated and with a place in the collective memory. Like the ghosts in *A Christmas Carol* by Charles Dickens (1843), the ghost architectures visualized in augmented reality (AR) can evoke reflections on the Past – demolished buildings – such as the Monroe Palace in Rio de Janeiro, which can be visualized through an augmented reality layer created by our lab; on the Present – showing hidden infrastructures or questioning reality, such as the case of Augmented EBA, a never-built art school pavilion that had an artistic intervention with an inauguration cocktail and an augmented reality model for visualization; or on the Yet to Come – showing future constructions, never-built architectures or utopic buildings, such as the case of the Porto Maravilha project, in which the AR experience helped researchers to understand the impact of the new urban regulation for the area. Augmented reality can also bring together buildings that were apart in space and time but have common themes and style, such as the Brazilian World Expo buildings of 1939, 1958 and 1970 that now can be part of an AR exhibition in the city of Rio de Janeiro, revealing the evolution of Modernist Brazilian Architecture. The concept of a "ghost city" represents the layer of information and memory that has always been upon cities, tacitly known by most of its inhabitants, and that now, once digitized, can be accessed – or revealed – by mobile technologies by virtually anyone, and that now can be part of image of the city.

INTRODUCTION

Mobile devices connected to the internet have effectively brought cyberspace into the public space of the city. The development of locative technologies has allowed the spatialization of information, making it specific to the user's position and reinforcing the role of the place in urban communication. The cameras in these devices aid in the opposite direction of this dialog, communicating the place with the cyberspace through images uploaded in social media.

Recent developments in devices to visualize ARs and the success of locative AR games raise questions about the possibilities of using this technology in building projects and urban designs. More than just a visualization method for professionals, the creation of urban hybrid spaces through the use of mixed-reality technologies can be used to teach architecture students, to present urban projects to the general public – increasing possibilities of participative processes of urban planning, to create interactive art installations or to visualize hidden urban infrastructure.

This chapter is based on examples of AR experiments of researchers and artists. The detailed experiments were organized by the authors and other researchers of the Laboratory of Urban Analysis and Digital Graphics of the Post-Graduation Program in Urbanism at the Federal University of Rio de Janeiro in Brazil. Since 2012, the theme has been present in our studies, and now these have been compiled and advanced in the research "Ghost Architectures: locative media experimentations in the city of Rio de Janeiro."

We focus on augmented experiences of art, architecture and culture regarding different temporalities: past, present and future. Cultural heritage practices in this research are defined as the management of values of heritage objects, which sometimes are memories of objects, with the intention of transmission across generations, and the idea of augmented heritage relates to the engagement with the visualized objects created with the use of augmented technologies. Without the possibility of being touched, but being visible to users, these objects started being named by us as digital ghosts, and we have explored the terminology ever since and started analyzing the interactions of users with the visualized objects from this perspective.

The objective of our studies is to explore AR as a media for urban understanding and to study ways of interaction with urban space mediated by digital locative technologies. Instead of developing new software or hardware, we focus our experimentations on low-cost options, usually exploring open-source or free apps already on the market and using smartphones for visualization, making it easy and affordable to our students or other citizens to replicate our steps. This solution is not as intuitive as head-mounted displays or transparent, as proposed by Murray (2011: 9-10); it requires more engagement from the user, who needs to install an application on a tablet or smartphone and walk around looking for the object to fit in their small screen. However, one of the benefits of this solution is that, after this first engagement, the user is already predisposed to interact with the object and to participate in the experiment in a more intense and less casual way.

THE CITY AS INTERFACE

In 1996, the visitors to the "Artifices" art festival of Saint-Denis in France saw a digital ghost sculpture. In a room, there was a white pedestal, and a portable screen leaning on a table next to the pedestal. The empty pedestal, when viewed through the screen, presented a statue of a calf on it; when walking around the pedestal, with the screen in hand, it was possible to see the statue from other angles. This was the installation "The golden calf" by the artist Jeffrey Shaw. In the screen display, in addition to the golden calf, the pedestal and its surroundings were also depicted as electronic models that mimicked the physical space of the showroom, and there was no camera in the back of the device to create a see-through effect in the screen. Shaw's work foreshadowed in many ways the relations of modern-day users and mobile devices, especially the hybrid spatiality created by overlapping specialized digital information to the tangible experience of the physical world.

More specifically, the installation dealt with the spatiality created by portable devices, raising an awareness of the digital layer of information that surrounds us, influencing the material world and our perceptions about it, and at the same time warning us that we may be idolizing false gods in empty vessels, replacing our own sense of reality by media, as pointed out by Lévy (1999: 45-46). Nevertheless, portable computing is a reality in the form of personal objects of both residents and visitors in most contemporary cities, with full-time connection to the internet renewing the flow of information available to a person's fingertips. More than that, embedded geo-location technology in these devices helps make this information location-aware; that is, available, promoted or demoted according to the user's geographical position, in addition to the usual territorial informational fences created by each country's legislation. When only fixed desktop screens were available, we already had the notion of a digital space; mobile portable screens added not only more opportunities to access this space, they helped develop the notion of a digital space mapped to the physical one.

Shaw's work provokes yet another reflection: it is the physical pedestal that shows the importance of the object to be visualized. The presence of the object is only noticed with the use of the interface, but it is the physical space destined for the virtual golden calf that indicates the importance of what will be observed. Therefore, it is necessary to question the relation of importance between environment and virtual object in cases of AR.

Mitchell (2005: 3) emphasizes that all communication is intrinsically related to its context. The city – and the specific space in it where the interaction takes place – is not a mute, neutral background but the very context that provides meaning for the information depicted. Moreover, in AR, the city is also the interface to the location of this information. Martjin de Waal states that the social construction of the city already configures it as an interface (2014: 7). Adriana de Sousa e Silva (2006) argues that the social construction of internet communication and the access to internet through mobile interfaces create hybrid spaces formed by the convergence of three distinct overlapping spaces: connected spaces, mobile spaces and social spaces (261). For de Sousa e Silva, this phenomenon happens because, with mobile devices, there is not the feeling of "entering" the internet; physical and digital spaces are perceived as one (2006: 263).

Manovich shifts the attention from the device and the application to the space in which the user is. With the advent of new media, navigable space becomes a media (2001: 251-252) and "augmented space" is defined as the "overlaying dynamic data over the physical space," usually in the multimedia format, localized and personalized (Manovich, 2005: 4). This factor brings a new paradox in urban communication: when space is media and the city provides context for data, place becomes increasingly more important as a value in itself; thus, making it more costly, in symbolic terms, to change the location of information.

AUGMENTED HERITAGE

Heritage is a modern development of the concept of the monument. This latter concept is found in various cultures, modern and ancient, while the former finds its origins in the 17th century (Choay, 2001). In both cases, the concepts relate to objects from the past that witness human permanence (and paradoxically our finitude) over time. Heritage, however, is also the management of these objects, both in the sense of preservation and, more subtly, in the attribution of contemporary values to them, as inferred from Riegl (1984), that is, their actualization – in opposition to the field of possibilities that characterizes the virtual (Lévy, 1996). Virtual heritage refers to digitally based heritage interpretive environments and the techniques used to create them (Refsland et al., 2000) to "record, model and visualize cultural and natural heritage" (Addison, 2006: 36).

Heritage deals with objects that bear witness to the past, to which values are attributed according to present perceptions and needs. Therefore, heritage object management deals not only with physical preservation, but also (and more importantly) with meaning to the present generations (Lynch, 1972). Heritage is the embodiment of values to a specific society.

Furthermore, heritage deals with the emotional responses that must be triggered by the presence of the object – or even in its absence, but in any case, the multiple connections people associate with the object either by learning or first-hand experience. Heritage must be experienced, and its religious roots are still present to some extent in present practices, bearing witness to our presence in the world despite our own finitude (Choay, 2001). Heritage can be described, and its narratives formally learned, but to raise awareness it must be part of someone's experiences, it must show the viewer something about himself or herself and the world he or she belongs to (Malpas, 2006). The aim of heritage is to form a collective framework for identity in the present.

Virtual (or digital, as it is also called) heritage works very much like MacCannell's (1999: 109-133) analysis of tourist activity in terms of Piercian semiotics: the marker, the sight and the tourist – where interpretive environments act as markers of the sights for the visitors. The layer of information provided is one of the very indications of the heritage status the object possesses.

Heritage space is characterized by the actions that take place in it, by those that may or have taken place in it, and also, to an extent, by those that cannot take place in it. Appropriate behavior – and the corresponding forbidden attitudes – are learned by example and by experiencing a culture from the inside, with rewards for following the appropriate patterns and denials when transgressing them. A set of mutually agreed regulations, written or not, constitutes the element of transformation of space, and becomes inscribed in the user's body. Heritage space representation, therefore, must take this into account, for appropriate behavior is part of the emotional setup for heritage values transmission. In our AR exploits here described, this induced behavior was so far limited to the setup of the user experience, the very instructions to access the works – but of course there are many other possibilities to be explored.

According to Azuma (1997: 356), the definition of an AR system (which we adopt in this chapter) is "1. Combines real and virtual, 2. Is interactive in real time, 3. Is registered in three dimensions." Regarding AR, the surrounding space is usually included in the representation automatically by means of the device camera. Immersion, in AR, is better described in terms of psychological immersion than perceptual immersion (McMahan, 2003), that is, the manipulation of the representational device instead of the suppression of one spatial system by another. It is also worth noting that current technologies, from non-standard apps to intermittent and sometimes imprecise GPS signals, imply that the user should actively search for something. This willingness to participate and experiment with the app means the user is more prone to engagement with the heritage object represented, but also that he or she is more aware of the representational device. The need to be at a specific location to obtain access to that information helps enhance the aura of the place – and that of the heritage object. This willingness implies also some level of body engagement with the surroundings; thus, dealing with issues of presence in terms of heritage values. It also means that the user has to perform a very specific, ergodic – non-trivial effort, as described by Aarseth (1997) – gestures to be able – perhaps to be worthy of it – to access the digital content.

GHOST ARCHITECTURES

In many cultures around the world, ghosts are spirits of dead people or animals that visit the physical world haunting or amazing the living. The presence of ghosts can be felt or seen but they cannot be touched, they are spatialized but not materialized. They do not necessarily come from the past, they can come from the future or even be from the present, but they run through time as they wish. In several folklore tales, ghosts represent ideas and feelings for the ones they visit, reminding them of problems from the past, raising hidden questions for the present or showing possibilities of alternative futures.

Cities are also made of collective memories and questions regarding their buildings or public spaces. We named "ghost architectures" buildings that persist in the memory of citizens even after they are gone – or even when they were never built in the first place but have strong influence as ideas. Augmented heritage is a way to access those buildings and the values they stand for in the construction of collective memory.

Like the ghosts in Charles Dickens' *A Christmas Carol* (1843), the ghost architectures visualized in AR can evoke reflections on the Past – demolished buildings; on the Present – showing hidden infrastructures or revealing cultural artifacts; and on what is Yet to Come – showing future constructions, never-built architectures or utopic buildings.

Ghosts of Cities Past

Throughout previous decades, architects and archeologists have developed graphic solutions to represent buildings or urban areas that have vanished in time. These solutions can be simple plans drawn in the floor showing where old churches used to be, such as the Maria-Magdalena-Kapelle and Virgilkapelle close to Vienna's cathedral; or, these solutions may be more complicated devices, such as the Ename 974 AR virtual heritage project (Pletinckx et al., 2000). This project involves a kiosk located next to the archeological excavations of the Ename Abbey where digital models of several hypothetical stages of development of the building were projected in the glass facing the ruins in such a way that visitors could see these images superimposed on the excavated foundations of the abbey. Another example is the AR visualization of a 3D model of the Berlin Wall in its original place, as organized by Gardeya (Spiegel, 2010). The observation of past events is also the proposal of HistoryPin (HistoryPin, 2017), which, through the geolocation in maps and the visualization of historical photos in the places where they were taken, seeks to create a global digital history through photographs.

Our first experiment in AR was with the Monroe Palace. Built in 1904, the palace was awarded the best foreign pavilion in the Louisiana Purchase Exposition, and later disassembled and rebuilt in 1906 in the city center of Rio de Janeiro, in an area known as Cinelândia. The building had several public functions over the years, and was, from 1925 to 1960, the Federal Senate of Brazil. After Brazilian federal capital was transferred to the city of Brasília in 1960, the building heavily underused and was practically abandoned. The building was scheduled for demolition for the expansion of the metro system, but public opinion changed the original plans. Nevertheless, the building was later demolished in 1976 by presidential order with no further explanations (Atique, 2011). Since then, the Monroe Palace has remained in the memory of the citizens of Rio de Janeiro and some suggestions to rebuild the palace occasionally appear.

As the Palace still has a relatively strong presence in the memories of many inhabitants of Rio despite its physical absence, we chose it for the experiment of developing an augmented marker (in the sense used by MacCannell, 1999) that could help trigger the many narratives about the building. The idea was that we could create the effect of the presence of the object (Lowenthal, 2005) – or, in this case, the presence of its surroundings for visitors. As the Cinelândia area is legally protected as cultural heritage of the city of Rio de Janeiro, the former surroundings of the palace remain preserved as they were when the palace was demolished, so it was be possible to visualize the 3D model in AR in real scale in its former location (Figure 1).

Figure 1: Photo montage of the Monroe Palace in Cinelândia current situation in 2003.

Source: Rodrigo Paraizo / LAURD-PROURB-FAU-UFRJ

The experiments with the Monroe Palace in AR were conducted in 2013 and 2014 (Medeiros, 2014). The Layar (Blippar, 2018) platform was chosen as the basis for the tests because it allows the creation of georeferenced augmentations with 3D models. The first test located a simpler version of the palace in the middle of Rodrigo de Freitas lagoon. Being a flat, open, and easily accessible surface, it was possible to have unobstructed views from several directions, as shown in Figure 2. Then, we moved the model to the original coordinates of the Monroe Palace in the city center of Rio de Janeiro. It was possible to view the entire building on the smartphone screen from a distance of approximately 100m from the georeferenced point of the model. The model, at times, seemed to be floating, something that was already expected, since the Layar application did not recognize differences of altitude, locating the model in the same horizontal plane of the observer. However, using the widespread mobile technology in 2014, the test showed that it is possible to have a sense of the scale and presence that the building once had in its surroundings, as shown in Figures 3 and 4.

Figure 2: Screenshot of Layar app with Monroe Palace 3D model geolocated in Lagoon Rodrigo de Freitas, Rio de Janeiro.

Source: Marina Lima Medeiros / LAURD-PROURB-FAU-UFRJ

Figure 3: Screenshot of Layar app with Monroe Palace 3D model geolocated in Cinelândia, Rio de Janeiro.

Source: Marina Lima Medeiros / LAURD-PROURB-FAU-UFRJ

Figure 4: Screenshot of Layar app with Monroe Palace 3D model geolocated in Cinelândia, Rio de Janeiro.

Source: Marina Lima Medeiros / LAURD-PROURB-FAU-UFRJ

We later decided to explore these reflections about the past by studying modern Brazilian pavilions of universal exhibitions – coincidentally, the Monroe Palace was in two world expos, in 1904 in Saint Louis and in 1922 in Rio de Janeiro. According to Pereira (2011: 7-8), the first universal exhibitions were built as efficient tools for educating the urban masses to the urban way of life, and the national pavilions were designed to summarize the culture of the countries. In the Brazilian case, the pavilions have also influenced the evolution of the country's architectural culture. We chose the 1939 pavilion for New York, by Lucio Costa an Oscar Niemeyer (Figure 5); the 1958 pavilion for Brussels, by Sergio Bernardes (Figure 6); and the 1970 pavilion for Osaka by Paulo Mendes da Rocha (Figure 7); all the architects are acclaimed master designers that influenced generations of Brazilian (and foreign) architects.

Figure 5: 3D digital reconstruction based on drawings and images of the Brazilian pavilion for the 1939 New York World Expo designed by the architects Lúcio Costa and Oscar Niemeyer.

Source: LAURD-PROURB-FAU-UFRJ

Figure 6: 3D digital reconstruction based on drawings and images of the Brazilian pavilion for the 1958 Brussels World Expo designed by Sérgio Bernardes.

Source: LAURD-PROURB-FAU-UFRJ

Figure 7: 3D digital reconstruction based on drawings and images of the Brazilian pavilion for the 1970 Osaka World Expo designed by Paulo Mendes da Rocha.

Source: LAURD-PROURB-FAU-UFRJ

Our goal was to explore AR as an educational tool, creating an exhibition of Brazilian pavilions from modern architects. In the case of Brazilian pavilions, the simultaneous presence of the three models has the primary purpose of comparing buildings hitherto separated in time and space for pedagogical matters (Figure 8). The technology employed draws attention to the ephemeral nature of the exhibitions. Furthermore, the contextual displacement of the buildings can reduce the understanding of the buildings seen alone, but allows us to compare their scales and obtain a synthetic reading of the Brazilian participation in world expos throughout that time.

Figure 8: Concept image depicting the visualization of the Brazilian pavilion of the Brussels World Expo in AR in the Federal University of Rio de Janeiro campus.

Source: LAURD-PROURB-FAU-UFRJ

The results of the experiments with the Monroe Palace and the Brazilian World Expo pavilions reveal that AR can be an instrument for discussing virtual heritage. In the case of the Monroe Palace, since the surroundings of the building were preserved from major changes, the visualization through the smartphone screen was a glimpse of the past, but limited since the small dimensions of the screen give the sensation of looking through a key hole, but at the same time ravishing for the understanding of the impact of the building on the landscape. For the Brazilian World Expo pavilions, the AR experience brought a comprehension that time-space in AR is not fixed and that it is possible to have a different World Expo with digital pavilions. This effect could be used in ludic ways to explore collective memories, enhancing the city image by creating augmented layers to be visualized by citizens and tourists.

Ghosts of Cities Present

Like a lens – or perhaps a modern-day dowsing rod – AR-enabled devices reveal information to the user. This feature can be used to help the user navigate through the city, to find subway stations or to assist in the maintenance of buildings and cities by revealing hidden infrastructures. The opposite may also happen, with users placing and "hiding" information that can only be found by other users with the same apps. This new form of communication is what happens with social media applications such as Skrite (Skrite Labs Inc, 2018) and WallaMe (WallaMe Ltd, 2018), which allow the user to spread geolocated messages, spatializing them in the streets or up in the sky. Urban arts can use AR to layer art over art, such as the Re+public app (Seiler, 2013), which shows animated and interactive 3D digital art over murals and graffiti, or the manifestAR action "We AR in MOMA," in which artists used AR to cover the paintings displayed in the museum with their own works.

This action of looking for the information can also be used to engage the user in performative arts, as in the case of the Augmented EBA, an art happening to which our laboratory contributed with the development of an AR experience. The acronym EBA stands for, in Portuguese, *Escola de Belas Artes*, which is the School of Fine Arts of the Federal University of Rio de Janeiro, which has changed location from different buildings during its history. The first building was designed by the French architect Grandjean de Montigny and was one of the first buildings in Brazil to be built with neoclassical aesthetics, but was demolished in 1938 (Pereira, 2008). Having been moved around public buildings in the city of Rio de Janeiro, EBA was finally installed in 1975 in a modernist construction designed by the Brazilian architect Jorge Machado Moreira – awarded Best Public Building in the Architecture Awards at the IV São Paulo Architecture Biennial of 1957. The building was originally designed to host only the Faculty of Architecture and Urbanism of the Federal University of Rio de Janeiro, but ended up hosting this faculty, the EBA and the University Rector's Office. To improve the facilities for EBA, the director of the school and the rector of the university planned an expansion for the building, with new rooms for ateliers, new laboratories and classrooms (da Luz, 2014), as shown in Figure 9. The company responsible for the projects and the construction of the building was chosen by public bidding in 2010. The construction began at the end of 2010 and should have lasted for one year. However, in 2011, irregularities were found in the bidding process and, since then, construction has been stopped.

Figure 9: 3D simulation of the Fine Arts School annex building in the campus of the Federal University of Rio de Janeiro.

Source: LAURD-PROURB-FAU-UFRJ

On 24th of November 2014, the completely virtual annex building of the School of Fine Arts of Federal University of Rio de Janeiro (EBA) was inaugurated, as a form of protest for the delay – and current abandon – in its construction. Professors and students from the course History of Computer Graphics and New Media of EBA promoted a happening in the form of a phony inauguration ceremony for the building, as if it were there, complete with speech, plaque, pulpit, cocktail party, documentation, ribbon cutting, formal invitation, as well as a website and a Facebook event. The building existed only through its representations (Figure 10).

Figure 10: Screenshot of Layar app with the 3D model of the annex building geolocated in the campus of the Federal University of Rio de Janeiro.

Source: LAURD-PROURB-FAU-UFRJ

Our laboratory worked with students from the Digital Modeling in Architecture course from the Faculty of Architecture and Urbanism to represent the building using AR. The project Augmented EBA proposed to investigate the possibilities of "other" realities, having as a starting point the lack of definition of the annex building. The Augmented EBA created the opportunity to put the question of construction of the building in a way that was both playful and political; showing the potential of AR to deal with matters of the present time in more than a functional way. The experiment also showed how the engagement with the AR system does not rely on high-tech devices but on the narrative and the poetics of the augmented space.

Ghosts of Cities Yet to Come

Augmented reality is already being used to present designs to private clients, usually in the form of digital scale models. However, this use can be extended to real scale models, placed in their future urban location, for clients and regular citizens to see and evaluate the relation of the design to its surroundings. One of the advantages of this approach is that many elements of the place are added to the perception of the design, such as temperature, winds, noise from the streets or street animation. To evaluate the type of assessment the general public could have for an urban project viewed in localized AR, we decided to visualize the Porto Maravilha project for the harbor area of Rio de Janeiro in AR.

The harbor of the city of Rio de Janeiro is a combination of natural hills and landfills built over the sea that have been added over the centuries. In this area, there are remnants of the historical evolution and social transformations that the city experienced from the Colonial Period to the current configuration of Rio de Janeiro as a metropolis. Today, with the development of industrial port activities and the use of cargo containers, there are several unoccupied warehouses and building lands in the region, as well as a large portion of state-owned land. Aiming to requalify its old industrial zones in downtown, the Municipality of Rio de Janeiro launched the "Porto Maravilha" Urban Operation in 2009.

The project is remarkable for its large size – five million square meters of area for urban renovation. City Hall decided make a consortium with private investors; a new urban legislation specific for that area allowed investors to pay to increase the maximum height for their buildings – raising limits from 60m to 150m, in some cases – and that money was used to finance infrastructure improvements in the area. Those new urban parameters will change the morphology of the area, now mostly composed of warehouses and small buildings.

The information about where and how the building heights would be affected was scattered through tables and maps, making it very difficult to figure out what the proposed new morphology of the neighborhood was. A 3D simulation or even 2D renderings could stimulate a more qualified discussion with the population about the project. Therefore, we decided to elaborate 3D models and section cuts of the proposed morphology and to verify our perception of these models in geolocated AR to understand *in loco* how the urban environment would change.

Using some of the new urban legislation parameters, such as new maximum height, new maximum built area and the setbacks, we modeled a few generic mass models of the future buildings if every one of them were built. We modeled these maximum envelopes as generic buildings in every plot available for transformation in the area. While other variables may influence urban morphology, we decided that these masses would be useful to understand the consequences of the proposed urban legislation. In addition, it is indeed one of the possible outcomes of the project, as shown in Figures 11 and 12.

Figure 11: 3D model of the current situation of Porto Maravilha's area in 2013.

Source: Marina Lima Medeiros / LAURD-PROURB-FAU-UFRJ

Figure 12: 3D model simulating new urban parameters for permitted maximum height, permitted maximum built area and setbacks proposed to Porto Maravilha's area.

Source: Marina Lima Medeiros / LAURD-PROURB-FAU-UFRJ

The process to organize the AR of Porto Maravilha was similar to the process of the experience with the Monroe Palace. At the end of 2013 and beginning of 2014, we created a geolocated layer in the Layar (Blippar, 2018) website for the Porto Maravilha tests. The major difference between the two projects was the number of points of interest (POI) created. In the case of the Monroe Palace, as a single building, only one POI was created. Since it is a simulation of an urban area with several buildings, it was necessary to create several POI for the Porto Maravilha layer. The towers were divided into groups according to the location and height, and each group was a different POI.

Figure 13: Screenshot of Layar app with 3D models of skyscrapers geolocated in Porto Maravilha's area.

Source: Marina Lima Medeiros / LAURD-PROURB-FAU-UFRJ

This approach helped to upload on the screen only the models that were close to the user, avoiding errors and poor real-time rendering. The results were not as good as the results with the previous experimentations, with only one 3D object to be seen. In the Porto Maravilha visualization, it is clear that the models of the buildings were not aligned to the street as they were supposed to be, and the scale of the volumes made this error even more perceptible, as shown in Figures 13 and 14. However, even with the errors, it was possible to realize the great impact that the new buildings will create in the morphology of the region. It is not possible to truly grasp the space that will result after the project is fully implemented, but being at the site to conduct the tests brought another impression of the place and the project. The degradation of the surroundings of Francisco Bicalho Avenue and the strong smell of canal sewage in the center of the avenue were a constant nuisance during the tests, a fact that allows a questioning of whether only building luxury towers will be able to create a true requalification of that space.

Figure 14: Screenshot of Layar app with 3D models of skyscrapers with textured façades geolocated in Porto Maravilha's area.

Source: Marina Lima Medeiros / LAURD-PROURB-FAU-UFRJ

In this experiment, the importance of the place in AR experiences stands out. Looking to the simulations in the virtual environment of the 3D modeler software, the impact of the Porto Maravilha project in the area was already clear; but, with the visualization in AR, other senses have a strong impact on the experience of the hybrid urban space. The weather conditions, the smell and the noise of the surroundings also impact the user's understanding of the project, making the AR with smartphone screen an excellent option to understand the relations of the proposed design with its surroundings.

CONCLUSION

A ghost city can be a collection of augmented heritage experiences in which location – and therefore place – becomes media itself, and it is part of the message. This layer of information and memory has always been upon cities, tacitly known by most of its inhabitants, and that now, once digitized, can be accessed – or revealed – by mobile technologies, by virtually anyone. This new medium of space – as pointed out by Manovich (2001: 251-252) – is starting to affect urban practices. On the one hand, we have locative media as part of our routines, creating another layer of meaning and information over cities and fostering urban images. On the other hand, applications in virtual reality and AR have been actively exploring the creation of highly immersive digital environments that may not discard the relevance of actual places, but – notably by force of networked distribution – certainly lead us to rethink what constitutes those places.

Although digital technologies tend to develop at impressive rates, the current state of commercially available AR is worth noting not only because of its achievements so far, but also because of its flaws and glitches, for they are also unexpected opportunities to reflect on the paths of development we want for these technologies. Currently, AR apps are not readily available in mobile devices – as are, for instance, email or instant messaging apps – that is, they are not part of the common core of a user's mobile software. Whenever AR apps reach this common status – with push warnings of locative content in the vicinities, for instance – that would mean the user's location is being constantly informed to yet another server, with all the concerns regarding data sharing and management that accompany this. Nevertheless, we could ask whether seamless AR viewing would reinforce or banalize heritage values transmission compared with our current situation.

There are other questions raised during the experience of this hybrid space of ghost cities: Who has the rights on a geolocation? Is the owner of a property also the owner of its digital coordinates? Some awkward situations have already happened with the popular game *Pokemon Go* (Niantic Inc., 2016); the game developers were asked to remove the location of the avatars from religious places. Will people allow developers to have any kind of message "posted" in front of their houses? Is it possible to make an augmented graffiti of protest with AR apps? Will the wall of your property be like a personalized wall of your social media profile? What will we see in public spaces? As social spaces, will they be filled with advertisements, like email boxes and websites? Or, will such spaces be augmented with ghost architectures that can enhance the collective memory about their heritage and be part of the image of the city?

REFERENCES

Aarseth EJ (1997) *Cybertext*. Baltimore / Londres: The Johns Hopkins University Press.

Addison AC (2006) "The vanishing virtual: safeguarding heritage's endangered digital record". In: *New Heritage: beyond verisimilitude* (eds T Kvan and Y Kalay), Hong Kong, 2006, pp. 36–48. Faculty of Architecture Univ. of Hong Kong.

Atique F (2011) O Patrimônio (Oficialmente) "Rejeitado: A destruição do palácio Monroe e suas repercussões no ambiente preservacionista carioca". In: *XXVI Simpósio Nacional de História ANPUH*, São Paulo, 2011, p. 14.

Azuma RT (1997) "A Survey of Augmented Reality". *Presence*.

Caudell TP and Mizell DW (1992) "Augmented reality: an application of heads-up display technology to manual manufacturing processes". In: *Proceedings of the Twenty-Fifth Hawaii International Conference on System Sciences*, January 1992, pp. 659–669 vol.2. doi: 10.1109/HICSS.1992.183317..

Choay F (2001) *A alegoria do patrimônio*. São Paulo: Unesp.

Cush A (2013) "Augmented Reality App Resurrects Every Bowery Wall Mural". In: *ANIMAL*. Available at: http://animalnewyork.com/2013/augmented-reality-app-resurrects-every-bowery-wall-mural/ (accessed 30 June 2018).

de Souza e Silva A (2006) "From Cyber to Hybrid Mobile Technologies as Interfaces of Hybrid Spaces". *Space and Culture* 9(3): 261–278. DOI: 10.1177/1206331206289022.

de Waal M (2014) *The City as Interface How New Media Are Changing the City*. NAI010 Publishers.

Dickens C (1843) *A Christmas Carol a Ghost Story of Christmas*. London: Chapman & Hall.

Flynn B (2007) "The Morphology of Space in Virtual Heritage". In: Cameron F and Kenderdine S (eds) *Theorizing Digital Cultural Heritage: A Critical Discourse*. Cambridge: The MIT Press, pp. 349–368.

HistoryPin (2017) *HistoryPin*. Available at: https://about.historypin.org/.

Layar (2018) Amsterdam: Blippar. Available at: https://www.layar.com/ (accessed 30 August 2018).

Lévy P (1996) *O que é o virtual?* São Paulo: 34.

———— (1999) *Cibercultura*. São Paulo: 34.

Lowenthal D (2005) *The Past is a Foreign Country*. Cambridge: Cambridge University Press.

Lynch K (1972) *What time is this place?* Cambridge, Massachusetts: MIT Press.

MacCannell D (1999) *The Tourist: a new theory of the leisure class*. Berkeley / Los Angeles: University of California.

Malpas J (2006) "Cultural Heritage in The Age of New Media". In: *New Heritage: beyond verisimilitude* (eds T Kvan and Y Kalay), Hong Kong, 2006, pp. 167–181. Faculty of Architecture Univ. of Hong Kong.

Manovich L (2001) *The Language of New Media*. Cambridge: MIT Press.

———— (2005) "The Poetics of Augmented Space: Learning from Prada". *Visual Communication*.

McMahan A (2003) "Immersion, Engagement and Presence: a method for analyzing 3-D video games". In: Wolf MJP and Perron B (eds) *The Video Game Theory Reader*. Nova York/ Londres: Routledge, pp. 67–86.

Mitchell WJ (2005) *Placing words: symbols, space, and the city*. Cambridge, Mass.: MIT Press.

Murray JH (2011) *Inventing the Medium: Principles of Interaction Design as a Cultural Practice*. 1st edition. Cambridge, Mass: The MIT Press.

Pereira MAC da S (2011) "A Exposição de 1808 ou O Brasil Visto por Dentro". *ARQTEXTO* 16: 6–27.

Pereira SG (2008) A Escola Real de Ciência, Artes e Ofícios e a Academia Imperial de Belas Artes do Rio de Janeiro. In: Ipanema RM de (ed.) *D. João e a cidade do Rio de Janeiro*. Rio de Janeiro: Instituto Histórico e Geográfico do Rio de Janeiro, pp. 383–390.

Pletinckx D, Callebaut D, Killebrew AE, et al. (2000) "Virtual-reality heritage presentation at Ename". *IEEE MULTIMEDIA* 7(2): 45–48. DOI: http://doi.ieeecomputersociety.org/10.1109/93.848427.

Pokemon Go (2016) Niantic, Inc. Available at: http://pokemongo.nianticlabs.com/en/.

Re+Public (2013) The Heavy Projects. Available at: https://www.heavy.io/ (accessed 30 August 2018).

Refsland ST, Ojika T, Addison AC, et al. (2000) "Virtual Heritage: Breathing new life into our ancient past". *IEEE Multimedia* 7(2) : 20–21. DOI : 10.1109/MMUL.2000.848420.

Riegl A (1984) *Le culte moderne des monuments : son essence et sa genèse*. Paris : Éditions du Seuil.

Skrite Social Sky Messages (2018) Skrite Labs Inc. Available at : https://www.skrite.com/ (accessed 30 August 2018).

Spiegel (2010) When Science Fiction Becomes Reality: Rebuilding the Berlin Wall with Augmented Reality. 6 July. Available at: http://www.spiegel.de/international/spiegel/when-science-fiction-becomes-reality-rebuilding-the-berlin-wall-with-augmented-reality-a-704970.html (accessed 30 August 2018).

WallaMe Augmented Reality (2018) Wallame Ltd. Available at: http://walla.me/

CHAPTER 5

Anonymous City, Anonymous Talking: Sarahah

Dr. Surhita Basu
Women's College, Calcutta
University of Calcutta, India

ABSTRACT

In January 2018, Katrina Collins from Australia started an online petition titled *Ban apps like Sarahah where my daughter was told to "KILL HERSELF."* Within a month, Google and Apple had to remove the Sarahah app from their stores. With more than 300 million users worldwide, the app was viral in many cities of India since mid-2017. After its removal, Stulish, a similar app, went viral in India in May 2018. This paper explores this intriguing repetitive popularity of anonymous messaging apps in the background of a growing phenomenon of urban isolation and anonymity, particularly in a city such as Kolkata that has its own rich tradition of community living or *para* culture and strong bonding over regular casual conversations or *adda*. With a pilot survey and in-depth interviews with 15 Sarahah app users based in Kolkata, this paper identifies different layers of urban and virtual anonymity, their interaction with each other, different dimensions of experiences of using the app, the nature of virtual familiar strangers, strong evidence for the online disinhibition effect, and the triadic relation between communicative freedom, sense of control and sense of insecurity in urban and virtual communication.

INTRODUCTION

Kolkata, the city of joy, was the capital of India under the British colony. This third-most populous metropolitan area of India (Demographia, 2018), now the state capital of West Bengal, thrives with its rich cultural heritage, strong colonial influence and identity conflicts spreading over space and time (Roy, 2010). The intellectual history of urban space originated from a sense of loss in the conflict between *Gemeinschaft* and *Gesellschaft* (Tonnies, 2001). Traditional theories of urban space and place identified this alienation more between the communities than within (Putnam, 2000). After the Second World War, theories of urban living placed higher emphasis on economic activities as cities became the center of consumption (Castells, 1977).

Gradually, theories on urban cultural transformation (Zukin, 1982; 1995) came to the forefront. Into this neo-Marxist evaluation of urban living was added the ICT revolution that launched the network society (Castells, 2010).

Digital communication has given into the hands of this alienated faceless society (Klinberg, 2015) the power of virtuality. The urban anonymous identity has crept into the virtual world, transcending the city landscape. Early studies on anonymous communication (e.g. Zimbardo, 1969) revealed the tendency of aggressive violence under the shield of anonymity. Previous researchers on online anonymous communication (Kling, Lee, Teich, & Frankel, 1999) and anonymous messaging apps such as Whisper, Secret and Yik Yak established concepts such as the online disinhibition effect (Suler, 2004) and anonymity sensitivity (Correa, Silva, Mondal, Benevenuto, & Gummadi, 2015). This virtual transformation of urban anonymity has traversed a long journey from Milgram's (1972) concept of *familiar strangers* to Schwartz's (2013) concept of *networked familiar strangers*. Into this dynamic composite was launched an online anonymous messaging platform, Sarahah, in November 2016 (Bell, 2017).

With more than 300 million users worldwide, Sarahah went viral in many cities of India by mid-2017 (Saha, 2017). However, in January 2018, Katrina Collins from Australia began an online petition titled *Ban apps like Sarahah where my daughter was told to "KILL HERSELF"* (Collins, 2018). Within a month, the petition attracted4, 69, 640 supporters, leading Google and Apple to remove the Sarahah app from their stores (Cassin, 2018). Interestingly, as the fad for Sarahah faded, in May 2018 Stulish, a similar app, went viral in India (Navbharat Times, 2018). This replacement of one app with another prompted the need to explore the nature and cause behind this repetitive popularity of virtual, anonymous communication in a developing nation and particularly in a city such as Kolkata that has its own distinct culture of *adda* (Chakrabarty, 1999; Chakravarty, 2017) or casual conversations. This present study explores anonymity as increasing urban reality in which virtuality becomes an extension of the existing phenomenon.

Method

An online pilot survey with convenient snowball sampling (Wimmer & Dominick, 2010) was conducted between May and July 2018 among Sarahah app users based in Kolkata to design the interview questionnaire and to identify potential interviewees. The objective of the pilot survey was to identify app users with different levels of exposure and with different ranges of opinions for or against the app. Seventeen questions in the pilot survey aimed to understand the frequency and purpose of the app usage in addition to users' opinion on the utility, applicability, importance and benefits of the app. The survey questionnaire includes a question on rating the app based on usage experience on a scale from 0 to 10, in addition to six opinion-based statements with response options ranging from strongly agreeing to strongly disagreeing with those statements. While selecting the sample for the interview, the survey respondents selected were those who were consistently positive or negative in their opinion toward the app over different questions. Furthermore, the respondents who were either strongly agreeing or agreeing, or strongly disagreeing or disagreeing with the statements were chosen. This approach ensured having those respondents in the interview sample who either had strong positive or strong negative opinions toward the app, enabling the researcher to gather valuable experiences and opinions during the course of the interviews. Thus, based on the extensiveness of app usage and intensity of opinion for or against the app, 15 survey respondents were selected for the interviews (Kvale, 1996), which were conducted between June and August 2018 with an average duration of an hour. The interview questions aimed to understand the interviewees' social and communicative backgrounds, their behavioral patterns of social media and app usage, and their opinions on various aspects of the app and, particularly, on anonymous communication. In the following section, fictitious names are used for the interviewees to protect their identities.

Findings

The number of collected responses from the pilot survey was 80. Out of 15 interviewees aged between 13 and 47 years old, 10 were female and five were male. The mean age of the interviewees was 28 years old. There were eight students ranging from eighth standard school to a master's degree program, in addition to seven working professionals. Out of the 15 participants, 13 grew up in a joint family setup. Six of the interviewees lived in old Kolkata or the northern part of city, two lived in the comparatively newly developed southern part, one lived in the old central part, one lived in the newly extended eastern part, and four lived in suburban Kolkata. Thematic analysis of the interviews offered the following diverse perspectives on urban and virtual living and communication.

"There Are Those 'Other' People in Our Neighborhood'

Kolkata still carries certain elements of community living, with resonances of the world of *Gemeinschaft* and the concept of *para* (Choudhury, 2017), or "neighborhood," has been integral to the city's identity. The word *para* in Bengali not only conveys the sense of a physical space, but also a sense of culture, a sense of bonding, a sense of security and a sense of community living among few families of a particular lane. However, the eastern metropolitan developments are incorporating a new cityscape where the concept of *para* is almost obsolete. One of the interviewees, Deep (personal communication, August 20, 2018), who lives in one such new locality of eastern Kolkata, Saltlake, stated, "There is no *para* in Saltlake. I don't know who live in the building opposite to mine. In a traditional *para,* if someone is sick, all people of that *para* will come to help; but in Saltlake, even if someone dies, others will come to know only when the body is brought out."Interestingly, in the same city, there still exists that traditional *para*. Sima (personal communication, June 13, 2018), who lives in north Kolkata, said, "In other areas, neighbors chat only during local festivals; but in our *para* it is the opposite. We not only know each other, but we know each other very well." However, she simultaneously pointed out a conflicting coexistence of two groups in that same *para*. Sima (personal communication, June 13, 2018) said, with much hesitation:

> In the same area lives a group of migrant laborers. We usually study in the evenings. But they play cheap movie songs loudly and chat loudly just outside our houses at that time. They are also quite dirty. They put cow-dung on their walls (for making dry cow-dung cakes to be used as cooking fuel), their children play on the streets, eating soil – it is like a slum area just beside our house. …There is also a conflict in arranging any festival in our para nowadays. If we want traditional music to play during our festivals, they will arrange a DJ night… However, if anyone gets into any trouble, then everyone, even those people will come to help.

This aspect of categorization and demarcation among the co-existing inhabitants of the same *para* highlights an interesting dimension of the cultural clash in urban localities (Chen, Orum, & Paulsen, 2013), the resulting avoidance of communicative norms, dissociation from the community and the rise of anonymity even in so-called traditional *para* setups.

"Now Anonymous People Live in My Childhood's Neighborhood"

Except two, all the interviewees, during their childhoods, had neighborhood friends with whom they spent their afternoon playtime. Interestingly, all the interviewees mentioned that their locality or their childhood *para* is not the same anymore.

According to India Brand Equity Foundation's (2018) report, India's real estate market size will jump from USD 126 billion in 2015 to USD 853 billion in 2028, and by 2031, 600 million Indians will be living in urban areas, rising from 434 million in 2015. The micro-level sociological implication of these figures is loss of bonding from one's immediate surroundings, as was already being felt by the interviewees. One of the interviewees, Som (personal communication, July 24, 2018), who lived in his 110-year-old ancestral house in Boubazar, one of the old localities of central Kolkata, explained:

> It is very expensive to maintain such big old houses nowadays. Most of the families cannot do anything but to sell it to the developers. Also, people are migrating these days for better opportunities, selling off the old houses. There are even people who just want to move to newly coming posh localities of Kolkata. The sense of rootedness that used to be there in my parents' generation is gone now.

The implication of this changing cityscape is a changing mindscape (Simmel, 1964) of the dwellers. All the interviewees stated that, in their childhood, they used to know almost all the people in their *para*, but now there are unknown people living in those newly developed high-rises in their childhood *para*. This way of living has replaced the traditional bond of community living with isolated and individualistic urban living, which is no longer the coexistence of conflicting sub-sets but the scattered habitation of anonymous individuals. Quite interestingly, anonymity was identified not only in a locality, but even within a single household.

"Now I Spend Less Time Talking with My Mother'

One of the interviewees, Nitu, who is a recent graduate, lives with her mother and brother in an apartment they moved into a few years ago. Nitu (personal communication, June 13, 2018) complained:

> When we return home in the evening, all of us sit in our own rooms engaged in social media. My mother spends a lot of time on social media. We hardly talk with each other anymore. The people of my generation still know how to handle it. But people of my parents' generation have gone completely crazy. …Parents don't tell their children to do something together anymore, at least to watch a movie together. Even when we go out, we are glued to our own screens sitting in the restaurants.

The same sentiment was echoed by Mou, who lives in suburban Kolkata with her in-laws and sees her husband only when he manages to come home from his out-station job. Mou, a self-acclaimed addict of online shopping, social media and online videos, stated that her addiction to the internet increased due to her loneliness. When her husband is away, they talk at least an hour every day over the phone. Previously, when her husband used to visit, they used to chat. Now, they just sit in the same room looking at their own mobiles. They are even busy with their mobiles when dining out together. Mou (personal communication, July 10, 2018) said, "We actually speak with each other a lot more when we are apart. But when we are together, we hardly talk to each other anymore."

Although not all, most of the interviewees described similar situations of growing anonymity among family members. However, many of them did not blame only social media or the internet for this. Chanda (personal communication, June 4, 2018), a 46-year-old psychology professor living with her octogenarian father and septuagenarian mother in their ancestral house in South Kolkata explained, "Due to socio-economic changes, people are nowadays spending more time at work. The work-life balance has been destroyed. This has increased the distance between people, even when living together."

The anonymity thus can be categorized into different layers as below:

I.   The first layer of anonymity exists in traditional *para* set-up amid the co-existing conflicting sub-sets of community

II.   The second layer of anonymity exists between those who were living in the traditional *para* and those who have shifted to the newly developed apartments in the same locality

III. The third layer exists among the habitants of newly developed areas that no longer constitute the concept of traditional *para*.

IV.   The fourth layer of exists among those living in the same house, either family members or friends

'Kolkata's Adda Has Shifted to Malls and Posh Cafes'

Although the culture of *adda* has been an essential characteristic of Kolkata, every interviewee stated that now the city is gradually losing this. Lina (personal communication, June 9, 2018), who is pursuing her career as a classical dancer and who lives with her parents in suburban Kolkata, pointed out:

> There has been a sophistication of Kolkata *adda*. Nowadays, people don't chat at street-sides anymore. They go to posh coffee-shops or malls as their whole life is on social media through selfies. It is much more appealing in photos that you are chatting in malls or in coffee-shops than at street-sides. So, even when they are chatting face-to-face, they are continuously updating on social media.

Almost all the interviewees believed that, due to lack of time and heightened work- or study-related pressure *adda* culture is fading. They stated that although the older generation still meets regularly to chat, the younger generation does not. Deep (personal communication, August 20, 2018), who lives in Saltlake with his elder brother and friends, exclaimed, "There is no street-side tea shop or outside porch of Saltlake houses. So, where will we meet for *adda*? ...My elder brother has to go to pubs, bars or weekend parties to chat with friends. Otherwise, where will one chat anymore?" This change of architecture and work culture affecting the community bonding of people in urban India provides a multi-faceted dimension of urban anonymity.

"There is a Social Media Take-Over of Kolkata's Adda"

In addition to the vanishing urban space for age-old *adda*, Kolkata is witnessing the transformation of *adda* culture into the virtual world. According to all the interviewees, the younger generation is extensively using social media and other online platforms to stay in touch and chat. Lina (personal communication, June 9, 2018) stated:

I talk a lot more on social media than face-to-face. I think people can express themselves better in social media because you can weigh your words and then choose the right expression. This is also non-intrusive, as you can talk with people when you want and when you are free. Not necessarily you have to make time out of your schedule to do so.

Social media is being used for sharing important information, for organizing a meeting among friends, for staying in touch, for knowing about other people's lives and off course to chat. People are also maintaining different dimensions of their social relationships through different sets of online groups. However not all interviewees believe that online conversation can be an alternative for Kolkata's *adda*.

"Chatting Online Lacks Spontaneity and Emotional Connectivity'"

Most of the interviewees believed that online communication could never replace face-to-face communication. Indra (personal communication, June 11, 2018), a 36-year-old English professor living in his ancestral home in north Kolkata, explained, 'Human communication is not only textual, but you have whole association and paraphernalia of body language, eye contact, physical presence etc. That's not possible in the virtual *adda*. I don't think whether that can be called adda in the first place.' Dev (personal communication, August 22, 2018) opined, 'One cannot do adda in social media. The depth is just not there. It is just comments and comments on comments, not conversation.'

Many of the interviewees felt that the virtual conversation has given a rise to fake emotions and fake expressions. Nitu (personal communication, June 13, 2018), illustrating this point, said, "You can chat online while you are doing many other things. So, actually, you are not much into the conversation." Lina (personal communication, June 9, 2018) echoed this opinion, "If you're writing "ha ha ha" in online communication, that doesn't necessarily mean you are actually laughing. You might not even know or read the message completely. But just to reply you write "ha ha ha…" So, the true feelings are not there in online communication."Sima (personal communication, June 13, 2018) said, "When talking face-to-face, you can understand a lot by looking at other. The reaction becomes spontaneous. But for online communication, one's reactions are measured. One can write something, then edit it out and then send. One can even delete what is sent."

Interestingly, online communication not only virtualizes human emotions, but also changes one's personality. Dev (personal communication, August 22, 2018) said, "I am definitely an extrovert, but I am introvert online. That is mainly because I don't find much satisfaction from online communication." Mou (personal communication, July 10, 2018) talked about an opposite case, "I have a friend who does not talk much. But it is surprising to see how much she talks online."

Virtual communication adds further layers to role-playing (Goffman, 1956), masks of identity and daily performances (Schechner, 1988). Many people become strangers to others in the virtual dimension, while many strangers become familiar, thus illustrating and extending the concept of familiar strangers (Milgram, 1972), adding further to networked familiar strangers (Schwartz, 2013). Virtual communication provides the platform to converse with strangers. However, the sense of the concept of strangers as used by Milgram (1972) is diversified here. Strangers are no longer only the people we see but donot talk to; strangers are also people we talk to. The otherwise extrovert personality turns introvert and hardly communicates in the virtual dimension. Conversely, introvert people who donot talk much face-to-face are much more talkative in online communication. This concept of urban anonymity is further complicated with the introduction of anonymous messaging apps, such as Sarahah.

"Sarahah Has Given an Opportunity to Express What Otherwise You Wouldn't"

For most of the interviewees, the utility of Sarahah was that it offered an opportunity to say something that was otherwise not possible in a face-to-face situation. However, many of the interviewees personally had not used the app for this purpose, but all the interviewees had used the app for other purposes. For Rini, a 13-year-old app user living in her ancestral house in suburban Kolkata, the initial reason for using the app was to provide feedback for the organizational requirements of the theater group where she performs. However, she soon started using it for personal feedback. In most of the cases, the messages she received were jokes or banter. All the other interviewees stated the same that most of the messages received and sent largely fall under the category of jokes, banter, quotes and funny messages. The app was hardly used for the purpose it was created for.

Still, there are users who have used it for its original purpose. For example, Lina said she used Sarahah because she could send messages to one of herschool teachers about not liking the subject he taught. She was happy when she found that the teacher had shared her message on his Facebook wall, expressing his pleasure to receive such an honest confession. Sampa, Nitu and Sree expressed similar sentiments. Sree (personal communication, August 23, 2018) stated:

For a long time, I wanted to say something to one of my university friends who spread rumors against me. Only because of Sarahah I was able to tell her what I wanted to say. She did not get that it was me. I wouldn't be able to do it otherwise as it would have created a tense and nasty situation.

In such cases, the virtual world has successfully provided a shield to people to break the barriers of the physical world and to extend their identities and personalities as desired (Suler, 2004). The social norms and situations that otherwise constrict human expressions have found an outlet in this virtual world by providing the safety of anonymity.

"Sarahah Made Me Feel Good About Myself"

Except for a few, most of the interviewees had sent and received positive feedback. Sampa (personal communication, June 9, 2018) explained, "Why use this platform to say anything critical to anyone! What if they get to know who it is? I don't want to get into any controversy." The sense of insecurity and lack of trust on online platforms are strong reasons why many of the users held back negative comments or any personal comments altogether. It is interesting to observe that many people act very carefully with their online identity and actions, not trusting the virtual world at all.

The experience of receiving such positive messages was overwhelming, at times to the level of competing with others. Lina (personal communication, June 9, 2018) said, "Sarahah messages have changed my perception about myself. I never knew that I am so much appreciated and loved by all. It has boosted my self-confidence." However, the exact opposite has also occurred.

"Sarahah Has Pushed Me Towards Depression"

A few of the interviewees had received negative messages that affected them to various degrees. Deep, who lost an academic year due to a poor result, was deeply hurt with a few messages he received consisting of personal attacks, sometimes even against his family members. He was depressed for a long time, which was exacerbated by his academic set-back. Although he has moved on, he said that the messages have stayed with him subconsciously. Deep (personal communication, August 20, 2018) said, "This app has given a shield to those who want to hide behind anonymity and say anything they want."

There were other interviewees who recalled how the updates from their acquaintances on social media showed the large number of negative messages received through Sarahah and the extent of angst it created among them. Sree (personal communication, August 23, 2018) said, "This app spreads a lot of negativity. Getting a chance, people are pouring out their long-kept anger. What is worse, it is shared and discussed openly on Facebook." Furthermore, anonymous messaging apps have influenced people's actions and relations with others.

"Sharing Sarahah Comments on Social Media is Ego-Booster"

The reason behind the popularity of this app was largely its feature of sharing messages received on social media. Most of the interviewees knew about Sarahah from Facebook. Explaining the feature, Lina (personal communication, June 9, 2018) pointed out, "Sharing the comments received through Sarahah on social media gives the users a 'celebrity-feel'. It's like, look how important I am." For Lina, the app was an addition to the already prevailing ego-centric selfie culture of social media. However, many selected the messages to share simply based on their fun quotient. For example, Kalyan (personal communication, June 11, 2018), a 32-year-old sociology professor who first moved from a rural area to Kolkata's suburban area in childhood and then to South Kolkata, said, "I shared those messages on social media which I think would be liked by all. It is basically for people to have fun together."

A few of the interviewees chose not to share the messages they received. Even while sharing the messages, people were quite selective. For example, Deep and Sampa did not share any negative messages they received. The app was widely used also as an online guessing game, on which one had to figure out who sent the message. As Lina (personal communication, June 6, 2018) said, "The fun of this app is the challenge of whether you can identify the sender. A lot of its attraction lies in this puzzle-solving game."

"I Identified the Sender by Writing Style and Context of the Message"

Although the app was developed for the purposes of anonymous feedback, interestingly the anonymity itself was an illusion. All the interviewees said that for most of the messages they received they were able to identify the sender and vice versa. The interviewees provided two main reasons for this:

- The first reason was due to writing style, including choice of language to write in, choice of words, spelling and even tone of the sentences. For example, Tanu, a 36-year-old college professor living in north Kolkata, said that she could identify a sender as he never uses any typing shortcuts and always spells the words in full.
- The second reason was the context of the message. In many cases, the interviewees were able to identify the message because the senders had already said it to them. For example, Ela, a postgraduate student who lives with her mother in a north Kolkata apartment, could identify the sender as her brother because it was the same banter that he usually shared with her.

This offers an interesting dimension of online anonymity which continuously interacts and synthesizes with the offline identity. The probability of identifying the anonymous sender of the messages is directly proportionate to the shared field of experience (Schramm, 1954) along with other factors. Interestingly in many cases the senders did not bother to try to hide their identity. In such cases the app users are not treating the app as anonymous messaging service, but just as another messaging service. However even when the users were trying to hide their identity, receivers were able to guess it in many cases.

Human identity thus evidently is a complex whole of many factors. Receiving anonymous messages online from people otherwise known activates in communicative experience that non-physical trait of identity which constructs someone's overall persona. However still in many cases the receivers were not able to identify the sender. In such cases it becomes evident that anonymity depends on the degree of association. Those who are in the social media network but still not well known constitute the network familiar strangers (Schwartz, 2013) who were difficult to identify. Thus, just like urban familiar strangers there are online familiar strangers: this becomes the virtual transformation of urban anonymity.

"I Stopped Talking with My Friend After the Sarahah Message"

As the anonymity of the message turns out to be non-functional, the messages sent and received via this app began to affect the lives of the users. Sampa (personal communication, June 9, 2018) recalled, "I have received messages that were not of good taste. I guessed who had sent them and confronted her, after which we stopped talking." Beyond the direct experiences, the secondary experiences of the interviewees through social media also illustrated similar instances.

In addition to hard feelings between friends, the app affected the lives of the users in other ways. For example, Indra (personal communication, June 11, 2018), who is a professor of English literature, recalled, "It appeared a huge number of female students have a crush on me. It made me reconsider my behavior and actions in class. This is also the primary reason why I uninstalled the app." Interestingly, the social or individual boundaries that made layers of human identity anonymous to others are unveiled in the virtual world, as proposed by the online disinhibition effect (Suler, 2004). However, these exposed traits affect the lives and actions of people in the physical world as well. Thus, there is continuous interaction between virtual and non-virtual identity, making virtuality only an extension of the urban reality.

"I Have Received Sexually Explicit Messages from Anonymous Sender"

The social stigma that compels individuals to suppress part of their identity, that social binding becomes obsolete in an anonymous virtual environment, unleashing traits of personality otherwise hidden. Unlike many of the interviewees, Sima accepted Facebook friendship requests from strangers. She shared her Sarahah link on Facebook like most of the interviewees, trusting the goodness of people. However, Sima (personal communication, June 13, 2018) said, "I repeatedly received messages stating, 'let's have sex' and 'let's have a one-night stand'. I was furious, scared and disturbed for days. I still wonder who sent these!"

Sima, who is an extrovert and tells everything to her parents, even recalls instances when a few men were disturbing her on her daily route which she reported to her parents, did not tell anything to her parents about the messages she has received through Sarahah. Sima (personal communication, June 13, 2018) explained, "In other cases I had nothing to do. But if I tell this to my parents, they would blame me, as I only added unknown people on Facebook and shared the Sarahah link. I just uninstalled the app." This anecdote is evidence that people choose to react differently in the virtual world. Anonymity, not only social or interpersonal, but virtual experiences, offer insights into the unknown dimensions of one's identity or what can be called the intrapersonal anonymity.

"I Have Received Political Threats"

Similarly, Deep, who is a member of his college's student union, said that there are two student unions in his college, each affiliated to adifferent political party. Since joining one union, he has received anonymous threatening calls from the other. He was scared at first, but later grew used to them. Even knowing the possibility of receiving threatening messages, he shared his Sarahah link on social media. Explaining the situation, Deep (personal communication, August 20, 2018) elaborated:

> The text messages you receive as anonymous threats have the least effect. More threatening are phone calls, and much more is telling it face-to-face. So, Sarahah messages I received, like "you have to leave this college by tomorrow," were ignorable. There is a difference between the real-world threats and such virtual threats.

Interestingly, in this case, the anonymity provides a security to both the receiver and the sender.

"I Will Freak Out If I Receive Anonymous Messages in Other Ways"

The anonymity that is welcomed virtually is otherwise shunned by all of the interviewees. Every interviewee acknowledged the existence of familiar strangers (Milgram, 1972) in their surroundings, but this is comfortable only from a safe distance. If these people approach to start a conversation or just to offer their opinion, none of the interviewees would welcome it. A few of the interviewees who already had experiences of receiving anonymous messages and phone calls never felt safe about it. Sima recalled an incident when she received anonymous mobile messages. Out of fear, she immediately informed her parents. Nitu, however, confronted the anonymous caller who used to call her every now and then. Ultimately, both Sima and Nitu changed their phone numbers. Deep (personal communication, August 20, 2018) explained, "If a stranger approached me on street and started talking to me, I would run in the opposite direction. That would be freaky. But the virtual world is safe." Even after such negative experiences and apprehensions, the interviewees chose to try Sarahah in which initiated the possibility of experiences they stated that they preferred to avoid. This choice highlights a sharp differentiation between virtual strangers and real-life strangers.

"Sarahah Gives the Power to Control Communication"

All the interviewees explained that, due to its virtuality, the conversation environment of Sarahah is safe. Sampa (personal communication, June 9, 2018) said, "If an anonymous person calls or sends a mobile message, that means the sender knows where you live, what your number is. But in the case of Sarahah, this threat is not there." All the interviewees shared their profile links through Facebook, believing that trustworthy people are in their friends list. Mou (personal communication, July 10, 2018) explained, "If any time I feel I do not want to receive messages, I can always uninstall. That is a big safety." Dev (personal communication, August 22, 2018), in the same tone stated, "I have full control here. I can leave any time I want without the possibility of anyone else trying to contact me. I am there because I chose it, not that others are pushing me into the situation."

Urban life has revealed trust issues and a sense of insecurity (Low, 2003; Davis, 2008) among people, even among familiar strangers. People are protective of their individual space, leading to restrictive social conversations. The virtual world offers the pleasure of freedom, breaking the shackles of such constraints. The sense of insecurity associated with the physical world is higher than that of the virtual world. Therefore, interaction with familiar strangers is high in the virtual world, as the sense of insecurity is less, and the sense of control is high. This dynamic relation can be presented as the following model:

$$\text{Communicative freedom} = \frac{\text{Sense of Control}}{\text{Sense of Insecurity}}$$

This model represents the reason communicating with virtual strangers is preferred to communicate with strangers in the immediate real-life environment.

CONCLUSION

In exploring the relation between urban and virtual anonymity, intricate layers of anonymity were identified among the dwellers of Kolkata. The anonymity at the micro-level begins with intrapersonal anonymity, in which one discovers different dimensions of one's identity in the online environment. The next level of anonymity occurs between family members, with a growing anonymity due to individuals' involvement in their own virtual worlds. Regarding the anonymity of familiar strangers, interestingly it has two dimensions: virtuality and non-virtuality. The familiar virtual strangers are welcomed more than the familiar strangers of the immediate environment due to the safety of physical distance and control over the situation, as opposed to the insecurities and distrust of urban relations. In the extension of urban familiar strangers there are two categories: unknown neighbors in the newly extended part of the city, where community bonding never occurs; and unknown neighbors in the newly constructed apartments of the old localities, where community bonding is gradually fading. The next layer of urban anonymity is between those sub-sets of people living in the same community but with certain cultural and economic differences. Interestingly, in rare instances, when people from the same community but from different sub-sets interact in the virtual world, the same coldness of the relation is transmitted. In such cases, it is the virtual transformation of urban anonymity.

This study, unlike traditional urban space theories (Chen, Orum, & Paulsen, 2013), focuses on intra-community anonymity more than inter-community anonymity. Virtuality, to some extent, has diluted inter-community anonymity by traversing beyond the physicality of the human relation. Anonymous messaging apps such as Sarahah work simultaneously to dilute and to harness urban anonymity while creating a new set of anonymity altogether. Further studies into this urban-virtual relation of identity and anonymity are necessary to illuminate the degree and direction of this relation.

ACKNOWLEDGMENTS

The researcher is thankful to Sushmita Chakrabarty for her help in collecting the pilot survey sample, and to Brahm Prakash Chaturvedi for his help with the pilot survey data collection and arranging the interview data transcription.

REFERENCES

Bell, K. (2017, July 23). *How Sarahah became one of the most popular iPhone apps in the world.* Retrieved August 05, 2018 from Mashable: https://mashable.com/2017/07/23/the-story-of-sarahah-app/

Cassin, E. (2018, February 26). *Sarahah: Anonymous app dropped from Apple and Google stores after bullying accusations.* Retrieved August 18, 2018 from BBC Trending: https://www.bbc.com/news/blogs-trending-43174619

Castells, M. (2010). *The rise of the networked society.* Oxford: Wiley-Blackwell.

———. (1977). *The urban question: A Marxist approach.* Cambridge: The MIT Press.

Chakrabarty, D. (1999). Adda, Calcutta: Dwelling in modernity. *Public Culture, 11* (1), pp. 109-145.

Chakravarty, S. (2017, December 01). *A brief history of Ādā – the Bengali fine art of discussion.* Retrieved August 10, 2018 from Quartz India: https://qz.com/india/1122129/adda-a-brief-history-of-the-bengali-fine-art-of-discussion/

Chen, X., Orum, A.M.& Paulsen, K.E. (2013). *Introduction to cities: How place and space shape human experience.* Hoboken, NJ: Wiley-Blackwell.

Choudhury, D. (2017). Realities and myths of public spaces: Conflict and participation in Kolkata. *International Journal on Emerging Technologies, 8* (1), pp. 337-343.

Collins, K. (2018, January). *Ban apps like Sarahah where my daughter was told to "kill herself."* Retrieved August 18, 2018 from change.org: https://www.change.org/p/app-store-google-play-ban-apps-like-sarahah-where-my-daughter-was-told-to-kill-herself

Correa, D., Silva, L.A., Mondal, M., Benevenuto, F.& Gummadi, K.P. (2015). *The many shades of anonymity: Characterizing anonymous social media content.* Association for the Advancement of Artificial Intelligence.

In D.E. Davis (Ed) (2008, Spring). Insecure and secure cities: Towards a reclassification of world cities in a global era. *MIT International Review*, pp. 30-41.

Demographia. (2018). *Demographia World Urban Areas 14th Annual Edition: 201804.* Demographia.

Goffman, E. (1956). *The presentation of self in everyday life.* London: Penguin Random House LLC.

IBEF. (2018, January). *Indian real estate industry: Overview, market size, growth.* Retrieved June 26, 2018 from Indian Brand Equity Foundation: https://www.ibef.org/download/Real-Estate-January-2018.pdf

Klinberg, E. (2015). *Alone in the city? The intellectual history of social isolation.* Department of Sociology. Northwestern University.

Kling, R., Lee, Y., Teich, A.& Frankel, M.S. (1999). Assessing anonymous communication on the internet: Policy deliberations. *The Information Society, 15,* pp. 79-90.

Kvale, S. (1996). *InterViews: An introduction to qualitative research interviewing.*Thousand Oaks, CA: SAGE Publications, Inc.

Low, S. (2003). *Behind the gates: Life, security and the pursuit of happiness in fortress America .*New York and London: Routledge.

Milgram, S. (1972). *The familiar strangers: An aspect of urban anonymity.* Washington: American Psychological Association.

Navbharat Times. (2018, May 25). *Sarahah* **केबादआया***Stulish* **ऐप, सोशलमीडियापरछाया.** Retrieved August 20, 2018 from Navbharat Times News: https://navbharattimes.indiatimes.com/tech/gadgets-news/new-stulish-app-has-gone-viral-on-social-media/articleshow/64315842.cms

Putnam, R.D. (2000). *Bowling alone: The collapse and revival of American community.* New York: Simon & Schuster.

Roy, M. (2010). *Historical background of Kolkata and its construction industry.* Kolkata: University of Calcutta.

Saha, S. (2017, August 10). *Sarahah app is going viral, and here is everything you need to know about it.* Retrieved August 18, 2018 from India Today: https://www.indiatoday.in/technology/features/story/sarahah-app-is-going-viral-but-what-is-it-and-how-does-it-work-1028966-2017-08-10

Schechner, R. (1988). *Performance theory.* New York: Routledge.

Schramm, W. (1954). How communication works. In W. Schramm (Ed.), *The process and effects of mass communication.* Urbana: University of Illinois Press. pp 3-26.

Schwartz, R. (2013). The networked familiar stranger: An aspect of online and offline urban anonymity. In K.M. Cumiskey, & L. Hjorth (Eds.), *Mobile Media Practices, Presence and Politics: The Challenges of being Seamlessly Mobile.* New York: Routledge. Pp. 135-149.

Simmel, G. (1964). The metropolis and mental life. In K.H. Wolff (Ed.), *The Sociology of George Simmel* (H.H. Gerth, & C.W. Mills, Trans., pp. 409-424). New York: Free Press of Glencoe.

Suler, J. (2004). The online disinhibition effect. *Cyber Psychology & Behavior, 7* (3). pp 184-188.

Tonnies, F. (2001). *Community and civil society.* (J. Harris, Ed., J. Harris, & M. Hollis, Trans.) Cambridge: Cambridge University Press.

Wimmer, R.D.& Dominick, J.R. (2010). *Mass media research: An introduction.* Boston: Cengage Learning.

Zimbardo, P.G. (1969). The human choice: Individuation, reason, and order versus deindividuation, impulse, and chaos. *Nebraska symposium on motivation.* Nebraska: University of Nebraska Press.

Zukin, S. (1982). *Loft living: Culture and capital in urban change.* Baltimore: Johns Hopkins University Press.

——— (1995). *The cultures of cities.* Oxford: Blackwell.

87

CHAPTER 6

Urban Walls and Virtual Bridges:
Social Capital and the Internet in Divided Cities

Dr. Francesca Savoldi
CICS.NOVA – Interdisciplinary Centre of Social Sciences
University of Lisbon, Portugal

ABSTRACT

This chapter summarizes research undertaken on the impact of internet use on "divided cities" – partitioned spaces characterized by community-based social contestation and segregation; whose nature depends on ethno-nationalistic conflict. The investigation in question used as its case study the city of Belfast, where a fractured urban fabric, characterized by defensive artifacts and eroded social cohesion (both consequences of conflict) coexist with a contemporary process of reunification. My argument is that, in this context, the internet is a tool that can enable new "walls" or "bridges" between separated communities and can have an influence on the urban transition of the city.

In particular, I observed how emergent communication technologies influence social capital in this specific partitioned urban context, and impacting patterns of local social interaction, which are conditioned by the high levels of urban segregation inherited from conflict. A critical approach to the concept of social capital was taken to characterize better those factors that promote reconciliation or feed division in that context.

Ethnographic work was carried out in Belfast, where surveys and interviews were conducted among the youth of Belfast. Using a qualitative-quantitative mixed method, supported by spatial analysis, I found indications that internet usage has a mixed influence on the transition of a divided city. From my research, it emerged that internet use has a catalytic effect on the dimension of bridging social capital, enabling inter-communitarian relationships and overcoming, to a certain extent, the limitations dictated by divided urban space. These findings are considered beneficial for the transformation of the divided city, given that they support the creation of shared spaces. In that sense, internet usage holds potential for accelerating integration in a divided city, and the internet usage should be considered for the creation of good practices in terms of urban agenda building.

However, a negative effect of internet usage was also observed, as this technology enables a new type of clash in the form of place-specific cyberbullying.

Keywords: Divided cities, Internet, Social Capital, Conflict, Segregation

1. Introduction: Divided Cities in the Internet Age

Divided cities are far from being a problem of the past. Political divisions materialized through physical segregation are an emerging global condition; fences and barriers are increasingly commonplace, often built as consequences of political conflicts and institutionalized sectarianism. This issue affects not only national borders, but the city's own space as well.

The diffused problems of urban *uncohesion*, gated communities and discourses of "us and them" that dominate the city space are pertinent to the contemporary urban policymaking agenda. The study of divided cities can illuminate the narrative forces driving urban polarization and contribute to the dialog surrounding the implementation of division as a political measure. The in-depth study of divided cities enables a greater understanding of the prolonged mechanisms of separation. Separation is often adopted as an initial and temporary emergency condition, but can, over time, become permanent, creating a more complex urban pathology that is increasingly difficult to eradicate.

This study reconsiders the issue of divided cities in the age of the "network society" – a term largely acknowledged for identifying the reshaped social morphology of society due to the social, political, economic and cultural changes caused by the spread of networked, digital ICTs. As claimed by Castells (2000), in the "rise of the network society," the spread of the internet, mobile communications and digital media, as well as a wide range of social software tools, has a key impact on production methods, relationships, the composition of society and, consequently, the layout of the city itself. Hence, there is an underlying consideration at the base of this research regarding how these factors, digital practices of communication in particular, are conditioning the situation of divided cities.

Based on the premise that, in divided cities, the division of urban space is inherent to social interaction – the latter also being key to any solution of integration – this study considers the internet to be a factor to examine in the reconfiguration of socio-spatial relationships. In particular, the investigation aims to observe whether, in this type of context, internet use promotes the interaction of reconciliation between separated communities ("bridges") or, on the contrary, generates new forms of confrontation or contributes to the maintenance of existing ones ("walls").

This issue is approached through the lens of social capital. Reframing the concept of social capital in the context of a divided city and carrying out an empirical enquiry on a specific case study, I analyze how the internet impacts inter-communitarian relationships and, thus, the transition of the divided city.

2. Conceptual and Theoretical Framework

2.1 Divided City as An Urban Category. Defining the Object of Analysis

What is a divided city? Van Kempen (2007), who argues "the undivided city is a myth and a utopia at the same time," describes divided cities as having a certain dichotomy to them, usually resulting from a divided society. He states that a clear connection can be established between a divided society and a divided city: if a society is divided, the urban space must also be divided. It is a matter of connection between social polarization and social inequality, on the one hand, and spatial segregation on the other.

If we consider the term "divided" in its literal meaning, we see that divided cities have been widespread across space and time, being associated to phenomena of segregation, urban inequality, urban apartheid, dual city, or contested city.

However, despite the generic usage of the word "divided" and the lack of consensus for a universal definition of what a divided city is, some authors have been more specific than others in defining it. Calame and Charlesworth (2012), who looked at the cases of Belfast, Beirut, Jerusalem, Mostar and Nicosia, described the divided city as "a physical crisis nestled within a political crisis carried forward by a raft of social ills" (p.171). Nagle (2013) describes it as being "defined by a violent conflict of ethno-nationalism and characterized by semi-permanent ethnic cleavages, high levels of endogamy and social segregation" (p.89). Björkdahl and Strömbom (2015) identified divided cities as areas where tensions occur along the contours of majority-minority relations in the urban space. Bollens, having spent his academic career living in and studying cities such as Jerusalem, Belfast, Beirut, Johannesburg, Nicosia, Sarajevo, Mostar and cities in the Basque region, describes divided cities as bipolar urban areas where political control is contested as identity groups push to create a political system that expresses and protests their distinctive group characteristics: "these are war-torn, hurt-filled, and often emotionally transcendent places" (Bollens, 2011, p.6).

I define the divided city as a partitioned urban area characterized by community-led political contestation and violence anchored in religious or ethnic clashes that dominate the identity construction of power that is also reflected by institutional mechanisms. These cities, often experiencing contested states, are dominated by severe patterns of segregation, as well as the materialization of boundaries and buffer zones through physical structures (walls, fences and other architectural devices).

In divided cities, boundaries are often built as the immediate political response to a situation of escalating violence. However, this physical partitioning often creates long-term effects that can remain for years after the physical boundaries are removed. Most of these short-term solutions become long-term problems, exacerbating sectarian and ethnic strife and generating difficulties that both differ from and outweigh the original socio-political problem. Their boundaries remain as violent reminders of exclusion, allowing the lines of physical division to become borders in a psychological sense. In the long term, partitioning typically exacerbates "urban diseases" and increases physical segregation within cities, creating racial enclaves, red zones and gated communities.

The division of urban space is usually consolidated through patterns of segregation, which tend to reinforce separation and differing access to certain resources, resulting in the feeding of inter-community conflict in some way.

Typically, divided cities suffer from the following 'urban diseases':

> Social: bad community relationships and negativity (hate, mistrust, fear, etc.), health problems (anxiety, stress, etc.), higher unemployment, higher crime rates (in particular sectarian crime, youth crime and acquisition crime in the form of drug sales and burglary), low educational attainment and social exclusion.

> Economic: greater public expenditure due to security, damage, policing, duplication of institutions and services; lack of private investment due to risk.

> Spatial: limited access to public services, leisure, commerce or resources in general; limited options of expansion based on community identity areas; visually defensive artifacts that dominate the urban landscape.

Divided cities commonly undergo long and complicated transitions. Considering that the impact of ICT in conflict transformation changes according to the stage of the conflict (Hattotuwa, 2004), I determined 'divided cities' according to the urban phase in which they are in to define our object of analysis. Considering the evolution of the conflict and the peace-building process, I distinguished three moments of a divided city.

1.   When the conflict is resolved, and the residual effects of the conflict are tenuous. In this case, when the division between communities is overcome, despite remaining signs of partition in the urban space (or vice versa), I believe that the effects of the internet would not be identifiable and would not be an important factor of change.
2.   When the city is affected by an ongoing conflict, characterized by a dynamic and acute state of violence and continuous/rapid changes in the urban space. In this case, due to the general volatile nature of the conditions dictated by the ongoing conflict and the many macro-variables associated to it, the impact of the internet would not be easily identifiable.
3.   When the city is in a situation of post-conflict and the urban space displays settled divisions (wall, clear signs of community

segregation, separated services/infrastructure, etc.), that influence and in some way control the daily life of its citizens, but which also harbor dynamics of peace-building. In this environment, in which there are forces interested in keeping the conflict alive while also maintaining public awareness and social efforts for reconciliation, the impact of the internet could have an evident and detectable role as a promoter of one position or the other.

2.2 Social Capital and the Internet in Divided Cities

The fractured urban fabric in divided cities has a clear link to the eroded social cohesion related to socio-political division. Relationships between communities have an essential role in shaping the social, the political and the spatial configuration of the city; so, interactions and networks between communities, which are subject to the influence of internet usage, determine in some way the configuration of the city and its urban transition.

This approach, which focuses on space, identity and community interaction, has an obvious and fundamental implication for the discourse of social capital.

The concept of social capital concerns the resources that social interaction can provide. However, the nature of resources can vary according to different approaches; there is no universal definition of social capital agreed upon by researchers across the social disciplines (Neves, 2012); each focuses separately on social capital's substance, origins or consequences (Adler and Kwon, 2002; Field et al., 2000; Robison et al., 2002).

The modern concept of social capital was defined by Pierre Bourdieu, who described it as "the sum of the resources, actual or virtual, that accrue to an individual or a group by virtue of possessing a durable network of more or less institutionalised relationships of mutual acquaintance and recognition" (Bourdieu, in Bourdieu & Wacquant, 1992, p.119). This definition was framed in a discussion about symbolic capital augmented by critical theories of class societies.

At a similar time – the late 1980s and early 1990s – James Coleman was also working on social capital; his notion is related to "rational-choice theory," combining both economics and sociology. In his approach, social context is characterized by the organization of relations between actors, which conform to the social structure. Coleman claimed, "social capital is defined by its function. It is not a single entity, but a variety of different entities having two characteristics in common: they all consist of some aspect of a social structure, and they facilitate certain actions of individuals who are within the structure. Like other forms of capital, social capital is productive, making possible the achievement of certain ends that in its absence would not be possible" (1988, p.98).

Among social capital's major proponents is Robert Putnam, who brought the concept to a mainstream audience with his work *Bowling alone. The collapse and revival of American communities* (2000). His conceptualization of social capital is an extended version of Coleman's idea; observing engagement and collective trust in different civil societies, he defined social capital as "features of social organisation such as networks, norms, and social trust that facilitate coordination and cooperation for mutual benefit" (Ibid). He has conducted empirical research and has formulated specific indicators.

Social capital can also be understood (and measured) through its dimensions. Putnam (2000) discusses two main dimensions that characterize different forms of social capital: "bridging," which is related to all social ties that, crossing different groups, gain access to external networks; and "bonding," which is related to strong social bonds within a homogeneous community or group, often associated with trust-building.

Putnam's view is particularly interesting for understanding social capital in divided cities; later in his work, he acknowledges the existence of a "dark side" of social capital. Observing the correlation between tolerance and social participation, Putnam found that the dimension of bonding might be restrictive in certain environments, causing intolerance and in-group thinking.

The dimension of bonding in divided cities has, in effect, an intrinsic duality due to out-groups' dynamics related to ethno-national conflict; here, the "dark side" of bonding can be understood as reinforcing hostilities between communities, reviving the conflict. To characterize better the dimension of bonding, this study conceptualizes a distinction between "positive bonding" – related to those close ties that generate trust and participation without reproducing the logic of the conflict – and "negative bonding" – related to those close ties that feed the logic in-group/out-group, exacerbating ethno-religious hostilities.

Once the meaning of social capital in divided cities was clarified, I then considered how internet usage is shaping social capital. Despite the rise in literature on this topic in the past decade, there is still no consensus among academics about the impact of the internet on social capital. However, as underlined by Neves (2013), three main paradigms emerged: functional, dysfunctional and neutral.

Certain authors claim that the use of the internet is producing a dysfunctional effect on society, in particular because it is eroding social capital (Kaplan, 2005), creating cyber-balkanization, fragmenting people into interest groups and fostering extreme perspectives (Sunstein, 2001), or because it brings about social fragmentation (Ruesch, 2011). With the same perspective, other authors claim that the internet takes people away from their physical or local communities (Slouka, 1995; Nie, 2001), isolating them instead of bringing them together (Stoll, 1995).

Some scholars have obtained opposite results, finding that internet usage was positively associated with the generation of social capital, because it makes users more socially active online and offline (Katz & Rice 2002), it increases tolerance to difference (Robinson, 2010), it fosters social engagement (Kouvo and Rasanen, 2005), it promotes political participation (de Zuniga, Jung and Valenzuela, 2012) and it supports increased contact with weaker ties, allowing the "wired resident" to overcome spatial, temporal, and social barriers to community involvement (Hampton

& Wellman, 2003; Hofer and Aubert, 2013); it also increases community resilience in situations of disaster survival and recovery (Aldrich and Meyer, 2014).

However, others have claimed that the internet has no influence on social capital (Franzen, 2003), arguing that, "the Internet is neither a threat to civil society and sociability nor its panacea" (Uslaner, 2004, p.48).

3. Case Study

3.1 The Division of Belfast

My research in 2015 focused on the case of Belfast, a divided city experiencing ethno-national religious conflict and that, at the time of this inquiry, was in transition toward reunification. This is a context where visible and invisible signs of division still mark the everyday life of citizens, from walls and barriers to an inherited mistrust and intolerance between the two dominant ethno-national communities. These communities coexist within a dynamic of reconciliation represented by a political and civil leadership that no longer considers the division as a solution, but a problem.

Ethno-national tensions, religion-based segregation and the periodic riots that characterized Belfast and Northern Ireland over two centuries resulted in a conflict known as The Troubles (1968-1998), which has its historical roots in the "plantation of Ulster" (a province of Ireland), which began in 1609 under the British Protestant order of King James I. After being a relatively small town during the 17th and 18th centuries, where English (Anglican) and Scots (dissenting Presbyterian) lived alongside the marginalized (Catholic) Irish population, Belfast grew as an industrialized city that experienced the crystallization of the struggle between Irish nationalism and the nationalism of imperial Britain.

After the partition of Ireland in 1920, Belfast became the capital of Northern Ireland; the consequences of discriminatory practices against the Catholic community during the following decade ended up being embedded in the social and physical fabric of the city, which increasingly assumed a sectarian geography. In the 1960s, protests against discrimination were increasingly affected by incidents within an atmosphere of escalating violence, which resulted finally in The Troubles. The conflict, which is sometimes described as a "low-level war," caused approximately 3,000 deaths, leaving the city deeply divided between Unionists/Loyalists (mostly Protestant) and Irish nationalists/Republicans (mostly Catholic).

Currently, the city is still affected by severe levels of systemic segregation; outside the "neutral" city center and a few other commercial neighborhoods, segregation permeates all areas of life both physically and psychologically. This situation includes housing, with over 95% of social housing divided into Catholic- or Protestant-only, and education – only around 5% of children attend integrated schools (Wainwright, 2013).

Several major walls (also known as peace-lines or peace-walls) still separate communities, especially those living in polarized and deprived working-class residential zones (Jarman, 2004). Mistrust is still high in Belfast, and the peace-walls are considered security for some of those who live with trauma and memories of violence. Other barriers of a different nature (brick, concrete, iron railings, corrugated steel, barbed wire and open-wire mesh) keep apart areas that have strong links between territory and ethno-political identity. Some gates between certain Protestant and Catholic zones close at the end of the day and sectarian murals of flags and other emblems, as well as some depicting paramilitaries with threatening messages, dominate the urban landscape.

Following the 1998 Good Friday peace agreement, several peace-building programs began to be implemented in Belfast, with the aim of creating the conditions for the reunification of the city through the reconciliation of its communities to transform the divided city into a "shared city." The main strategy of the peace plans was to create a framework of social cohesion through mediation at community level, trying to build positive relationships between communities and promoting respect. The social capital concept is, hence, a transversal discourse that permeates Belfast's peace-building process.

The analysis of the characteristics of Belfast as a divided city, including the expressions of its internal division and the adopted measures for the normalization of its urban condition, which I framed according to social capital discourse, was necessary to identify what I have been calling in figurative terms "walls" and "bridges." These terms were, therefore, useful for adapting and measuring the dimensions of social capital and to observe how they are influenced by the internet usage.

3.2 Fieldwork: Research Method and Data Collection

My transversal study in Belfast considered that the effects of the internet could not be isolated nor proved as the unique cause of change. However, it was possible to observe the internet's effect through the comparison between social capital online and offline; I also observed potential variations in social capital, according to different levels of internet usage.

The research strategy counted on a mixed method that combined qualitative and quantitative analysis, according to a pragmatic epistemological approach.

A survey was conducted among the youth of Belfast, with the support of a local umbrella youth organization. The questionnaire was composed of queries concerning different variables: socio-demographic identity, internet usage and social capital – the last variable observed both in the virtual and physical spheres. The indicators related to social capital were created through an adaptation of the matrix developed by Williams (2006), reshaping the questions according to the context. Characterizing internet usage, I developed a method that combined time and characteristics of connectivity with online activities; two main classes of users were identified among the respondents of the survey (moderate and heavy).

A total of 384 questionnaires were collected according to a convenience sample randomly distributed through the supporting local organization. Respondents were aged between 15 and 30 years old; 40% of whom were residents from highly segregated areas of the city, with a particular concentration from areas adjacent to the major walls.

Another survey, accompanied by interviews, was conducted among 23 social workers of the partner organization, which was analyzed qualitatively. The aim was mainly to perceive the expectations of community workers regarding the impact of the internet on youth social capital and to obtain contextual clues about possible furthers indicators of social capital.

A series of complementary interviews were conducted with different local stakeholders, including academics, local authorities and Non Governmental Organizations.

3.3 Analysis and Results

The analysis of the main survey was developed in two stages. In the first section, I carried out a descriptive analysis in which I compared young people's responses for every social capital indicator, both in the online and offline environments. The aim was to identify differences between the two environments to verify whether internet usage was enabling bridges (expressed by the bridging and positive bonding dimensions of social capital) or walls (negative bonding) between communities. Spatial distribution of respondents was also considered to detect any pattern of answers.

In the survey, 20 questions characterized the three dimensions of social capital considered by this research (answers used the Likert scale).

Fragmented results emerged from this analysis; although, I could observe how online interaction was related to higher levels of bridging, while for bonding (negative and positive), no substantial difference between the online and offline spheres was found.

In relation to the bridging dimension, my findings showed that:

> Internet usage was fostering youth's interest in knowing the characteristics of the "other" local community, overcoming the restrictions imposed by the socio-spatial division (in particular residential and scholar segregation);

> Using the internet, youths of Belfast displayed an increased interest in knowing about what was happening in different neighborhoods of the city;

> Interacting online appeared beneficial for increasing the will of youths to explore different urban areas, expanding their spatial practices;

A spatial pattern of responses was observed: those youths who resided close to the major peace-walls benefited from internet usage more than others in terms of increasing their bridging social capital.

Concerning the dimension of positive bonding social capital, internet usage did not appear to be a factor of substantial impact:

- Social capital's indicators (trust, social support and access to limited resources) were clearly more reproduced in the offline sphere than the online one.
- An exception was observed, however: one of the indicators showed that the internet is enabling the creation and maintaining of strong links between young members of different communities (especially among those who live near the peace-walls).
-

In relation to negative bonding the Internet also did not turn out to be a fundamental impact factor:

- According to the responses of a only small minority, the internet appears to be an enabling platform for the reproduction of intra-community identity, the expansion of feelings of sectarian victimization, as well as a platform for organizing anti-social activities.

The second section of the analysis aimed to verify whether a higher level of internet usage was more associated with a higher level of social capital, or vice versa. To verify any association between these two variables, I carried out a quantitative analysis; the results are to be considered as a simulation of a statistical analysis, since a sample of convenience was used, which means that it is representatively limited.

In this section, I identified different levels of social capital (in its online and offline dimensions) through the latent class analysis (LCA), followed by descriptive statistics. The association between different levels of internet usage (moderate and heavy users) and social capital were measured using the independent chi-squared test.

From the results, no statistical association between the variables was found; however, a certain linear trend was observed. It emerged that social capital generated through online and offline interaction relates differently to internet usage. The main finding revealed that more intense internet usage is positively related to those social capital dimensions that represent what I have defined as "bridges" (bridging and positive bonding), being positive for the peace-building process – although this is verified only for virtual social capital.

These findings coincide largely with the expectations of the surveyed and interviewed community workers of the organization that supported this study. Those community workers considered that internet usage is positively impacting social capital, broadening the social horizons of young people in Belfast and fostering curiosity and tolerance about cultural differences (especially with the "other" community). The internet had no influence on strong social ties.

During the interviews, social workers also expressed a particular concern about the issue of bullying (and its online modality, cyberbullying), defined as a deviant behavior related to interpersonal connections, which in Belfast can be linked to the post-conflict condition. As this phenomenon can be framed by social capital discourse and it is obviously subject to influence by internet usage, I created an additional indicator included in the main survey.

The results of the descriptive analysis for this indicator suggest that virtual space is a more prolific environment compared with the physical world for the spread of verbal abuse – which among the youths of Belfast also assumes a sectarian character. A question of note could be whether the increase of online verbal offenses work as a venting practice that substitutes other forms of violence, or as a further form of violence.

CONCLUSION

The aim of this investigation was to understand the role of the internet in reconfiguring socio-spatial relations in divided cities, using social capital as an analytical tool.

Through an extensive on-field research in Belfast and combining different methods of analysis, this research found that the internet is not a neutral factor in the transformation of territorial divisions between ethno-national communities of a divided city; in effect, the results reveal that the internet exerts a certain influence on social capital, impacting local social dynamics and, thus, the city's urban transition.

My findings reveal that:

1) Internet usage had a catalytic effect on generating the social capital component defined by the bridging dimension, which facilitates the expansion of local networks encouraging cross-community contacts, promotes new forms of integration and enhances an extended spatiality, contributing to the narrative of the "shared city."

Due to the nature of the internet, which is characterized by different restrictions compared with the physical sphere, its usage can, to a certain extent, overcome the lack of opportunities for social cohesion that the urban condition of a divided city imposes.

The observed spatial pattern is a further expression of this effect; in fact, in the considered case study, young people living in the most spatially constrained areas (near the major peace-walls), ended up benefiting more from internet usage in terms of gaining this type of social capital.

2) There was, however, no fundamental consequence of using the internet on the dimensions of negative and positive bonding. This finding means that online interaction does not improve solid community support, nor it endorses a general attitude to keep the conflict alive.

3) This research identified also a negative effect of the internet, as it is largely enabling cyberbullying, which in a divided city assumes sectarian connotations. However, the consequences of this phenomenon on urban transition need deeper study.

In summary, having demonstrated that internet usage holds great potential for social cohesion within a divided city at least according to social capital discourse an urban agenda in such a context should foster the construction of inter-communitarian dialogue through emergent communication practices.

REFERENCES

Adler, P.S. & Kwon, S-W. (2002). Social Capital: Prospects for a New Concept. Academy of Management. *The Academy of Management Review* 27, pp. 17-40.

Aldrich, D.P. and Meyer, M.A. (2014). Social Capital and Community Resilience. *American Behavioral Scientist*, 59(2) pp. 254-269

Björkdahl, A. and Strömbom, L. (2015). *Divided Cities: governing diversity*. Nordic academic Press, Lund

Bollens, S.A. (2011). *City and Soul in Divided Societies*. London: Routledge

Bourdieu, P. and Wacquant, L.J.D. (1992). *An Invitation to Reflexive Sociology*. Chicago: University of Chicago Press.

Calame, J. and Charlesworth, E. (2012). *Divided Cities: Belfast, Beirut, Jerusalem, Mostar, and Nicosia*. Philadelphia: University of Pennsylvania Press

Castells, M. (2000). *The rise of the network society*. Blackwell Publishing Ltd, Oxford.

Coleman, J.S. (1988). Social Capital in the Creation of Human Capital. *The American Journal of Sociology* 94, S95-S120

De Zúñiga, G., Jung, H.N. & Valenzuela, S. (2012). "Social media use for news and individuals' social capital, civic engagement and political participation." *Journal of Computer-Mediated Communication*, 17, pp. 319-336.

Field, J., Schuller, T. & Baron, S. (2000). "Social capital and human capital revisited." in *Social Capital: Critical Perspectives*. Edited by Stephen Baron, John Field, and Tom Schuller. Oxford University Press: Oxford, pp 226-242

Franzen, A. (2003). Social Capital and the Internet: Evidence from Swiss Panel Data. *Kyklos*, 56, pp. 341-360.

Hampton, K. & Wellman, B. (2003). "Neighboring in Netville: How the Internet Supports Community and Social Capital in a Wired Suburb." *City & Community*, 2 (4) pp. 36-43

Hattotuwa, S. Untying the Gordian Knot: ICT for Conflict Transformation and Peacebuilding. *Dialogue*, 2 (2), 2004, pp. 39-68

Hofer, M. & Aubert, V. (2013). "Perceived bridging and bonding social capital on Twitter: Differentiating between followers and followees." *Computers in Human Behavior*, 29, pp. 2134-2142.

Jarman N. (2004). *Demography, development and disorder: Changing patterns of interfaces areas.* Institute for conflict research Belfast.

Kaplan, D. (2005). "e-Inclusion. New Challenges and Policy Recommendations." Retrieved from http://ec.europa.eu/information_society/eeurope/2005/doc/all_about/kaplan_report_enclusion_fi nal_version.pdf Accessed October 21st, 2013.

Katz, J.E. & Rice, R.E. (2002). *Social Consequences of Internet Use: Access, Involvement, and Interaction.* Cambridge, MA: MIT Press.

Kouvo, A. & Rasanen, P. (2005). "Does the Internet have an impact on sociability? A comparison of four European countries." Conference: *4th International Conference of ESREA Network on Education and Learning of Older Adults (ELOA): Learning Opportunities for Older Adults: Forms, Providers And Policies*, in Vilnius, Lituânia

Nagle, J. (2013). "Unity in Diversity": Non-Sectarian Social Movement Challenges to the Politics of Ethnic Antagonism in Violently Divided Cities. *International Journal of Urban and Regional Research,* 37 (1) pp. 70-92

Neves, B.B. (2012). *Social Capital and Internet Usage: A Study in Lisbon.* PhD dissertation. Technical University of Lisbon, Portugal. ISCSP-UTL

———— (2013). "Social Capital & Internet Use: The Irrelevant, the Bad, and the Good." *Sociology Compass*, 7(8), pp. 599-611.

Nie, N.H. (2001). "Sociability, interpersonal relations, and the Internet: Reconciling conflicting findings." *American Behavioral Scientist*, 45 (3), pp. 420-435.

Putnam, R. (2000). *Bowling Alone: The Collapse and Revival of American Community.* New York: Simon & Schuster.

Robison, L.J., Schmid, A.A. & Siles, M.E. (2002). "Is social capital really capital?" *Review of Social Economy* 60, pp 1-21.

Robinson, J. & Martin, S. (2010). "IT Use and Declining Social Capital?" *Journal of Social Science Computer Reviews*, 28(1), pp 45-63.

Ruesch, M. (2011). A peaceful Net? Intergroup contact and communicative conflict resolution of the Israel Palestine conflict on Facebook. *First Global Conference on Communication and Conflict*, Prague, 2011

Slouka, M. (1995). *War of the worlds: Cyberspace and the high-tech assault on reality.* New York: Basic Books.

Stoll, C. (1995). *Silicon Snake Oil: Second thoughts on the Information Highway.* New York: Doubleday.

Sunstein C. (2001). *Republic.com.* Princeton University Press, Princeton, NJ, United States

Uslaner, E.M. (2004). "Trust, civic engagement, and the Internet." *Political Communication*, 21 (2), pp 232-242.

Van Kempen (2007). "Divided cities in the 21st century: challenging the importance of globalisation." *Journal of Housing and the Built Environment*, 22 (13), pp 21-31.

Wainwright, R. (2013). *Borders and Barriers-The Belfast Peace Lines.* Retrieved from http://www.richwainwright.com//foreign-assignments/borders-and-barriers-the-belfastpeace-lines/ accessed January 6th, 2014.

Williams, D. (2006). "On and off the 'net': Scales for social capital in an online era." *Journal of Computer-Mediated Communication*, 11(2), pp 593-628.

CHAPTER 7

Karachi's Urbanization:
Challenges and Prospects for a Thriving Digital Culture in Urban Life

Dr. Sadia Jamil
Khalifa University of Science and Technology
Abu Dhabi, UAE

ABSTRACT

Urban population in South Asia is growing at a very rapid pace and is expected to rise by 250 million by 2030, as per World Bank latest estimates. This pace of urbanization provides South Asian countries with the potential to change their developing economies to be part of the developed nations' group regarding both prosperity and livability. However, the region continues to struggle to make the most of the urbanization-led opportunities. One major reason is that its urbanization has been messy and hidden. Messy urbanization is reflected in the widespread existence of slums and sprawl, and in the lack of basic infrastructure and amenities for the public. With the advent of technology, it is widely opined that technology can help to resolve urbanization-related issues and can help South Asian countries to transform its major cities into smart cities, or at least a better place to live for its urban dwellers. Perhaps this is not the case for Karachi, which is the gateway of Asia and the economic hub of Pakistan. The city's urbanization is both rapid and messy, and it is not known to what extent the city's residents have benefited from the ICT development to cope with urban life challenges and their social interaction. Therefore, drawing on the *theory of technological determinism*, this study aims to explore major challenges and problems relating to the growth of digital culture in Karachi, the biggest urban city and economic hub of Pakistan. This study also addresses how and to what extent the proliferation of ICT infrastructure has transformed the public's lifestyle and patterns of urban social interactions among the city's dwellers. To achieve these aims, this study uses the quantitative method of *survey* and the qualitative method of *focus group discussion* and offers a thematic analysis of gathered data.

Key words: Urbanization, digital culture, urban life, urban social interactions

INTRODUCTION

Today, more people live in urban areas[1] than in rural areas worldwide. Particularly, countries in Africa and Asia are urbanizing more rapidly than other regions of the world and are expected to be "56 to 64 per cent urban by 2050" (United Nations, 2014). The case of Pakistan is noteworthy because the country is recognized as one of the most urbanized countries of South Asia. The Pakistani rural population is migrating to urban cities much more quickly than any other country in the region, resulting in an urban population growth of 3% annually. "The United Nations Population Division estimates that, by 2030, nearly half the country's population will live in urban areas" (Kugelman, 2014). There are a few key reasons for Pakistan's rapid urbanization, including migration from rural areas for better livelihood, safety issues due to war and conflict (especially in the tribal areas, Khyber Pakhtunkhwa and Baluchistan provinces) and an increase in population due to high birth rates (Kugelman, 2014).

The matter of concern is that Pakistan's urbanization[2] is "messy and hidden" (World Bank, 2015). The country's cities are growing beyond the administrative boundaries constituting "ruralopilies," which comprises almost 60% of urban Pakistan (Qadeer, 2000). Particularly, urban population dwelling in the southern port city of Karachi is facing the challenges of an increased crime rate and security risks, economic crises (especially poverty and unemployment), water and air pollution, poor urban land management (i.e. absence of land record system and data on used land), inadequate housing and health conditions, as well as poor sanitation, transportation and education facilities (Qureshi, 2010).[3]

Nevertheless, in the past 15 years, the penetration of ICT infrastructure and the proliferation of the internet and other digital technologies in Karachi and its suburb areas are remarkable developments, despite the challenges associated with the city's messy urbanization. Concentrated efforts have been made by the Authorities to foster

---

[1] UNICEF suggests that, "an urban area can be defined by one or more of the following: administrative criteria or political boundaries (e.g., area within the jurisdiction of a municipality or town committee), a threshold population size (where the minimum for an urban settlement is typically in the region of 2,000 people, although this varies globally between 200 and 50,000), population density, economic function (e.g., where a significant majority of the population is not primarily engaged in agriculture, or where there is surplus employment) or the presence of urban characteristics (e.g., paved streets, electric lighting, sewerage)".
See details at https://www.unicef.org/sowc2012/pdfs/SOWC-2012-DEFINITIONS.pdf

[2] "By definition, **urbanization** refers to the process by which rural areas become urbanized as a result of economic development and industrialization. Demographically, the term urbanization denotes the redistribution of populations from rural to urban settlements over time. However, it is important to acknowledge that the criteria for defining what is urban may vary from country to country" (Peng et al., 2000).

[3] Pakistan's cities contribute relatively less to the country's economy than in the neighbouring country of India (i.e. "58 percent of India's GDP comes from its 30 per cent urban population").

digital culture [i] through the development of ICT networks, the introduction of Broadband Policy (in 2004) and the establishment of a National Data Base and Regulatory Authority (in 2002) for maintaining the online records of citizens' national identification, their mobile SIMS and other data (Jamil, 2020). Karachi's public usage of the internet and mobile phones has also considerably increased in terms of access, subscriptions and level of content and services during the past decade (Jamil, 2019). The prime reason for the internet's influx in Karachi is the introduction of high-speed internet and mobile broadband services (3G and 4G LTE). These developments have had a "catalytic effect" on the Karachiites' use of social media. People now actively use new media technologies (such as mobile apps, video games, graphics and animations) and social media (such as Facebook and Twitter) to share their opinions, experiences, suggestions and feedback on any topic (Jamil, 2019; Jamil and Gifty Appiah-Adegi, 2019; Asia Media Foundation, 2010).

From an optimistic point of view, Karachi's technological developments can be viewed as potential drivers of progress and its development as a smart city, based on the assumption that a thriving digital culture can have a positive impact on almost all aspects of public life, such as personal identity, safety, education, economic betterment and so on. However, it is important to realize the technical and social challenges associated with the growth of digital culture in the city.

Thus, drawing on the *theory of technological determinism*, this study aims to explore the key challenges and issues relating to the penetration of digital culture [4] in Karachi. The study also investigates how and to what extent the proliferation of ICT infrastructure has altered the public's lifestyle and their patterns of urban social interactions. [5]

The survey findings reveal that 94% and 90% of respondents viewed *improper management of ICT infrastructure* and *high cost of internet and mobile phone services,* respectively, as the key areas of issues for the growth of digital culture in Karachi. Furthermore, 82% of the survey respondents regarded *poor service accessibility and quality* as a challenge for the proliferation of digital technology in the city. These findings are confirmed by the focus group participants, who suggested that the management of ICT infrastructure is poor in the city and that the internet and mobile phone subscription fee is not affordable for many people. Therefore, people do face problems in mobile and internet service accessibility. These issues also highlight that internet and mobile phone service quality is not as good as in neighboring

---

[4] In this study, **digital culture** refers to the public's use of communication technology (such as internet and mobile phones), social media (such as Facebook, YouTube and Twitter) and new media technologies (such as mobile apps and services, e-content, digital audio, video, animations and graphics, etc.) in everyday life.

[5] **Social interaction** means the establishment of a relationship between two or more people that leads to reaction between them. Social interaction and communication can be a physical topic, a regard, or a conversation, and the relationship between people that requires the definition of events and appropriate activities. Social interaction is the result of the role of the people in space and their membership in group and social networks (Akbari, 2015, p. 1156; Daneshpour, Abdolhadi and Charkhian, 2007, p. 186).

countries such as India and Bangladesh, despite the introduction of 3G and 4G technologies.

Some focus group participants, from Karachi's Central, Malir and Korangi districts, mentioned the socio-cultural constraints (including linguistic barrier, a lack of economic resources and content restriction by the Authorities and PEMRA[6]) as key factors that affect the public's use of the internet and smart phones. Overall, all the focus group participants agreed that the proliferation of ICT infrastructure has transformed the public's lifestyle and their ways of urban social interaction to a relatively large extent. Nevertheless, the participants urged the proper management of ICT infrastructure and the formulation of effective policy guidelines by the Authorities to improve the quality of urban life and to facilitate easy and affordable public access to internet and mobile phone services, thereby fostering the digital culture in Karachi.

To explain these findings in detail, this article briefly reviews literature on the *theory of technological determinism* and the *process of urbanization* in Karachi. The article then explains the methodology of the study and discusses the findings. Finally, the conclusion is presented.

Literature Review

Theory of Technological Determinism

The theory of *technological determinism* emphasizes technology as the chief driver of social change, progress and development (Miller, 2011, p. 3). The proponents of this theory view the potential power of technology in shaping people's lives, the way they think and how they interact with each other. The technological determinists' perspective of "technology as the tool of progress" is based on the idea that technological advancement can solve social problems, and this is the way that society develops and moves forward (Marx and Smith, 1994). However, critics of technological determinism assert that technology depends on the socio-economic structure within which it is implemented or operated (Winner, 2004). The author also thinks that technology cannot be considered as a "solo determinant" of change and progress, and its consequences are shaped by social, political, cultural and economic settings. In the case of Karachi, both contextual factors and urbanization-led problems can affect the potential power of technology in facilitating a thriving digital culture in the city. Therefore, this study seeks to investigate the ways technology is transforming public lives and how it reshapes the patterns of their urban social interaction in the city.

---

[6] PEMRA means Pakistan Electronic Media Regularity Authority.

Karachi City: A Brief Overview

Karachi[7] is one of the important cities of the world due to its population size, urban expansion rate and geo-strategic position. The city is the capital of Pakistan's Sindh province and it is the business hub of the country because economic activity in the city is central to the country's economy, constituting "20 per cent of total national output and 30 per cent of total industrial output" (Haq, 2014, p. 1). As a major revenue-generating city, with six districts, Karachi contributes considerably to Pakistan's economy and the provincial revenues. The city, with its massive potential to "serve" the Sindh province and Pakistan overall stands out as a "globalized complex in competition with other regional centres" of similar context and infrastructure (Qureshi, 2010, pp. 306-307).

Urbanization in Karachi

Pakistan is the most rapidly urbanizing country of South Asia. The country's urbanization rate is 3% annually, which is higher than the neighboring South Asian countries of India, Bangladesh and Sri Lanka. The population of Karachi alone has increased 80% from 2000 to 2010, which is the "biggest rise of any municipality in the world" (Kugelman, 2014). Karachi's rapid urbanization has resulted in an enormous stress on the city's capacity to provide adequate urban services to its residents (Kugelman, 2014). The city's inhabitants are confronted with gross problems of security risks, poor housing and land management; the emergence of slum areas (*kachi basti*); severe water and electricity shortages; a polluted environment; and inadequate sanitation, education, transportation and health facilities (Khuro and Mooraj, 1997; Hassan, 1999; Kazmi et al., 2008; Qureshi, 2010).

Karachi's urbanization is inevitable because of heavy migration of rural population from all over Pakistan and high birth rate, resulting in heaps of problems that clearly suggest that urbanization is happening badly. However, past studies have shown that urbanization can go well with positive outcomes and social progress. For example, Kundra (2014: 3) suggests:

---

[7] "Karachi was setup in 1728-29 by Hindu fishermen and merchants at the northern coast of the Arabian Sea. Former names of the city had been 'Kalachi Jo Goth' or 'Kalachi Jo Kuh', which later became 'Kalachi' (sometimes referred to as Kolachi) until the beginning of the twentieth century. In 1839, the British Army occupied Karachi and its strategic importance was immediately identified as it became the first airport of the undivided India (subcontinent) in 1843 and an important administrative seat for the British Empire. The British developed the irrigation system in the whole province during these years. Later in 1870, it was connected to Punjab with the railway link for mobilizing agricultural products to the port and within the country. So, these three main factors such as: irrigation system, railway link along with air and sea ports became the reasons for the development of Karachi as the main attraction for the people around. In 1869, Karachi became the largest exporter of wheat and cotton to Indian territories. In 1947, the independence year of Pakistan, Karachi became the first capital of the newly founded Pakistan (West). In 1958, it was decided that the capital should be shifted to Islamabad. But Karachi remained the capital of Sindh province" (Qureshi, 2010, p. 307; Hassan and Mohib, 2007).

Urbanization is a process of urban growth leading to the rise of a city or a social process whereby cities grow, and societies become more urban. In other words, urbanism is perceived as the product of societal change, the manifestation of certain economic and social systems at work.

When analyzing the case of Karachi, the city's process of urbanization can go well, and prolific transformation and long-term benefits can be achieved through social inclusion, economic viability, technological advancement and environmental sustainability to ensure preservation of environment. Particularly, today, many countries recognize the role of technology in meeting the goals of urban development. In this regard, Sharma and Sinha (2010, p. 8) highlight some very good international examples, stating:

> Governments of many countries are taking the lead in developing the next generation of cities driven by technological solutions. For example, South Korea is building a new city with state-of-the-art schools, hospitals, apartments, office buildings, and high-end cultural amenities. Masdar City, the world's first carbon neutral, zero-waste city, is an initiative of the governments of Abu Dhabi intended to position the country as a leader in renewable energy and sustainable technology component can enable the designing of smarter cities that offer a better quality of life for their residents while being more sustainable and cost efficient. It is not only the residents that stand to benefit from this trend; governments can meet their objectives faster and more cheaply.

Unfortunately, in Karachi, the process of urbanization is messy. Furthermore, the importance of well-planned ICT infrastructure and the potential role of technology in the city's urban planning and progress is not the priority of the authorities. The literature review reveals that, to meet Karachi's multiple challenges, five master plans have been prepared since 1923. None of these plans has been substantiated legally, however, which has resulted in the development of widespread slum areas (*Katchi Abadis*) in the city (Hassan, 1999; Hassan and Mohib, 2003). The Karachi Strategic Development Plan (KSDP) 2020 is the most recent urban development master plan that has a legal standing under "Section 40 of the Sindh Local Government Ordinance 2001" (City District Government Karachi, 2007). Ironically, Karachi's urban development is very slow, and the authorities' planning is ineffective by virtue of a lack of coordination among the various agencies liable for the formulation and implementation of projects and plans. This administrative inefficiency can also affect the proliferation of digital culture in Karachi and its growth as a smart city. There are no local studies that provide qualitative and quantitative insights into the key challenges that impinge the facilitation of digital culture in the city; thus, this study aims to fill this gap in the literature.

Methodology

This study investigates two research questions, namely: (i) what are the key areas of issues that are impinging on the growth of digital culture in Karachi? (ii) Has the proliferation of ICT infrastructure transformed the public's lifestyle and their pattern of urban social interaction in Karachi? To explore these questions, the study uses the quantitative method of *survey* and the qualitative method of *focus group discussion*. Using *simple random sampling,* [8] the study incorporated a total of 100 male and female survey respondents aged between 25 and 60 years old. These survey respondents were chosen from six districts of Karachi, namely Karachi Central District, Karachi East District, Malir District, Karachi South District, Karachi West District and Korangi District. Fifteen survey respondents were selected randomly from five districts of Karachi, and 25 survey respondents were chosen from Karachi Central, which is the largest district of the city.

Moreover, for the first research, the multiple-choice survey[9] questionnaire sought to identify the challenges and issues relating to the rise of digital culture in Karachi across five key themes: (i) improper management of ICT infrastructure; (ii) poor service accessibility and quality; (iii) the high cost of internet and mobile phone services; (iv) ineffective policy guidelines; and (v) socio-cultural constraints (i.e. language barrier, content restriction by the authorities and PEMRA, a lack of education and economic resources). For the second research question, the closed survey questionnaire explored respondents feedback in terms of "agree" or "disagree" to ascertain whether the proliferation of ICT infrastructure has transformed the lifestyle of the public and their methods of social interaction in Karachi.

Using purposive sampling,[10] the study includes responses from 12 journalists in two focus groups categorized on the basis of gender (i.e. six male and six female journalists in each focus group). The selected focus group participants were full-time employees of local Urdu and English-language newspapers and television news channels[11] in Karachi. Purposive sampling[ii] was used to include the feedback of Karachi's journalists about the city's urbanization and the challenges associated with the proliferation of digital culture in different districts. To ensure confidentiality, the

---

[8] **Simple random sampling** is an impartial and unprejudiced representation of a group. It is recognized a neutral method to choose research participants or a sample from a larger population, since every person of the population has an equal chance of being selected.

[9] In this study, **multiple-choice survey questionnaires** were used so the survey respondents could select the key areas of issues that affect the rise of digital culture in Karachi.

[10] **Purposive sampling** refers to the "selection of certain groups or individuals for their relevance to the issue being studied" (Gray, Williamson, Karp and Dalphin, 2007, p. 105).

[11] This study includes 12 Karachi journalists from the 12 most influential media organizations in Pakistan including: (i) Express Tribune, (ii) Dawn newspaper, (iii) The News International, (iv) Daily Jang, (v) Daily Express, (vi) Daily Nawa-e-Waqt, (vii) SAMA Television News, (viii) ARY Television News, (ix) Geo Television News, (x) Dunya News channel, (xi) Ab Tak News channel, and (xii) AAJ news channel.

names of the participating journalists in the focus group discussion have been replaced with numbers (ranging between 1 and 12). Furthermore, the study uses *relative frequency statistics*[12] to present the survey results in the form of percentages, and *thematic analysis*[13] to present the findings of the *survey,* and *focus group discussion* data under two different themes that emerged from the research questions of this study.

Findings and Discussion

Key Areas of Issues that Affect the Growth of Digital Culture in Karachi

Karachi's urban population is growing more rapidly than any other city in Pakistan. The city is stretched to its extreme limit, battling to provide basic facilities and services to its residents. While authorities at federal and provincial levels do allocate funds to resolve the city's widespread problems, the adoption of alternative approaches is indispensable for the long-term growth of the city. Proliferation of technology and digital culture can help in reshaping or at least improving the public's quality of life in Karachi. However, there are certain challenges that impinge the facilitation of digital culture in the city. For instance, 94% and 90% of the survey respondents highlighted the *improper management of ICT infrastructure* and the *high cost of internet and mobile phone services,* respectively, as the key areas of issues that affect the growth of digital culture in Karachi. Moreover, 82% of the survey respondents considered *poor service accessibility and quality* to be a major problem. Many survey respondents (79%) regarded *ineffective policy guidelines* as a problem area. On the other hand, some survey respondents (39%), especially from the Karachi Central, Malir and Korangi districts, mentioned socio-cultural constraints, including the linguistic barrier, a lack of economic resources and content restriction by the authorities and PEMRA. Figure 2, below, illustrates the key issue areas that impinge on the growth of digital culture in Karachi (i.e. the first research question of the study.)

In this study, the focus group discussion data largely validate the survey findings and reveal that local authorities lack proper planning and strategies to manage the country's ICT infrastructure. Moreover, people are unable to use mobile phone and internet services due to high tariffs and taxes. A senior male journalist from a television news channel stated:

---

[12] A **relative frequency** is the fraction of times an answer occurs. To find the relative frequency, divide each frequency by the total number of students in the sample – in this case, 20. Relative frequencies can be written as fractions, percentages or decimals (Dean and Illowsky, 2010: 1).
[13] **Thematic analysis** helps to classify data under relevant themes to interpret the various aspects of research topic (Boyatzis 1998; Braun and Clarke 2008).

I do not deny the efforts of the Government in developing the ICT sector in Pakistan. Nevertheless, I must say that the Government lacks effective policies and plans to expand the ICT infrastructure and to enable more people to use mobile phone and internet services..In Karachi, internet and mobile phone services are often interrupted due to messy urban planning and infrastructure and the Government's suspension of internet or mobile phone services during religious events of Moharam and Rabi-ul-Awal...Then, one must take into account high internet and mobile phone tariffs...people cannot afford WiFi services with heavy taxes...These are just a few deadlocks in the transformation of Karachi as a smart city and the promotion of digital culture in the city, apart from heaps of urban life challenges such as poor education, health, transportation and living facilities. (Focus group: Participant 10)

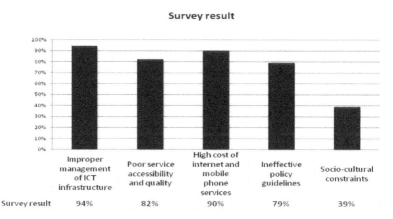

Survey result

	Improper management of ICT infrastructure	Poor service accessibility and quality	High cost of internet and mobile phone services	Ineffective policy guidelines	Socio-cultural constraints
Survey result	94%	82%	90%	79%	39%

Key areas of Issues Identified by Karachiites that affect the growth of digital culture in Karachi

Similarly, some focus group participants view socio-cultural constraints as the main problem area regarding the growth of digital culture in Karachi. For example, according to a female journalist of an Urdu-language newspaper:

Pakistan is a conservative country. So, one main problem is societal conservatism for the effective use of internet and mobile phones...Many women living in small cities and rural areas cannot use mobile phones and the internet freely due to family restriction..And this happens even in a big city like Karachi...Many people are not fluent in English to use mobile applications and seek information through the internet...the linguistic barrier is a problem..However, above all, I would say literacy rate has dropped in

Karachi and, overall, in Sindh Province that is very important for facilitating a thriving digital culture in the city. (Focus group: Participant 9)

Thus, drawing on the theory of technological determinism, this study suggests that technology depends on economic and cultural factors for the growth of digital culture in Karachi. The author believes that the political factor is also important because any ICT-related planning and implementation process in the city requires political stability and rational decision-making ability by the ruling authorities.

Impact of Proliferation of ICT Infrastructure on the Public's Lifestyle and their Patterns of Urban Social interaction in Karachi

The survey findings suggest that the majority of people (89%) who reside in six districts of Karachi "agree" that ICT development has changed the way they live their lives and interact with each other. Feedback from the focus group participants substantially confirms the survey findings. For example, the majority of the focus group participants (i.e. four out of six participants in the male focus group, and all the participants in the female focus group) "agree" that the proliferation of ICT infrastructure has altered the public's lifestyle and their ways of social interaction in Karachi. However, a few focus group participants (i.e. two male focus group participants) suggested that there is no major impact on the public's lifestyle. For example, a local television news producer stated:

> See! Municipal authorities play a very important role in the provision of basic infrastructure, maintaining the law and order situation in society all over the world. Good governance and innovative paradigms are both required to resolve issues and to facilitate urban and technological development. Funds are not allocated adequately, nor is the role of technology recognized by the municipal government in Karachi. I reside in Karachi Central District – where unplanned building construction, scattered garbage, severe water and electricity shortages, and poor transport and health facilities have made people's lives miserable. Basic infrastructure is in such a shabby condition that it often affects the internet and mobile services provision to the masses. Even for electronic identification at NADRA [National Data Base and Regulatory Authority], people from Karachi Central District have to go into other areas. So, the situation of Karachi is worst, not only because of rampant urbanization, but there is no clear policy and effective measures to tackle the issues arising due to the rapid influx of migrants into the city…Despite the growth of ICT infrastructure, I do not see any major impact of the technological development on the public's lifestyle in Karachi as they are living a miserable life when it comes to basic facilities. (Focus group: Participant 4)

In response to Participant 4's comments, a female journalist, who is an employee of a local English-language newspaper and a resident of Karachi West District, highlighted the ways ICT infrastructure has transformed the public's lifestyle in the city and the ways they interact with each other. She suggested:

> I partly agree with the point of views of Participant 4. We must acknowledge the Government's efforts in developing a centralised electronic system of maintaining citizens' national identification and their mobile SIMS card record online through the National Data Base and Regulatory Authority (NADRA). This is a security measure that can help in dealing with the increasing crime rate and terrorists' activities. Currently, the NADRA offices in Karachi are facing the problem of a heavy public influx and, at times, they do have problems in providing fast service. But it does not mean that we ignore the Government's efforts entirely...The Broad Band Policy (2004) and the introduction of 3G and 4G internet services have transformed the public's lifestyle considerably. You can see how much Karachiites are dependent on mobile apps and internet for online shopping and banking, e-learning, flight, train and taxi bookings, mobile health and food services...Now people's interaction is less physical and they are well connected through the technological web of Skype, WhatsApp, Twitter, Facebook, IMO and other social interaction sites. Yes, we are indeed far behind the developed nations and some developing countries (like neighboring India), where technologically innovative smart cities are providing quality life to citizens, but we should remain optimistic to reach that benchmark. (Focus group: Participant 5)

The author believes that Karachi's urbanization is both promising and problematic. The process aids Pakistan's economy through better revenue output; nevertheless, if not managed adequately, it may result in further aggravated situations regarding service delivery and the quality of urban life in the city. Technology-based solutions and the promotion of digital culture can help reshape Karachi as a smart city where all basic infrastructures—power supply, energy, water and waste management, transportation, health or education or communication—are planned and built with the use of technologically advanced materials and are maintained with integrated networks. By technology-based solutions, the author means the use of energy management softwares, integrated security management, smart meters/grids for power supply, high-tech communication networks, the introduction of GPS-enabled bus and train systems, [iii] online health, education, transportation and community services. Many countries worldwide have adopted technological solutions for the development of smart cities and the promotion of digital culture, including Songdo city in South

Korea, Masdar City in Abu Dhabi, and Ahmedabad in Indian Gujrat[14] (Sharma and Sinha, 2010, pp. 10-11).

Considering the current situation of Karachi, the aforementioned solutions may sound idealistic given the wide range of challenges that hamper the city's capacity to facilitate the public's access to and use of digital technology. A male local television news channel's journalist highlighted the deadlocks in the facilitation of digital culture in Karachi:

> Karachi's ICT infrastructure does enable interaction and interconnectivity between and across homes and office buildings. So, you can say that technology is rehashing the public's lifestyle and their mode of interaction to quite some extent. But the quality and service delivery are questionable in the city. Let me tell you how. Mobile and internet services are not accessible for every resident of Karachi, and even the quality is not good despite high service cost with the bulk of associated taxes....Additionally, the authorities do not even seem interested to invest in technologies that resolve power and water crises, to lessen energy consumption, to increase recycling of waste, to produce clean water and renewable electricity, and to promote a healthy environment – these are all essential for improving urban life in Karachi. (Focus group: Participant 8)

The focus group participants' responses suggest that they envisage a potential role of technology in transforming the public's lifestyle and their modes of social interaction. For example, a male reporter from a local Urdu-language newspaper revealed:

> I live in Malir District of Karachi, where the Sindh government started working on Arfa Karim's[15] IT City project in 2016. The Sindh's Ministry for Science and Technology is also developing a geographical information system which will contain the information related to city maps, roads, plots, population density and other indicators. These are some good initiatives that give us hope for the urban development of Karachi, notwithstanding the challenges...Penetration of mobile phone and the increased use of the internet has altered the pattern of social interaction among Karachiites, as it is more online now instead of face-to-face communication. Earlier, people used to have weekend town- and farm-house gatherings here, but now you will see

---

[14] "The city of Ahmedabad in Gujarat, India, has deployed a GPS-enabled Bus Rapid Transit System (BRTS) solution to meet its transportation needs in a sustainable fashion (see sidebar on Ahmadabad, p. 13). Ahmadabad BRTS is modelled on the hugely successful Transmilenio of Bogota and the BRTS of Curitiba, Brazil. These solutions aim not only to reduce congestion, but also to improve public transport and minimize environmental impact" (Sharma and Sinha, 2010, p. 11).

[15] Arfa Karim IT city was started in Karachi's Malir district by the Sindh Ministry for Science and Technology. The project aims to develop the IT sector in the city.

comparatively fewer people attending Mushairas, Ghazal nights, concerts and community functions. This can be seen as one of the implications of technology. In addition, urban life in Karachi is very hectic due to heaps of routine problems. Therefore, keeping in touch on text message or a phone call or WhatsApp is far easier for people than physical interaction... This implies that people, like in many other cities of the world, can be physically isolated in Karachi, but they are well-tied technologically regardless of time and space. Now people are actively using mobile apps and online services for banking, health, education, transportation and social purposes. So, I see a thriving digital culture in Karachi that is not only changing the public's lifestyle, but also it will bring more positive outcomes for its progress as a smart city. (Focus group: Participant 6)

Furthermore, drawing on the *theory of technological determinism*, this study reveals that the focus group participants viewed "technology" as a vital tool for resolving Karachi's urbanization-led problems and for transforming the public's lifestyle in the city. Nevertheless, the author believes that technology alone cannot perform a miracle and that the proliferation and the use of technology depends on the certain factors: a sound system of governance for effective management of ICT infrastructure, service delivery, useful policies and city administration, active civic engagement, and equal participation of all stakeholders including corporate and civil society to work together with the authorities for municipal management and to achieve long-term technological gains. One classic example of civic engagement and participation is the recent establishment of the Karachi-based *National Incubation Centre* (NIC) in May 2018, which serves as a technology hub for events, workshops and seminars, as well as being a digital platform to access Pakistan's leading mobile phone and internet services, and a common place for learning, fund raising (for various causes) and business expansion. The author emphasizes that more such efforts for operationalizing the idea of civic participation and corporate collaboration with local governance for technology-driven solutions of urban issues, the advancement of ICT infrastructure and the promotion of digital culture in Karachi are needed for its progress as a mega and smart city.

CONCLUSION

This study suggests that the rampant urban expansion and multiple challenges associated with the growth of ICT infrastructure and digital culture in Karachi demands radical and proactive actions by the city council, Sindh provincial and federal authorities. This approach means the conceptualization and implementation of a wide range of policies and practices around new, socially inclusive, environmentally friendly and technological paradigms. Technology has a key role to play in resolving Karachi's urbanization-led problems, and the residents of the city acknowledge this fact. Thus, the author asserts that authorities needs to pay attention to issues that impinge upon the proliferation of technology and digital culture in Karachi for its better future as a smart city, which can serve as an engine of economic and industrial growth by attracting foreign investment in the global competitive landscape.

REFERENCES

Arif, M. G., and Hamid, S. (2009). "Urbanization, City Growth and Quality of Life in Pakistan". *European Journal of Social Science*, 10 (2), 196-215.

Asia Media Foundation. (2010). *New Media in Pakistan*. Retrieved at http://culture360.asef.org/wp-content/blogs.dir/1/files/2011/11/ASEF-New-Media-in-Pakistan-WEB.pdf

Boyatzis, R.E. (1998). *Transforming qualitative information: Thematic analysis & code development.* Thousand Oaks, CA: Sage Publications.

Braun, V., and Clarke, V. (2008). "Using Thematic Analysis in Psychology". *Qualitative Research in Psychology, 3* (2), 77-101. Retrieved at http://www.tandfonline.com/doi/pdf/10.1191/1478088706qp063oa

Caragliu, A., Del Bo, C., and Nijkamp, P (2009). "Smart cities in Europe". *Serie Research Memoranda 0048*. VU University Amsterdam, Faculty of Economics, Business Administration and Econometrics.

Cohen, B. (2006). "Urbanization in developing countries: Current trends, future projections and key challenges for sustainability". *Technology in Society*, 28, 63-80.

Daneshpour, Abdolhadi, S., & Cahrkhian, M. (2007). "Public Spaces and the Influential Factors on Collective Life", *Bagh-e Nazar Magazine*, 4, (7), 19-28

Dean, S., and Illowsky, B. (2010). *Sampling and Data: Frequency, Relative Frequency and Cumulative Frequency.* Retrieved at https://www.saylor.org/site/wp-content/uploads/2011/06/MA121-1.1.3-3rd.pdf

Gray, P.S., Williamson, J.B., Karp, D.A., & Dalphin, J.R. (2007). *The research imagination: An Introduction to qualitative and quantitative methods.* New York, NY: Cambridge University Press.

Haq, M. (2014). *The Rise of Karachi as a Mega City: Issues and Challenges.* Retrieved at https://mhrc.lums.edu.pk/sites/default/files/user376/the_rise_of_karachi_as_a_mega_city_0.pdf

Hasan, A. (1999). *Understanding Karachi: Planning and reform for the future.* Karachi, Pakistan: City Press.

Hasan, A., and Mohib, M. (2003). "Urban Slums Reports: The case of Karachi, Pakistan". In UN-Habitat. Global Report on Human Settlements 2003, The Challenge of Slums, Earthscan, London; Part IV: 'Summary of City Case Studies', pp. 195-228

Jamil, S. (2020). A widening digital divide and its implications for democracy and social inequalities in Pakistan. In Massimo Ragnedda and Anna Gladkova (Eds), Digital Inequalities in the Global South. London: Palgrave Macmillan, pp. 59-78.

———— (2019). Mobile Phone Usage and its Socioeconomic Impacts in Pakistan. In X. Xu (ed.) *Impacts of Mobile Use and Experience on Contemporary Society.* Hershey, PA: IGI Global, pp. 112-127.

Jamil, S., and Appiah-Adeji, G. (2019). Journalism in the era of mobile technology: the changing pattern of news production and the thriving culture of fake news in Pakistan and Ghana. World of Media – Journal of Russian Media and Journalism Studies, 3, pp. 42-64. Retrieved at: https://doi.org/10.30547/worldofmedia.3.2019.2

Kazmi, S., Mehdi, R., and Arsalan, M. (2008). "Karachi: Environmental challenges of a mega city". In Misra, RP (ed.) *South Asian Mega cities.* New Delhi, India: Cambridge University Press, pp. 23-36.

Khuhro, H., and Mooraj, A. (1997). *Karachi Megacity of our Times*. Karachi, Pakistan: Oxford University Press.

Kugelman, M. (2014). *Pakistan's urbanization: a challenge of great proportions*. Accessed at http://www.dw.com/en/pakistans-urbanization-a-challenge-of-great-proportions/a-18163731

————. (2014). *Pakistan's Runaway Urbanization: What Can Be Done?* Retrieved at https://www.wilsoncenter.org/sites/default/files/ASIA_140502_Pakistan%27s%20Runaway%

Kundra, S. (2014). *Process of Urbanization*. Retrieved at https://www.researchgate.net/publication/303697345_Process_of_Urbanisation

Marx, L., and Smith, R. (1994). *Does Technology Drive History? The Dilemma of Technological Determinism*. The United States: The MIT Press.

Miller, V. (2011). *Understanding Digital Culture*. London: Sage.

Peng, X., Chen, X., and Cheng, Y. (2000). "Urbanization and its consequences". *Demography* Vol. II. Retrieved at http://www.eolss.net/Eolss-Sampleallchapter.aspx.

Qadeer, M. (2000). "Ruralopolis: The Spatial Organization and Residential Land Economy of High Density Rural Regions in South Asia". *Urban Studies* 37(9): 1583–1603.

Qureshi, S. (2010). The *fast-growing megacity Karachi as a frontier of environmental challenges: Urbanization and contemporary urbanism issues*. Retrieved at https://www.researchgate.net/publication/228652446_The_fast_growing_megacity_Karachi_as_a_frontier_of_environmental_challenges_Urbanization_and_contemporary_urbanism_issues

Rostow, W. (1960). *The Stages of Economic Growth: A Non-Communist Manifesto*. Cambridge: The University of Cambridge Press.

United Nations. (2014). *World Urbanization Trends 2014: Key Facts*. Retrieved at https://esa.un.org/unpd/wup/publications/files/wup2014-highlights.pdf

World Bank. (2015). *Leveraging Urbanization in South Asia: Managing Spatial Transformation for Prosperity and Livalibility*. Retrieved at http://www.worldbank.org/en/region/sar/publication/urbanization-south-asia-cities.

CHAPTER 8

Living a Watched Life in Kuala Lumpur: Normalization of Surveillance in Urban Living

Yvonne Hoh Jgin Jit
University of Malaya and Universiti Tunku Abdul Rahman, Malaysia
and
Amira Firdaus
University of Malaya, Malaysia

ABSTRACT

Cities, since time immemorial, have been the focal point of convergence for people, businesses, government apparatus and the activities associated with change and innovation, and power and control. One under-studied intersection of this city-centric convergence of entities and activities is that of surveillance. Training the eye on the Malaysian urban metropolis of Kuala Lumpur, one of many Global Cities (Sassen, 2001) and Alpha World Cities (Globalization and World Cities Research Network, 2016)), we explore modern and postmodern surveillance phenomena, and the normalization of surveillance in urban, networked Malaysia. Surveillance is a deliberate act of collecting information with "focused, systematic and routine attention to personal details for purposes of influence, management, protection or direction" (Lyon, 2007, p.14). The core act of surveillance is, plainly put, the act of watching in order to control, as exemplified by state surveillance in Malaysia through policing and political surveillance. Social media now empower ordinary people to exert lateral surveillance upon the state. Social surveillance is also facilitating civic and political engagement among ordinary people. With a new government still finding its footing after the May 2018 historic win by the opposition coalition, *Pakatan Harapan*, surveillance in Malaysia is undoubtedly still evolving. Nevertheless, as long as freedom of expression and access to online digital tools remain, lateral and social surveillance will continue to be practiced by Malaysia's networked urbanites.

INTRODUCTION

With 76% of the population in Malaysia living in urban areas, based on data reported by market research company Statista in 2017, the country is one of the most urbanized in East Asia, with rapid growth in urbanization over the past decade. The UN, in its report "2018 World Urbanization Prospects," predicts that Malaysia will be 86% urbanized by 2050. Kuala Lumpur, as its capital, is the largest city in Malaysia, with 1.8 million people (Department of Statistics Malaysia, 2018). In this chapter, the discussion on Kuala Lumpur includes the Greater Kuala Lumpur area, which is populated by more than 7.2 million people.

Kuala Lumpur – population and surveillance (See Table 1)

Table 1: Kuala Lumpur and Urban Malaysia

Kuala Lumpur	Capital of Malaysia
Greater Kuala Lumpur	Covers 10 municipalities in Kuala Lumpur, Putrajaya and Selangor state
Population	Kuala Lumpur: estimated 1.8 million as of 2018 Greater Kuala Lumpur: estimated 7.2 million as of 2016 Population statistics only include Malaysian nationals. Kuala Lumpur and Greater Kuala Lumpur are also heavily populated by expatriates, international students, undocumented persons, refugees and foreign workers
Urbanization in Malaysia	76% (as of 2017) Kuala Lumpur: 100% Putrajaya: 100% Selangor: 94.1% Penang: 90.8% *State urbanization rates are based on the latest National Census in 2010 by the Malaysian Department of Statistics
Internet penetration	Malaysia: 76.9% (as of 2016); 24.5 million Internet users in urban areas: 67.2% Internet users in rural areas: 32.8%
Internet access devices and broadband use	89.4% access Internet through mobile smartphones 36.3% access Internet through laptops and notebooks 29.3% access Internet through desktops 18% access Internet through tablets 28.5 million mobile broadband subscriptions in 2016
Social media use	97.3% Malaysians use Facebook 56.1% Malaysians use Instagram 45.3% Malaysians use Youtube Other platforms used by Malaysians include Wechat, Google+, Snapchat, Twitter, etc

Kuala Lumpur and Greater Kuala Lumpur include both Kuala Lumpur, located within the Klang Valley, and Malaysia's administrative capital, Putrajaya (both federal territories), as well as parts of Selangor state sitting within the Klang Valley. Kuala Lumpur is the center of political and civil society, as well as business, education and culture, and is a central node in both international and domestic transportation networks.

As is the case with many large cities, Kuala Lumpur residents include wealthy and middle-class Malaysians, as well as others who struggle to make a living, commonly known in Malaysia as the "B-40" or "Below 40" group, referring to those in the lower 40% income bracket. In addition to Malaysians who live and work in Kuala Lumpur, the city also plays host to myriad groups and communities, both cosmopolitan and subaltern. Kuala Lumpur is a focal point for diplomats, expatriates, international students, and tourists. Both legal and illegal migrant workers from Indonesia, Bangladesh, Nepal and other developing countries provide the city and the country with its "3D" workforce, doing "dangerous, dirty and demeaning" work that locals shy away from. An estimated 160,000 refugees and asylum seekers use Kuala Lumpur as a transit point to more permanent residential status in other countries – a destination many never reach, leaving them vulnerable in Kuala Lumpur to state and criminal exploitation, always being watched and sometimes hunted.

From state surveillance, government and corporate collection of big data, closed circuit televisions (CCTVs) and speed cameras dotting the city's building complexes and highways, to police patrols, neighborhood watches, building and living community guards and subaltern vigilante/underworld watchmen, these big city residents are always under surveillance in one way or another.

State Surveillance

Surveillance, at its most fundamental, is a deliberate act of collecting information or, as Lyon (2007, p.14) puts it, "focused, systematic and routine attention to personal details for purposes of influence, management, protection or direction." Historically, surveillance powers lie in the hands of the ruling powers, for whom surveillance is used as a form of management and control. As observed by Monahan (2010, p.91), "surveillance at its core is about control." Control is exerted through the collection of information obtained during surveillance, for instance, police surveillance of suspected crime. It is through surveillance that society can be managed and control, and to do so, the core act of surveillance is, plainly put, the act of watching in order to control.

This control can also be understood through the study of Jeremy Bentham's design of the panopticon. Its design illustrates the idea of the power of a few over the many through its use of the watchtower (which hides the identity of the watchers – the people with surveillance powers), and the prisoners who are visible to the tower – the watched. The concept of the panopticon emphasizes power relations between the watcher and the watched. According to Foucault (1977/1995), the presence or perceived presence of surveillance sustains "the automatic functioning of power" in its visibility (the watchtower or the metaphoric watcher). The panopticon is seen then as a form of power in which the birth of "disciplinary societies" comes forth, whereby the use of surveillance through panoptic power is used to wield control and to impose constraints to regulate society. A "disciplinary society," which is controlled and regulated through the use of a panoptic system, is naturalized to the fact of being under constant surveillance and self regulates to be accepted as legitimate and law-abiding citizens.

Traditional notions of surveillance revolve mostly around state or governmental surveillance and are often interpreted as negative. In a similar vein as Foucault, Fuchs (2011, p.136), taking a negative stance on internet surveillance, succinctly describes surveillance as being connected to "harm, coercion, violence, power, control, manipulation, domination, disciplinary power, involuntary observation." In particular, Fuchs highlights the internet as the ultimate tool of negative surveillance tool. The American Government, for example, exploited the internet to spy on its own citizens and on other countries. The American people and the world now know this, thanks to government contractor and whistleblower, Edward Snowden, and Wikileaks' surveillance of the surveillant. This turning-the-tables watchdog act might perhaps be thought of as positive surveillance, in which the power of surveillance is turned against the state – "the watcher" – giving power to the masses – "the watched." This is a form of empowerment through the use of surveillance, further discussed in this chapter.

Apart from the more "nefarious" use of surveillance for espionage purposes, state surveillance also includes some slightly more defendable intentions, such as policing for public safety and the management of population activity. From CCTVs to the use of biometric systems to track citizens, systematic surveillance is now a "routine and inescapable part of everyday life" (Lyon, 2010, p.107).

The discussion of modern surveillance in urban Malaysia fittingly finds a starting point from Kuala Lumpur City Hall's 1996 introduction of video surveillance to monitor and manage traffic congestion in the city center (Malaysian Multimedia and Communications Commission, 2008). Kuala Lumpur later adopted a Safe City Program in 2004, which saw more CCTVs installed to combat crime in public places.

The Malaysian Commission for Multimedia and Communication (MCMC) noted that Malaysia was, in 2004, still in the early stages of implementing video surveillance in public spaces. In 2008, 113 areas in Kuala Lumpur city were monitored by police CCTV in an initiative led by the Ministry of Housing and Local Government. By 2016, *The Sun Daily* reported that the Kuala Lumpur Police Chief at the time, Tajudin Md Isa, said that police were monitoring 309 security cameras in the city, while another 691 security cameras were monitored by City Hall (IFSEC Southeast Asia, 2016). This thousand-strong city security camera provision in Kuala Lumpur cannot be compared, however, to the 30,000 cameras in the city of Shanghai, a fact highlighted by the Kuala Lumpur Police Chief in his bid to install more security cameras in the city to combat crime. In 2017, the federal government announced that

200 "hotspots" would be installed with auto-tracking high definition CCTV nationwide. In the same year, the Government began collaboration with Chinese technology firm Huawei to develop video and facial analysis technology to aid policing work using surveillance cameras (Laili, 2017).

In January 2018, Chinese digital giant Alibaba announced that it is aiding Malaysia to develop a smart city system known as Malaysia City Brain, designed to "harness artificial intelligence, big data and cloud technologies" (Soo, 2018), effectively creating an ultra-smart surveillance system that, when (if) completed, will be used in a wide range of public sector services, including security. A few months later, in April, reports surfaced of Malaysian auxiliary police officers wearing body cameras with facial recognition capabilities developed by Chinese firm YITU Technology (*New Straits Times,* 2018).

China has grown rapidly in surveillance technology for policing and state control, with the British Broadcasting Corporation (BBC) reporting that, in its efforts to build the biggest surveillance network in the world, China has already installed 170 million cameras nationwide, with another 400 million to be installed within the next three years (2017). The same report stated that the massive and rapidly expanding surveillance system is used not only to prevent crime, but also to predict it. While crime prevention is desirable, one might argue that surveillance technology that predicts the probability that an individual may commit a crime is eerily reminiscent of the science fiction film *Minority Report,* in which otherwise-innocent people are incarcerated based on computer-driven predictions that they will commit a crime. The previous *Barisan Nasional* (National Front)-led Malaysian Government's intention to adopt China's surveillance technologies raises potentially difficult moral/ethical dilemmas.

However, it should be noted that most of these programs were announced before the historic change of government on May 9, 2018. Any changes by the new Malaysian Government regarding its surveillance policies remain to be seen. However, it is, thus far, highly likely that the current Malaysian Government will continue in the same vein, as there have been no announcements of any changes to policy. Strong indications of the close ties between the Malaysian Government with the Chinese Government and leading business figures are apparent with the continuation of the many collaborative efforts.

In fact, one of the first visits that Prime Minister Dr Mahathir Mohamad received from top Chinese business figures was that from Jack Ma, the founder of Alibaba Group, at the Prime Minister's office in June 2018, one month after the general election. One month later, Dr Mahathir returned the favor during a visit to China, meeting Jack Ma at his Hangzhou headquarters as his first stop. The Chinese e-commerce giant, which boasts more than 500 million shoppers on its platforms, spearheads the development and use of big data and cloud computing by tracking the digital footprints of its customers to work more effectively to continually change the shape online retailing, finance and manufacturing.

Surveillance Beyond the City

Government surveillance exists first in service of the people but can also be used as a political weapon. State surveillance goes beyond urban policing, through video surveillance, and includes surveillance against terrorism – much of it focused on the dark net and open social media, as well as political surveillance, particularly on the media and the online public sphere.

Arguably, as is the case in using urban city surveillance to combat crime, state surveillance is also an attempt to keep the public and the country safe (i.e. surveillance to protect national security). The global and regional rise of terrorism has necessitated many nations to implement anti-terrorism policies in recent years. However, unlike the general public acceptance of urban city CCTVs, a divide exists within Malaysian society regarding the threat of terrorism as a justifiable reason for the Government to spy on its people and others deemed as threats to national security. While there is general consensus on the need to combat terrorism, many fear that draconian measures to do so may impinge upon rights of free speech and privacy, reminiscent of post-9/11 American politics and the American Patriot Act.

The US Government's draconian reaction to 9/11 was often cited by the Malaysian Government at the time as validation of its own surveillance practices. These practices include controls over media and free speech, as well as the colonial-era Internal Security Act (ISA) and its successor, the Security Offences (Special Measures) Act 2012 (SOSMA) to detain people without trial if suspected of threatening national security. Malaysia argued that America, which had been highly critical of Malaysian Government censorship of media and public discourse and purported draconian laws, is no different – worse, in fact – in its transgressions of democratic and individual rights, for example, through its detainment without trial and clandestine torture of terror suspects and prisoners of war.

Traditionally, the Malaysian Government has maintained that it is important for media to play the role of government partner in the national development and preservation of national unity, peace and harmony in a multi-racial society. This developmental media ethos supported political surveillance and censorship by the state as a means of preventing critical voices from inciting racial-tensions. It should be noted that the online sphere is where much critical discourse occurs, in part due to government control of media (until recently). Consequently, electronic trails and big data offer tremendous opportunities for the state to engage in political surveillance of the online public sphere, as well as on political opponents and individual netizens.

State Online Surveillance

Malaysians enjoy high internet penetration, with 20 million internet users (as of 2014) in a country of almost 30 million. Within this growing number of users, a significant majority, as of 2015, are aged 15 to 35 (Malaysian Multimedia and Communications Commission, 2015), a demographic highly attuned to social media. Over 62% of the population access social media daily, making Malaysia one of the most "socially engaged" nations in the world (TNS Global, 2014). Online media hold a prominent presence in local public consciousness. Malaysia's high internet and social media penetration is the result of a decades-long state initiative to grow an information-based economy with a knowledge-based workforce.

While Malaysian media are traditionally controlled by the state through political media ownership and laws restricting free speech, the internet in Malaysia is free from censorship. The recently ousted but long-ruling *Barisan Nasional* (National Front) pledged a free online sphere in the 1990s to attract foreign investment, and generally kept this promise while it was in power.

Panoptic State Surveillance

This current age, in which technology has rapidly changed and is increasingly permeated into everyday life, has led to accessibility of surveillance tools to the general public. From telescopes and bulky cameras in the early 19th century, which were a significant part of media and documentation of history, to the current period of mobile cameras and CCTVs on every street corner in the typical metropolitan city, surveillance is now not solely in the hands of governments or even rich corporations, but available to anyone who has a camera of any form. This factor leads to the next trajectory of surveillance: the encroachment of surveillance into the everyday life of society.

According to a country profile about Malaysia compiled by the Open Net Initiative (ONI) in 2012, protection of privacy is highly regulated in the commercial sphere, wherein the dissemination of personal information for commercial purposes is prohibited. The state, however, retains extensive rights to use personal data for surveillance and legal action. Regulatory bodies such as the MCMC are empowered to search and seize private electronic data. All ISPs must be licensed by the MCMC, indirectly enabling the MCMC the right to access all ISP-held user information. In addition to using such data for security and crime surveillance (e.g. monitoring terrorist and organized crime syndicates), the Government can also conduct political surveillance using online data.

The ONI report (2012) concluded that Malaysians were generally "accustomed to monitoring and surveillance by the government." While most forms of state surveillance are benign or inconsequential for the average Malaysian, political surveillance sometimes leads to arrests of prominent bloggers and political writers. Reporters Without Borders (2011) noted that Malaysian bloggers and political writers were under strong pressure, with a number of politically motivated arrests since 2010.

The Communications and Multimedia Act (CMA) 1998 empowered the MCMC with broad powers in managing and overseeing online communications, from licensing to monitoring online postings, for instance, investigating and charging netizens who post (politically) offensive content. Section 211 of the CMA decrees that the posting of "false information" is an offense that, upon conviction, can result in a fine of up to RM50,000 (approximately US$12,000) or "imprisonment for a term not exceeding one year." In early 2016, the *Barisan Nasional* Government further proposed amendments to the CMA to tighten control over online discourse through blogger and online news site registration, as well as tougher penalties for online offenses. Although the internet is free from censorship, netizens must be wary of numerous laws prohibiting the dissemination of official (state) secrets, public incitement, slander, etc. These state acts of political surveillance undoubtedly contribute to an increased panoptic sense of being watched and the fear and uncertainty that accompanies it, especially for outspoken netizens.

Spyware Surveillance?

The Citizen Lab at the University of Toronto – an ICT, human rights and global security research center – named Malaysia as one of 25 countries it detected with servers running FinFisher, a sophisticated cyberspying system (Perlroth, 2013). Citizen Lab researchers Marcus Morquis-Boire and Bill Marczak said that, in the aforementioned article in *New York Times*, governments use such software primarily for political surveillance, rather than crime prevention. The Citizen Lab wrote that, while it cannot confirm whether the Malaysian Government was using FinFisher to spy on its people, it felt that there is the possibility that someone from the Government is involved as the software is sold to governments only.

The Citizen Lab suggested also that the modus operandi in the Malaysian case seemed to target Malay speakers who are interested or involved in the 13th Malaysian general election as the software was tagged to a document with a title related to the matter. The MCMC did not confirm or deny the allegations. However, when local news portal *The Malaysian Insider* published this story, the MCMC filed investigations against the portal, citing that the article was poorly researched and not fact-checked. *The Malaysian Insider*, a news portal owned by The Edge Media Group (which, incidentally, owns *The Edge Malaysia,* which has investigated and covered extensively the 1Malaysia Development Berhad or 1MDB, scandal that implicated the then Prime Minister Najib Razak), ceased operations in 2016.

Surveillance as Empowerment

The theoretical perspective of surveillance has shifted dramatically from one of control and power to a more postmodernist form of surveillance as an emancipatory tool. As described by Lyon (2007), modern surveillance theory centers on "classical treatments" that focus on the bureaucratic, the state apparatus and a more machine-like approach toward management and control.

Postmodern surveillance theory differs from classical treatments in that it has moved away from state or corporatist powers and toward the everyday surveillance that lies in the hands of those who have the technology to do so. This theoretical shift of surveillance from modern to postmodern conceptualizations of the (state) watcher and the watched (public) lies in the now-interchangeable roles of the former and the latter. Anyone can be assumed to watch and be watched. For example, web users embrace the idea of the many watching the many; thus, extending the concept of surveillance from panoptic to social. Unlike the control logic of uni-directional panoptic surveillance, "social surveillance" offers the possibility of interchangeable roles between the watcher and the watched (Joinson, 2008; Tokunaga, 2011; Marwick, 2012). Surveillance is not a force exerted upon the watched, but an activity that watched and watcher consensually participate in (i.e. "participatory surveillance") (Albretchslund, 2008). In contrast to the vertical exertion of panoptic surveillance, "lateral surveillance" (Andrejevic, 2005) allows for more participatory peer-to-peer monitoring in which people watch their acquaintances, friends and family in everyday life.

Here, opposition to surveillance that spoke of freedom of expression, particularly the idea of a political public sphere, is empowered by social surveillance and social media as surveillant tools, in which civic engagement, activism and use of surveillance become a form of empowerment. Studies by Shilton (2010), Wilson and Serisier (2010), Fuchs (2011), Leistert (2012), Reeves (2012) and Trottier (2015) identified that surveillance power in the hands of the public can turn into useful tools to balance the power between the traditional masters of surveillance and those who traditionally had no access to those tools to raise the voice of the minority or the ruled. Reeves, in particular, describes not only how surveillance can work against the ruling hegemony, but also with state powers as well. For many years, the political opposition and some civil rights groups in Malaysia have been expressing their unhappiness over the governmental control of most mainstream media, as well as the alleged self-censorship of media producers and journalists. Part of the reason for such practices, according to detractors, is due to governmental control through monitoring and surveillance. As such, these groups of people are particularly dependent on the Web 2.0 platform as their media channel for expression and communication.

Contextually, the socio-political environment in Malaysia has been one that is skewed toward a classical approach of state and corporate use of surveillance, with some controlled movement toward surveillance as a form of empowerment. Again, due to the change of governments, there might be some changes in the near future as the new ruling coalition, *Pakatan Harapan* (Coalition of Hope)[16], campaigned and won on a reformist agenda, promising greater freedom of expression and amendments to many of the country's more draconian and restrictive laws.

---

[16] As of March 2020, the Coalition is no longer the government, with power changes and breakaways from the coalition muddying the political situation in Malaysia

Empowering Social Change and Embracing a Watched Life

As previously discussed, when surveillant tools fall into the hands of the people, surveillance power becomes an empowering tool. In line with Andrejevic (2005), Reeves extended the study of lateral surveillance by researching the US Department of Homeland Security program "If You See Something, Say Something" and dissecting the Government's strategy of redirecting the responsibility of surveillance to the public. As part of the initiative to "harness the sensory capacities of citizens," this use of lateral surveillance has combined traditional policing strategies and the concept of peer-to-peer monitoring. As such, the public becomes part of the monitoring system, together with the state's surveillance apparatus. This willingness among the public to cooperate likely stems from the normalization of surveillance in general society. Lyon (2015) points to the 9/11 attacks on the US as a turning point for the narrative about surveillance by the American Government. People regard surveillance as normal and necessary because only the "new heightened security measures and information collection" can keep people safe from terrorist attacks. Such normalization of a previously jaundiced view of surveillance makes it an acceptable part of daily life.

Non-Governmental Individuals (NGIs)

As a tool of empowerment, surveillance has also become a useful method for activists and concerned citizens. So-called NGIs are independent and non-politically aligned individuals who work on issues or problems to help others in their communities. In Malaysia, NGIs are a growing group of people who are, in their own unique ways, trying to improve situations or solve problems within their own communities. These NGIs include prominent individuals such as Syed Azmi Alhabshi, who is often covered by the media and invited to give talks and speeches about his work, and Rayyan Haries, a young man who has traveled to areas such as the Philippines after Typhoon Haiyan to help victims and the island of Lesbos during the Syrian refugee crisis. There are also many lesser known people who dedicate their free time to causes such as animal rescue or helping the less fortunate.

Many of these NGIs, well known or otherwise, use social media for social surveillance to connect with people who need help, as well as to spread the word about the work that they do. Often, people who are watching the NGIs' postings help share and exchange information, as well as do their part in assisting. The constantly interchanging roles of watcher and the watched are particularly prominent in this domain. Take the previously mentioned Syed Azmi, for instance. Operating out of Kuala Lumpur, he has approximately 176,000 followers on his Facebook page, on which he frequently posts to share his experiences and his projects, shining light on the many cases that he is handling at any given moment. As Syed Azmi has grown more prominent with his NGI work, many people use this platform to connect and share information. One of the very successful projects that he started with a few others was FreeMarket, a project that began out of helping underprivileged and marginalized people in Kuala Lumpur.

The concept of this project is that people can give and take anything for free at the FreeMarket. This group, spearheaded by Syed Azmi, met in 2014 through a local community Facebook page for Taman Tun Dr Ismail, in a suburb in Kuala Lumpur. From there, they started organizing local community events that eventually led to FreeMarket. Now, FreeMarket has been held many times by the group or other people who copied the concept in many urban and rural areas in Malaysia, and in several other countries as well. The fact that this very local event managed to take flight in so many different places is due to the use of social media for the monitoring and gathering of information by many watchers who share similar interests.

Social Surveillance and Elections

In highly urbanized Malaysia, where 67% of internet users are from urban areas such as Kuala Lumpur, George Town, Ipoh, etc., Malaysians (particular those aged between 25 and 34 years old) are among the most active Facebook users in the world. In the 2018 general election, which brought a historic change of government, much was touted about the extraordinarily high usage of social media during the run-up to polling day on May 9, 2018. Not only were there the usual political discussions and sharing of news and rumors alike, on the night of polling, when results were being announced both online and through traditional media, users from various cities live-streamed from the polling grounds through Facebook. The live streams that were particularly of interest included calls for citizens to go to specific polling stations to monitor allegations of wrongdoings by members of the Malaysian Election Commission (EC) and the Malaysian police, widely suspected of stealing ballots to change the elections results.

Social media users from several cities, for example, Ipoh (of Perak state) and Klang (of Selangor state), used social media to galvanize others to scrutinize ballot counting and to thwart alleged ballot stealing by the then-governing party, the National Front. These users utilized their mobile devices and social media accounts as tools of empowerment through social surveillance, making it possible to circumvent what they consider to be political transgressions. This is how surveillance is enacted in which citizens become the watcher, performing their duties of civic engagement and political participation.

In the highly contested and close 14th General Election on May 9, 2018, when trust for news was at a low of 30%, and over 72% of those polled relied on social media for news (Reuters News Report 2018), social media platforms, such as Facebook, Twitter and WhatsApp, were important surveillance tools for the people to scrutinize and share political information. In a report by the Centre of Applied Data Science (CADS) in Malaysia, their research on Malaysians using Twitter during the general elections noted that social media usage was possibly a contributing factor to the wins by the Malaysian Islamic Party (PAS), because other than having strong grassroot engagement, the states they won (Terengganu and Kelantan) had low internet penetration. These states are lower in their urbanization levels, with the latest 2011 statistics by the Department of Statistics Malaysia placing Kelantan at the bottom of the table with 42%. There is a sense that engagement through online social media is higher in urban cities as the penetration is higher in these areas.

CONCLUSION

Observably, in this age, normalization of surveillance is enhanced through the exposure of people to the culture of surveillance. To discuss this issue, one must return to the principal use of surveillance – to control. As previously discussed, surveillance is employed to maintain and manage populations and, in its panoptic form, the simple acknowledgment of the existence of surveillance works to enhance security in any surveilled area. For instance, shops with signs of "CCTV in operation" are meant to deter shoplifting. Such surveillance, used as "social control," is often rationalized through a rhetoric of crime prevention, particularly in urban spaces. Discussing urban surveillance, Coleman (2005) turns to the concept of primary definition (Hall et al., 1978) to describe how positive views of surveillance arise from discourses centered around urban experiences and spatial order. He concludes that a primary definition of surveillance as "a set of technologies beneficial for the public interest" (Coleman, 2005) and a part of city space contributes to its general acceptance.

Coleman's 2005 discussion is also reflected in today's world, in which the emergence of "smart cities" has seen the alignment of the idea of a more efficient, sustainable and safe city shift to one in which surveillance is often widely normalized. A 2017 report produced by London-based organization Privacy International notes that smart cities are "oriented around citizen feedback and data collected by devices" in which the use of surveillant technologies is rationalized to promote "very specific visions of urban organization." One concern highlighted by the report is surveillance's encroachment upon privacy of citizens, in which personal information is no longer adequately protected.

Despite close state surveillance and the threat of prosecution during the *Barisan Nasional* era – or perhaps *because* of it – Malaysian civil society flourished in the relatively free online public sphere. While the media's watchdog role was inherently inexistent until the 1990s rise of the internet, the free internet enabled Malaysian citizen journalists, political observers, bloggers and online news sites – many based in and around Kuala Lumpur – to metaphorically exert civil society surveillance over the Government. This massive lateral surveillance, particularly by urban-based netizens in Kuala Lumpur and other major Malaysian cities, is widely credited for affecting real political change.

Surveillance and the (be it traditional) use of state apparatus or surveillance on digital platforms very much depend on the politics of the day. Policies and laws drawn up by the government determine how and how much surveillance will be used, not only by the state but also the types of surveillance a typical person on the street is able to procure and the results of surveillance that can be wielded. The government of the day will also address the types of surveillance technology that will be brought into the country and normalized in its usage. As discussed previously in this chapter, China's use of surveillance technology and cloud computing in both state and commercial sectors is probably one of the widest ranging in the world. Malaysia's close ties are apparent in its adoption of and collaboration with some of the technology in its policing and urban management efforts.

In May 2018, for the first time since independence 61 years earlier, the *Barisan Nasional* Government was elected out of office and replaced by the former opposition coalition, *Pakatan Harapan*. The new government is promising not only to uphold internet freedom but to also promote greater freedom of expression and a free media. However, with the historic change of governments in 2018, the impact of the change in state surveillance practices remains to be seen. At the time of writing, the new Government has been in power for a little over a year and, so far, there has been little indication in a change of approach in the use of surveillance in policing and urban management. Dr Mahathir Mohamad, the resurgent nonagenarian premier, received a welcome and official visit by Jack Ma, the founder of e-commerce giant Alibaba shortly after the general election. Mahathir reciprocally visited Alibaba headquarters in China in August 2018. Alibaba, whose cloud computing platform is set to be implemented in Kuala Lumpur's smart city initiative, seems to be continuously enjoying good business ties with Malaysia, despite the change of leadership.

The new Government, which promised to repeal the much-maligned Anti-Fake News Act 2018, has yet to make any significant changes in media policies. The Anti-Fake News Act 2018, which was hastily gazetted as law one month before the general election, was seen as an effort to stifle dissemination of information both on- and offline. The Act's loose legal definitions allow any information not verified by the Government to be deemed fake news. The Act is seen by many as a tool for the former Government to wield against dissenters, particularly those highlighting the former Prime Minister Najib Razak's alleged transgressions in the 1MDB scandal. The repeal of the Act, taking two rounds of tabling at the Senate after being passed in the Parliament, was finalized in December 2019.

The robust environment of social media in which the NGIs are actively participating in social surveillance for civic engagement and political participation should continue growing in its use and influence. As long as the media laws do not regress, and the popularity of social media continues, social surveillance will only continue to grow. Should the promises of the new Government regarding freedom of expression and freedom for the media eventually materialize, then the use of social surveillance for activists to monitor the performance of politicians and state officials, and the use of social media as a digital public sphere, will continue to be an important part of Malaysian civic life with the vibrant use of social media for surveillance and public expression and discussion.

REFERENCES

Albrechtslund, A. (2008). "Online social networking as participatory surveillance". *First Monday, Vol. 13*(3). Retrieved from http://firstmonday.org/ojs/index.php/fm/article/view/2142/1949.5

Andrejevic, M. (2005). "The work of watching one another: Lateral surveillance, risk and governance". *Surveillance & Society 2*(4). 479 – 497.

Axyrd, S. (2018, May 5). *Machine learning algorithms dive into GE14 battle on Twitter-verse.* Retrieved from https://www.digitalnewsasia.com/digital-economy/machine-learning-algorithms-dive-ge14-battle-twitter-verse

BBC. (2017, Dec 10). *In your face: China's all-seeing state.* Retrieved from https://www.bbc.com/news/av/world-asia-china-42248056/in-your-face-china-s-all-seeing-state

Citizen Lab. (2015). *Short background: Citizen Lab research on FinFisher presence in Malaysia.* Retrieved from https://citizenlab.ca/wp-content/uploads/2013/05/shortbg-malaysia1.pdf

Coleman, R. (2005). "Surveillance in the city: Primary definition and urban spatial order". *Crime, Media, Culture, Vol. 1*(2). 131 – 148.

Department of Statistics, Malaysia. (2011). *Population distribution and basic demographic characteristic report 2010 (updated 05/08/2011).* Retrieved from https://www.dosm.gov.my/v1/index.php?r=column/cthemeByCat&cat=117&bul_id=MDMxdHZjWTk1SjFzTzNkRXYzcVZjdz09&menu_id=L0pheU43NWJwRWVSZklWdzQ4TlhUUT09

———— (2018). *Federal Territory of Kuala Lumpur.* Retrieved from https://www.dosm.gov.my/v1/index.php?r=column/cone&menu_id=bjRlZXVGdnBueDJKY1BPWEFPRlhIdz09

Foucault, M. (1979). *Discipline and punish: The birth of the prison.* Harmondsworth: Penguin.

Fuchs, C. (2011). New media, Web 2.0 and surveillance. *Sociology Compass, 5*(2), 134 – 147.

Globalization and World Cities. (2017, Apr 24). *The world according to GaWC 2016.* Retrieved from http://www.lboro.ac.uk/gawc/world2016t.html

IFSEC Southeast Asia. (2016, Feb 29). *Police want better CCTV.* Retrieved from https://www.ifsec.events/sea/visit/news-and-updates/kl-police-want-better-cctv

Joinson, A.N. (2008). "'Looking at', 'Looking up' or 'Keeping up with' people? Motives and Uses of Facebook". In *Proceedings of the 26th Annual SIGCHI Conference on Human Factors in Computing Systems* (pp. 1027- 1036). New York.

Laili. I. (2017, Nov 9). *200 hi-def CCTV cameras for 'modern policing' to prevent crimes Deputy PM.* Retrieved from https://www.nst.com.my/news/nation/2017/11/301202/200-hi-def-cctv-cameras-modern-policing-prevent-crimes-deputy-pm

Leistert, O. (2012). "Resistance against cyber-surveillance within social movements and how surveillance adapts". *Surveillance & Society, 9* (4), 441 – 456.

Lyon, D. (2007). *Surveillance studies: An overview.* Cambridge, UK: Polity Press.

————. (2010). Surveillance, power and everyday life. In Kalantzis-Cope, P., & Gherab-Martin, K. (Eds.). *Emerging digital spaces in contemporary society.* London: Palgrave Macmillan, pp. 107 – 120.

————. (2015). *Surveillance after Snowden.* Cambridge, UK: Polity Press.

Malaysian Communications and Multimedia Commission. (2008). *Video surveillance in public spaces.* Retrieved from https://www.mcmc.gov.my/skmmgovmy/files/attachments/Video_Surveillance_Public_Spaces.pdf

———— (2015, Aug 25). *Communications and media pocket book of statistics 2015.* Retrieved from https://www.mcmc.gov.my/skmmgovmy/media/General/pdf/CM-Q4-2015_BI.pdf

————— (2017). *Internet users survey 2017.* Retrieved from https://www.mcmc.gov.my/skmmgovmy/media/General/pdf/MCMC-Internet-Users-Survey-2017.pdf

Marwick, A. E. (2012). "The public domain: Social surveillance in everyday life". *Surveillance & Society, 9*(4), 378 – 393.

Monahan, T. (2010). "Surveillance as governance: Social inequality and the pursuit of democratic surveillance". In K.D. Haggerty, & M. Samatas (Eds.), *Surveillance and democracy* (pp. 91 – 110). New York: Routledge.

New Straits Times. (2018, Apr 16). *AFSB first in Malaysia to integrate body-worn cameras with facial recognition technology.* Retrieved from https://www.nst.com.my/lifestyle/bots/2018/04/358122/afsb-first-malaysia-integrate-body-worn-cameras-facial-recognition

OpenNet Initiative. (2012, Aug 7). *Malaysia.* Retrieved from https://opennet.net/research/profiles/malaysia#footnote820f8nnp2

Perlroth, N. (2013, March 13). "Researchers find 25 countries using surveillance software". *New York Times.* Retrieved from https://bits.blogs.nytimes.com/2013/03/13/researchers-find-25-countries-using-surveillance-software/

Privacy International. (2017, Oct). *Smart cities: Utopian vision, dystopian reality.* Retrieved from https://privacyinternational.org/sites/default/files/2017-12/Smart%20Cities-Utopian%20Vision%2C%20Dystopian%20Reality.pdf

Reeves, J. (2012). "If you see something, say something: Lateral surveillance and the uses of responsibility". *Surveillance & Society, 10*(3/4), 235 – 248.

Reporters without borders Countries under surveillance: Malaysia. (2011, March 11). Retrieved from http://www.rsf.org/malaysia-malaysia-11-03-2011,39718.html

Reuters Institute for the Study of Journalism. (2018). *Digital news report 2018.* Retrieved from http://media.digitalnewsreport.org/wp-content/uploads/2018/06/digital-news-report-2018.pdf?x89475

Sassen, S. (2001). *The global city: New York, London, Tokyo (2nd ed.).* Princeton, NJ: Princeton University Press.

Shilton, K. (2010). "Participatory sensing: Building empowering surveillance". *Surveillance & Society, 8*(2), 131 – 150.

Soo, Z. (2018, Jan 29). *Alibaba helps Malaysia implement smart city programme.* Retrieved from https://www.scmp.com/tech/china-tech/article/2131006/chinas-alibaba-helps-malaysia-implement-smart-city-programme

Statista. (2018). *Malaysia: Urbanization from 2007 to 2017.* Retrieved from https://www.statista.com/statistics/455880/urbanization-in-malaysia/

TNS Global. (2014). *Malaysian Internet users amongst the most socially engaged in the world.* Retrieved from http://www.tnsglobal.com/press-release/malaysian-internet-users-amongst-the-most-socially-engaged-world

Tokunaga, R.S. (2011). "Social networking site or social surveillance site? Understanding the use of interpersonal electronic surveillance in romantic relationships". *Computers in Human Behavior, 27*, 705 – 713.

Trottier, D. (2012). "Interpersonal surveillance on social media". *Canadian Journal of Communication, Vol 37.* 319 – 332.

United Nations. (2018). *World Urbanization Prospects.* Retrieved from https://esa.un.org/unpd/wup/Country-Profiles/

Wilson, D., & Serisier, T. (2010). "Video activism and the ambiguities of counter-surveillance". *Surveillance & Society, 8*(2), 166 – 180.

CHAPTER 9

Digital Governance and Digital Literacy: Examining the Portuguese Case

Lucinda Caetano
FCT, CIAUD at the University of Lisbon, Portugal
José Crespo
CIAUD, FA at the University of Lisbon, Portugal
and
Rodrigo Cury Paraizo
Graduate Program in Urbanism
Federal University of Rio de Janeiro, Brazil

ABSTRACT

In a globalized world, our daily lives are increasingly visible (and lived) in social networks, and digital technologies are being used to create various opportunities for the citizen to interact with the institutions at the different political, economic and social levels. From local to regional and national governments, from administrative to political, there is an increasing number of channels for different levels of participation. There is a worldwide trend in the adoption of digital technologies by public administration in the form of mobile, web-based applications, digital modeling and simulations, and interactive platforms.

Portugal is no exception, to the extent that the country's legislation contemplates the use of collaborative territorial management platforms. In the daily routine for local administrations, however, such technologies and platforms are rarely used. The participation of the general public in Portugal is already very low, digitally assisted or not; however, 33% of the total population is not considered proficient in the use of digital technologies for participatory tasks, a digital divide that can pose a great risk in the near future as several processes will become entirely digital. Digital illiteracy is now greater than "regular" illiteracy during the period of the Portuguese dictatorship, and there is no visible effort to enable the population to overcome this division. Smart cities, however, to be more than a buzzword, must be as smart as the ability of their citizens to appropriate technologies to solve their own problems.

This chapter analyzes the Digital Governance in Public Administration of the continental territory of Portugal, at national, regional and municipal levels, observing different digital information tools related to the public administration, political activism and the integration of public institutions and their research purposes, such as municipalities, public associations, and universities.

Another aspect that is explored concerns the different typologies of participation and digital governance, ranging from the improvement in the provision of public services from the consumer perspective, to semi-active and active participation, such as participatory budgeting, at national or local level. This chapter also intends to verify the efficiency of digital communication in fostering participation, either at the content level or at the operational level.

In summary, this chapter discusses and explores the various facets of digital governance, with a focus on the main objective of increasing public participation levels for the collective construction of the city or, as Henri Lefebvre (2008) points out, to guarantee The Right to the City and the Right to Participation. We understand that the political will of government agencies is not enough to ensure participation; universities and civil society associations acting as intermediary governance agents have a key role in assisting digital literacy and simultaneously stimulating active public participation by making citizens active in the collective construction of cities.

FRAMEWORK

In a global society in which the New Urban Agenda of the UN Conference (HABITAT III, 2016, p. iv) presents "a paradigm shift based on the science of cities; it lays out standards and principles for the planning, construction, development, management, and improvement of urban areas" with the objective of inclusive and sustainable urban development and the universal right to the city.

The objectives of the New Urban Agenda are expressed in the Europe 2020 Strategy, which serves as a reference framework for European Union, national and regional activities and has as one of the main objectives Digital Governance through optimization of resources and the provision of efficient public services, using as tools for this paradigm shift ICT and public participation.

In the Portuguese case, the transposition of European directives into national urban policies led to the publication of strategic diplomas – Sustainable Cities 2020 [1]; the revision of some legal systems of territorial planning, such as the new law of general bases of public policies of land, territorial planning and urban planning [2]; the new legislation on Territorial Management Instruments (RJIGT) [3]; the change to the legislation on urbanization and construction (RJUE) [4]; the production of specific initiatives for Modernization and Administrative Simplification – such as the Simplex Program [5]; the Network of Participatory Municipalities (RAP) within the project *Portugal Participa – Caminhos para a Inovação Societal* [6]; the evaluation of the Municipal Transparency Index (ITM) by association with Transparency International of Portugal [7]; the creation of experimental projects by the Agency for Administrative Modernization (AMA), such as LabX [8]; the centralization of territorial information in the General Directorate of the Territory (DGT), including the

Collaborative Territorial Management Platform (PCGT) [9]; and the use of tools inherent to Participative Democracy, such as the Participatory Budget, both at the municipal level and at the national level [10] and the capture of ideas for implementation by the Public Administration, or by civil society organizations, as used in some municipalities.

CONCEPTS AND DEFINITIONS

Our theoretical framework explores the concepts inherent to Digital Governance, ICT and Public Participation.

Governance

One of the most "innovative" concepts, referred to in most strategic documents at local, European and national level, is "governance," which is frequently linked to a form of government based on transparency and public participation.The concept of governance is so broad that one can start from the generic and even simplistic view of Dente et al. (2005, apud CRESPO, 2013), who define it as "government activity." This definition is based on an interpretation that relates the meanings of "governability," "governance" and "government," in which "governance" corresponds to the government's ability to set goals and to make decisions for the implementation of necessary actions in its "governance" process and course.

Crespo (2013, p. 94), in analyzing this conceptual pluralism, which defines "governance" as "a set of actions, practices and processes that connote the exercise of government," while "government" refers to the "field of political institutions and organizational structures." On the other side of the spectrum is Kooiman (2003) apud Hall (2011), who defines governance as the "totality of theoretical conceptions about governing." In other words, governance comes to mean the totality of theoretical conceptions about the various "ways of governing"; that is, it is more concerned with the underlying ideologies than with the actions, practices and processes used in the activity of governance, being, therefore, the opposite of the definition referred to by Crespo (2013).

In his study, Hall (2011) analyzes governance as a key concept in public policies, especially in tourism policies, categorizing typologies and fundamental elements, defining governance structures into four distinct categories: Hierarchy, Communities, Networks, and Markets. Using this grid of analysis as a reference, governance starts from a situation of absolute control (Hierarchies), through the Market and Networks, until it reaches a situation of self-regulation (Communities) or "non-government."

Information and Communication Technologies

According to Luís Borges Gouveia (2004, p.12), ICTs are "a set of technologies associated with digital and that allow the storage, processing and communication of information, in digital, but also their conversion for the purpose of human understanding"; or, using the definition of Beynon-Davies (2002, apud GOUVEIA, 2004, p.12), they bring "together the technology used to support the collection, processing, distribution and use of information. The Information technology consists of hardware, software, data and communications technologies." (our translation)

Digital Governance

Returning to Hall's typological grid (2011), in the case of digital governance, we would have the same spectrum that varies from Hierarchy to Market and Networks and reaching Community. In other words, the demand may come from the government (top-down model), or mixed situations, or directly from the community (bottom-up model), such as the phenomenon of public data applications in Brazil, which, according to Marcelo Fontoura (2014, p.6), "lies at the intersection between the idea of government transparency and online participation, especially the work of hackers or the 'smart city bee' which is a digital startup, created by experienced professionals and experts in smart cities, whose goal is to accelerate the development of smart and livable cities and smart communities around the world" (our translation [11].

Of course, according to Chourabi et al. (2012), IT enables public transparency and opens new possibilities for democratic participation by enabling citizens to become more participatory and active in decision-making processes in their neighborhood and city. However, this change can only occur if there is "simplified" information sharing and if the Public Administration allows an active public participation; that is, if we are in the presence of a digital platform that promotes the interaction.

Public Participation

According to the literature on the subject, there are different types and definitions of active and passive participation.

The OECD considers participation to be active when:

> citizens are actively involved in decision-making and policy-making. Active participation means that citizens themselves play a role in formulating policies, for example when proposing policy options. At the same time, the responsibility for policymaking and the final decision lies with the government. Engaging citizens in policymaking is an advanced bidirectional relationship between government and citizens, based on the principle of partnership' (OECD, 2002, p.22).

However, according to other authors, real active participation implies the empowerment of civil society, that is:

supposes dynamic interaction among all external and internal participants, or technicians and community, through every phase of the process, from the earliest phases of defining strategies to decision-making. In this type of participation, communication and dialogue among those involved is promoted, in the form of conversation, open or small group meetings, as well as collective work sessions, facilitating a result conforming better to local objectives and to empowerment of communities.' (Vasconcelos, 2007, apud Raposo et al., 2017, p.11).

In these terms, what the OECD calls "active participation" would be more appropriate to define as "semi-active participation", because it refers to participation processes where public opinion, when evaluated, is only adopted, if considered relevant by the Public Administration.

On the other hand, it will be passive if it is:

> associated with actions such as information and consultation of populations, and generally corresponds to the final phase of processes, after the determinant decisions have been made by technicians and politicians. Cases in point are public audiences where those present can be heard, can get information and clear doubts about the process under discussion, yet do not take part in decisions (Vasconcelos, 2007, apud Raposo et al., 2017, pp.10-11).

Portuguese legislation on territorial management instruments, prior to Decree-Law 380/99 of 22 September (which established the Legal Regime of Territorial Management Instruments), was based on the logic of civic rights and duties, based on the four types of links between Public Administration and citizens, as shown in Table 1, below, so that public participation has always been associated with a passive format.

Table 1: Types of Public Participation

The duty of publicity	The duty of participation	The right of information	The right of participation
The Public administration has a duty to keep citizens informed	The citizen has the duty to participate in public inquiries requested by the Public Administration	The citizen has the right to request information and clarify doubts	The Citizen has the right to speak in the forums provided for in democratic regimes

Source: Caetano (2017, p. 60)

The publication of Decree-Law 380/99 presents evaluation as one of the basic pillars of public participation, changing it to a model that advocates semi-active participation based on information, participation and evaluation. Currently, the publication of Decree-Law 80/2015 further strengthens public participation. In the current model, the participation undergoes three phases. In the first phase, the Municipality has the duty to disclose all the information relating to the Territorial Management Instruments through Social Communication, Collaborative Territorial Management Platforms and websites. In the second phase, citizens have the right to make suggestions, observations or complaints and/or ask for clarifications (at the beginning, during and at the end of the procedure), to make proposals to draw up planning contracts with the Municipality and to intervene in the public discussion periods. In the third phase, the Municipality has a duty to evaluate contributions and to respond to citizens in writing or in person.

The Territorial and Administrative Characterization of Portugal

Portugal, a member of the European Union, is located in the Iberian Peninsula, with an approximate population of 10 million inhabitants and a population density of 112.5 inhabitant per km^2 (varying between 5 inhabitants per km^2 (Alcoutim/ Algarve) and 7,362 inhabitants per km^2 (Amadora in the Lisbon Metropolitan Area), with the most populous municipality being Lisbon, with 506,892 inhabitants, in the Portuguese territory (including the mainland and the archipelagos of the Azores and the Madeira) of 92,000 km^2, according to data from 2014.[12]

The structure of administrative division [13] in districts and municipalities was approved by Decree-Law in 1964, but superimposed on this structure there is another one for statistical purposes, denominated as the Nomenclature of Territorial Units for Statistical Purposes (NUTS) [14], approved in 1986, due to the country's integration into the European Community. The NUTS were organized into three levels of subdivisions, called NUTS I, NUTS II and NUTS III (see Figure 1).

The political-administrative structure emerged with the Constitution of the Portuguese Republic in 1976 and later revisions [16], determining the autonomy of local power, constituted by municipalities and parish councils (308 municipalities, of which 278 are on the continent, 19 are in the Autonomous Region of the Azores and 11 are in the Autonomous Region of Madeira). The number of parish councils (lower-level administrative divisions) after the revision was implemented in 2013 [17] was reduced to 4,259.

In 2013, the Government promoted a macro-territorial division, giving the possibility to the municipalities to associate themselves for the joint management of their territories, creating legal instances denominated metropolitan areas (AM) and intermunicipal communities (CIM). In Portugal, there are two metropolitan areas (Lisbon and Porto) and 21 intermunicipal communities [18]. Urban development in Portugal as a public policy for territorial development (for the past 20 years) is the responsibility of the General Directorate of the Territory, through the approval of the Territorial Planning Policy and strategic documents.

Figure 1: Delimitation of NUTS

Source: PORDATA, Contemporary Portugal Database [15]

The promotion of urban development in the implementation of urban policies at local level is done by municipalities through municipal or intermunicipal territorial plans. In recent years, metropolitan areas have gained relevance in urban development, such as the network programming of collective equipment, mobility and transport.

WHAT ARE THE MECHANISMS OF DIGITAL GOVERNANCE AND WHAT IS THE ANALYTICAL METHODOLOGY?

This research analyzes digital governance in Portugal at the three hierarchical levels of national, district and municipal, seeking to relate possible factors and evaluation criteria that provide clues about the index of transparency and citizenship promoted by the public administration. The resources for analysis were electronic media, namely the institutional websites and the digital platforms of the national and municipal Public Administration.

National Digital Governance Mechanisms

The analysis at national level was based on the observation of two different situations – action and evaluation. In terms of action, we observed three mechanisms of participation existing at national level, namely, the status of the Portuguese Plan of Action under the Open Government Partnership [19]; the existing content and the interactivity proposed for citizen participation in the Collaborative Territorial Management Platform (PCGT), integrated in the digital platform of the General Direction of the Territory; and the methodology adopted and the results of the two editions of the Participatory Budget of Portugal (2017 and 2018).

The evaluation sought to collect data from national observatories on the behavior of municipalities within the scope of local governance, specifically the integration or otherwise in the RAP and the ITM, analyzing average results at national and district levels and articulating the values with the evaluation criteria used.

Regional and Municipal Digital Governance Mechanisms

The digital governance evaluation in the municipalities of the Portuguese Continent used the averages by district of the predefined parameters: the ITM (based on the 2017 assessment); the eventual political change; the percentage of abstention in the municipal elections of 2017; the integration in the RAP and the use or otherwise of participatory budgeting. The data were collected from the websites of the 278 Municipalities and Institutions of the Central Administration.

The methodology of analysis of municipal digital governance was based on the data collection of all municipalities following a pre-established matrix with predefined parameters to delineate the situation of the country and each region. Following the global analysis, we selected a relevant case study based on the municipalities with the highest and lowest ITM in each region. The intention is to understand the relation of the various mechanisms of participation among themselves and in the promotion of more efficient citizenship.

DISCUSSION OF RESULTS

National Mechanisms for Participatory Action

The Portuguese Plan of Action in the Open Government Partnership

The Letter of Intent of Portugal (December 13, 2017) can be found on the website of the platform and refers to the actions to be implemented in the scope of transparency and accountability of governance and public participation. The document mentions two approaches.

The Letter of Intent refers, on the one hand, to the Participatory Budget of Portugal as a pioneering action worldwide and, on the other hand, reinforces the focus on the co-creation of public services through the "Simplex + Project"; the LabX Public Administration Experimental Laboratory and the National Open Data Portal [20]. The document justifies the national commitment regarding the adoption of the 2020 Strategy for ICT: Strategy for Digital Transformation in Public Administration in Portugal [21], whose measures are based on the articulation of data and online availability to citizens of public services of the Public Administration National

Administration. It should be noted that these measures, while important for the transparency and accountability of the Public Administration, are focused on the "consumer" of public services and not on citizenship or active civic participation.

The Portuguese Plan of Action in The Collaborative Territorial Management Platform

The Collaborative Platform for Territorial Management (PCGT) is an instrument for citizenship that, in the scope of consultation and public participation of the instruments of territorial management, was created in the Decree-Law of 2015, whose implementation was the responsibility of the General Directorate of the Territory. The present (2018) analysis of the content on the platform reveals that it is still embryonic. This is because documents and updates are lacking--both in the territorial instruments in force and in those in preparation.

The Participatory Budget of Portugal (2017 And 2018)

The Participatory Budget of Portugal (OPP) emerged in 2017 with a double approach, allowing the presentation of proposals at both national and regional levels. In the first edition, the ideas had to be presented face-to-face in the 50 participatory sessions that took place throughout the country, covering about 2,500 people. The organization by regions was based on NUTS II and took place in four areas of public management – culture, agriculture, science and adult education – whose overall value was three million euros.

The 900 proposals submitted were reduced to 599 projects submitted to a vote, and 38 projects (two at the national level and 36 at regional level) were selected through 80,000 votes. The major theme of these projects was culture, and the region with the most winning projects (seven) was the Lisbon Metropolitan Area. The second edition, which finished on September 30, 2018, maintained the same approach – national and regional – but changes occurred, increasing the scope of all areas of public administration and the overall value to five million euros. The presentation of the proposals could be made in person or through a digital platform. In this edition were presented 1,417 proposals (about 30% more than in the previous edition). Concerning the 692 projects that were voted on, 273 were national and 419 were regional, with the central region holding the largest number of voting projects (118), with culture remaining as the prevailing theme for the projects (79 national and 150 regional).

National Evaluation Mechanisms

The Participative Municipalities Network

The creation of the RAP was within the framework of the "Portugal Participates – Paths to Societal Innovation" project. The RAP aims to be a collaborative structure that brings together all Portuguese municipalities committed to the development of participatory democracy mechanisms at the local level.

The Membership will only take effect once the enrollment has been formalized and an annual contribution in cash is guaranteed, the amount of which varies according to the amount of the Institution's budget. The coordination is arranged by an association of the civil society IN LOCO in partnership with the University of Coimbra and the municipalities of Cascais, Porto, Odemira, and Funchal, with 53 municipalities as members, according to the document on the website. The news related to the "Portugal Participa" website give notice of Participatory Budgets (OPs) of the acceding municipalities. However, according to the query made to the websites of the 278 municipalities, not all the members included in the listing have OPs in progress. We have doubts about the updating of the data, and this situation has repercussions for the presented results.

The Municipal Transparency Index (ITM) 2017

The Portuguese representative of the ITM announce on its website the annual evaluation carried out by the Portuguese municipalities, whose relationship between the score, levels and content is shown in Table 2.

Table 2: The Score Related to Levels of Transparency

Degree	Level	Content
100	Level I	All information is provided
92.9	Level II	All 'determinant' information and more than 50% of the 'important'
85.7	Level III	All the information 'determinant' and between 25% and 50% of the 'important' information
78.6	Level IV	All 'determinant' information and less than 25% of 'important' information
71.4	Level V	More than 50% of the 'determinant' information and more than 50% of the 'important' information
64.3	Level VI	More than 50% of the 'determinant' information and between 25% and 50% of the 'important'
57.1	Level VII	More than 50% of the 'determinant' information and less than 25% of the 'important' information
50	Level VIII	Between 25% and 50% of the 'determinant' information and more than 50% of the 'important' information
42.9	Level IX	Between 25% and 50% of the 'determinant' information and 25% to 50% of the 'important' information

Degree	Level	Content
35.7	Level X	Between 25% and 50% of the 'determinant' information and less than 25% of the 'important' information
28.6	Level XI	Less than 25% of 'determinant' information and more than 50% of 'important' information
21.4	Level XII	Less than 25% of 'determinant' information and 25% to 50% of 'important' information
14.3	Level XIII	Less than 25% of 'determinant' information and 10% to 25% of 'important' information
7.1	Level XIV	Less than 25% of 'determinant' information and less than 10% of 'important' information
0	Level XV	No information is available

Source: Excerpt from the ITM 2017 evaluation [7]

The evaluation carried out in the municipalities shows that, in the 18 districts of mainland Portugal, the average of the ITMs is between Levels VII and X, with the districts of Beja and Guarda having the lowest level of transparency. Portugal is at Level VIII, so that between 25% and 50% of the "determinant" information and more than 50% of the "important" information are available on municipal websites. However, there are municipalities with higher and lower values. In 2017, the three municipalities with the highest score – Level III – were Alfândega da Fé, Vila do Bispo and Vila Nova de Cerveira, and the municipality with the lowest score – Level XIV – was Pedrógão Grande.

Regional and Municipal Mechanisms

The Portuguese mainland, with 88,600 km^2 and about 10 million inhabitants, has an average density of 115 inhabitants per km^2 and is administratively organized into 278 municipalities, of which only 20% have more than 50,000 inhabitants. The analysis of civic participation revealed that almost half the population did not vote in the last local power elections (2017) and that there was political change in only 17% of the municipalities.

In terms of the presence of digital platforms in the local Public Administration, the situation is generally assured, since at national level there are only two municipalities without an autonomous site, although one is represented in the Portal do Cidadão and another in the National Portal of Municipalities and Town Councils.

The analysis of municipality websites revealed that, when there are associations of municipalities, it is easier to access digital tools, in addition to reducing costs and standardizing the design, facilitating manipulation by users. We consider it important to mention the cases of the geographic information platforms of the Alto Alentejo and Cova da Beira Associations (NUTS III) that guarantee access to all member municipalities. In the same way, for a long time, the territorial platforms of the municipalities of the Algarve were assured by the Portal of the Association of Municipalities of the Algarve (AMAL); only in more recent times have the municipalities implemented autonomous platforms.

The diagnosis of the presence of territorial portals found that 78% of the municipalities (196) had active and accessible portals in August 2018: 15% have under construction sites or with a previous requirement of a login or download plug-in. In these terms, if we add the number of municipalities that have fully accessible territorial portals to those that are subject to conditionality, only 14% of municipalities do not have their own territorial portals. Nevertheless, some municipalities still have on their site the link to the National Territorial Information Service (SNIT), made available by the General Directorate of the Territory, although it is still not complete or updated, as previously mentioned.

The data collected show that the parameters that are related to the ITM are those that show how municipalities are engaged in tools of active participation, such as the integration in the RAP and the existence of Participatory Budgets (OPs), as verified in Table 3, which presents the values resulting from averages by district.

However, this rule has its exception in the Castelo Branco District, which, although there are no participatory budgeting processes and only two municipalities integrated in the RAP, scored well in the ITM.

Table 3: Relationship of the ITM with Other Parameters of Analysis

Districts	Quantity of municipalities	ITM 2017 (Degree)	Political changes (%)	Voters in the 2017 elections (%)	RAP (number)	OP's (%)
Aveiro	19	50.00	21.00	57.00	4.00	21.00
Beja	14	35.70	29.00	62.00	2.00	7.00
Braga	14	42.90	21.00	64.00	3.00	21.00
Bragança	12	42.90	17.00	61.00	2.00	17.00
Castelo Branco	11	50.00	0	61.00	2.00	0
Coimbra	17	57.10	0	56.00	5.00	41.00
Évora	14	42.90	7.00	59.00	0	14.00
Faro	16	50.00	6.00	47.00	3.00	25.00
Guarda	14	35.70	36.00	62.00	1.00	21.00

Districts	Quantity of municipalities	ITM 2017 (Degree)	Political changes (%)	Voters in the 2017 elections (%)	RAP (number)	OP's (%)
Leiria	16	50.00	38.00	54.00	2.00	50.00
Lisboa	16	50.00	0	49.00	7.00	44.00
Portalegre	15	42.90	13.00	65.00	0	0
Porto	18	57.10	28.00	58.00	2.00	33.00
Santarém	21	50	10.00	55.00	3.00	14.00
Setúbal	13	42.90	23.00	46.00	0	0
Viana do Castelo	10	50	20.00	59.00	3.00	20.00
Vila Real	14	57.10	21.00	58.00	3.00	29.00
Viseu	24	50	17.00	59.00	2.00	8.00
Average for 18 districts	**15.44**	**47.62**	**17.06**	**57.33**	**2.44**	**20.28**

Source: Elaborated by the authors

It is important to note the distinction between the presence of digital tools in Public Administration and the use of these tools within the digital governance framework, according to several different points of view: from the point of view of the consumer offering better public service; from the perspective of passive public participation that provides public information to ensure greater transparency and accountability of the public administration; and from the perspective of active or semi-active public participation that promotes active citizenship, including the management of participatory instruments.

Considering that the focus of this research is the analysis of active public participation in the local Public Administration, in addition to the averages by regions, we used a sampling technique with the municipalities that, in each district, obtained a greater or lesser degree of administrative transparency (evaluation of 2017) relating the evaluation to other important parameters in terms of civic participation. The other parameters under analysis are whether the population is smaller or larger than 50,000 inhabitants; whether the RAP is integrated; whether there was political change in

2017; whether participatory budgeting processes are in progress; whether it has a territorial platform that is autonomous and totally accessible; and whether the meetings of the Municipality or Municipal Assemblies are being transmitted live or via video on social networks.

According to the analysis performed in the 34 municipalities with the highest ITM scores (varying from Level III to Level VI), and in the 33 municipalities with the lowest ITM scores (ranging from Level X to Level XIV), it was verified that the factors that influence the evaluation are the mechanisms that promote civic participation; the other parameters having little or no relevance. However, some municipalities (both the 10 with highest ITM and the eight with lowest ITM) are outside the norm, which is why we consider it important to carry out a more detailed analysis of the exceptions. In relation to municipalities that, despite having the participatory tools listed, obtained low scores, it is worth mentioning some issues. For instance, given the unreliability of updating the information contained on the RAP website, it is not known whether the municipalities of Terras de Bouro, Tomar, Ponte da Barca, Amadora and Nelas were effective members in 2017, on the occasion of the ITM evaluation.

Regarding Carrazeda de Ansiães, its Participatory Budget was set 2018, therefore not active in 2017, at the time of the evaluation. The Municipality of Caminha only began the online transmission of the Municipal meetings and the Municipal Assembly sessions in 2018, and although there was no political change, different governance processes were created. Finally, the municipalities of Vila Franca de Xira and Amadora are unusual cases, because although there are participatory processes in progress, there is no emphasis on civic participation or municipal transparency on their websites. In addition, they are complex territories with high population indices, with Amadora being the municipality with the highest population density of the country – 7362 inhabitants per km^2.

Regarding the municipalities that obtained high scores, in spite of not having the participative tools listed, we present a detailed analysis in Table 4.

Table 4: Analysis of Municipalities "non-standard" with higher Transparency index

Municipality	Relevant factors
Alvito	Emphasis on the website on municipal transparency
Vila de Rei	Emphasis on the website on municipal transparency
Vila do Bispo	Emphasis on civic participation website
Batalha	The mobile application deployment
Fronteira	Existence of Municipal Councils in various areas of governance
Paços de Ferreira	The Municipal Budget was opened to public participation through an online questionnaire, The

Municipality	Relevant factors
	mobile application deployment, emphasis on the website on municipal transparency
Salvaterra de Magos	Existence on the Electronic Complaint Book site and in 2017 (the year of evaluation) and a Participatory Budget process was under way
Sines	Emphasis on the website on civic participation and municipal transparency
Arcos de Valdevez	Emphasis on the website on municipal transparency
Cinfães	Publicity on the website of the Code of Conduct and Adhesion to the project "Simplex"

Source: Elaborated by the authors

CONCLUSIONS

Based on the evaluation of the results obtained, we verify that Portuguese public policies reflect the commitment of the Portuguese Government to equip the Public Administration with tools of ICT to provide better public services and increasing transparency and accountability in public management.

In this sense, as demonstrated in national and local terms, the digital devices in the Public Administration are in operation or in the process of operation in practically the whole territory. However, as far as active citizenship is concerned the results are yet far from desirable, for a variety of reason: from the lack of a participatory tradition, to the lack of interest or distrust of citizens regarding politics, and the lack of digital skills of a large majority of the population. For some reason, In this particular case, the investigation identified only two municipalities that have Digital Service Mediators, which could help overcome this problem.

To understand the relationship between digital devices and active citizenship, or participation in matters of public interest, from the perspective of user participation, we used the classification in the three categories proposed by Vítor Domício de Meneses (2017, p.84), namely: Information Devices, Mobilization/Activism Devices and Didactic/Research Devices.

In this classification, Meneses defines Information Devices as the most traditional typology regarding governmental information portals, whose objective is related to the sharing of information "so that the citizen can follow the events and can act. However, there is not always room for user interaction." (2017, p.85) (our translation) Meneses stresses that:

> Mobilization /activism provide their users with the possibility of connecting with other citizens (mobilization) and as well as with decision-makers (pressure and feedback).

149

The transformation of the behavior of passive citizens, as consumers of information, into active citizens, who are part of a larger movement of mobilization and activism, is only possible if the relationship between digital platform and user is changed." (2017, p.88) (our translation)

Although organized citizens usually create these devices, in the case of this investigation one could also consider Participatory Budgets as Mobilization / Activism Devices.

The Didactic/Research Devices, according to Meneses, resemble the "Information" typology:

however, by inserting interactivity mechanisms and allowing analyses, comparisons and configurations in data display (...) Generally created through the association of companies and private institutions, these devices, although also aimed at sharing information to empower citizens, also have a didactic and research concern." (2017, p.92) (our translation)

One Didactic/Research Unit in Portuguese territory is the CIAB – Information Center, Mediation and Arbitration of Consumption of Vale do Cávado – which is an institution formed by municipalities, the University of Minho, associations and State Institutions to arbitrate. Arbitration is defined as "a form of administration of justice in which the conflict is submitted, by determination of the law or by agreement of the parties, to the judgment of individuals" [22].

In short, from the research carried out, it seems important to emphasize that there is still a long way to go regarding the emphasis on "digital literacy," the simplification of technical language in digital information transmitted (especially in the territorial scope), and the alteration of the format so that the manipulation/presentation of contents can be realized from the perspective of the user.

The problems are varied and range from the hermetic technical language that prevents a more consistent participation, especially in the scope of territorial management tools, to the nomenclature and the complex and unintuitive workflow of the services provided in the digital platforms that do not promote a real interaction.

Finally, it should be noted that in at least 10% of the municipalities we found projects or actions that are innovative or relevant in terms of citizenship, which can be inspiring for changes in terms of digital governance. These actions range from the collection of ideas or projects to the contest of ideas and proposals, to funding ideas to be implemented by collectives or citizens. In addition, we have verified other interesting situations, such as itinerant encounters with the population, the placement of Public Projects to Public Discussion (although not required by law), including the selection of a winning idea selected from several versions of public projects presented to the public. Other, more generalist and long-term initiatives include the creation of observatories and the production and dissemination of manuals on Citizenship and Participation; the adoption of a participatory process through the Local Action Group for the elaboration of the Strategic Program 2020; the use of forums with the boards for decisions on the municipal budget or its placement in public scrutiny to assist in decision-making; and the adoption of meetings with the population for information and debate on municipal intervention.

While these municipal initiatives are inspiring and helpful in the process of joint urban policymaking, we understand that the political will of government agencies is not enough to ensure participation. Universities and civil society associations acting as intermediary governance actors play a key role in assisting digital literacy, while at the same time they can encourage participation to realize the right of everyone to the city.

NOTES

[1] Sustainable Cities 2020 RCM 61/2015, August 11

[2] The new Law of general base of public policies of land, territorial planning and urban planning Law 31/2014, May 30

[3] The new legislation on Territorial Management Instruments (RJIGT) Decree-Law 80/2015, May 14

[4] The change to the legislation on urbanization and construction (RJUE) Decree-Law 555/99, 16 December, with the subsequent changes, in terms of republication in the Decree-Law 136/2014, September 9

[5] The Simplex Program https://www.simplex.gov.pt/ Accessed 23 August 2018

[6] Network of Participatory Municipalities (RAP) http://portugalparticipa.pt/Home/Network/ Accessed 23 August 2018

[7] The Municipal Transparency Index (ITM) https://transparencia.pt/itm-2017/ Accessed 23 August 2018

[8] LabX https://labx.gov.pt/ Accessed 23 August 2018

[9] The Collaborative Territorial Management Platform (PCGT) http://www.dgterritorio.pt/sistemas_de_informacao/snit/igt_em_curso__pcgt/pec_/ Accessed 23 August 2018

[10] The Portugal Participatory Budget https://opp.gov.pt/ Accessed 23 August 2018

[11] The bee smart city https://hub.beesmart.city/strategy/smartivist-accelerate-smart-city-development Accessed 4 May 2018

[12] According to the National Statistics Institute https://www.ine.pt/xportal/xmain?xpgid=ine_main&xpid=INE&xlang=en] Accessed 23 August 2018

[13] The structure of administrative division of Portugal Decree-Law 46139, 31 December 1964

[14] NUTS RCM 34/86, March 26

[15] PORDATA https://www.pordata.pt/NUTS.aspx Accessed 23 August 2018

[16] The 7th Revision of the Constitution of the Portuguese Republic was approved by Constitutional Law 1/2005, August 12

[17] Reorganization of parish councils approved by Law 22/2012, May 30, and implemented by Law 11-A / 2013, January 28

[18] AM and CIM Law 75/2013, September 12

[19] Open Government Partnership https://www.opengovpartnership.org/ Accessed 23 August 2018

[20] The National Open Data Portal https://dados.gov.pt/pt/datasets/ Accessed 23 August 2018

[21] The TIC 2020 Strategy RCM 108/2017, 16 julho https://tic.gov.pt/ Accessed 23 August 2018

[22] CIAB http://www.ciab.pt/pt/ Accessed 23 August 2018.

REFERENCES

Caetano, L., O. (2017). Public Participation in Territorial Management. A Construction of Citizenship. In *Proceedings of the Incubators conference at the KU Leuven Urban Living Labs for Public Space. A New Generation of Planning? Faculty of Architecture, Brussels, 10 11 April 2017.* © KU Leuven. E-BOOK | ISBN 9789082510898.
https://arch.kuleuven.be/english/research/publications/publications

Chourabi, H., Nam, T., Walker, S., Gil-Garcia, J. R., Mellouli, S., Nahon, K., Pardo, T. A., e Scholl, H. J. (2012). Understanding smart cities: An integrative framework. In *System Science* (HICSS), 2012 45th Hawaii International Conference on, pp. 2289–2297. IEEE.

Crespo, J. L., (2013) Governança e território. Instrumentos, métodos e técnicas de gestão na Área Metropolitana de Lisboa. Doutoramento em Planeamento Regional e Urbano UTL, Lisboa.

Fontoura, M. C. da (2014) Hackers e participação: uma análise de aplicativos de dados públicos do Brasil e seus criadores. Tese de Mestrado pela Faculdade de Comunicação Social da Pontifícia Universidade Católica do Rio Grande do Sul. Porto Alegre.

Gouveia, L. B. (2004) *Local e-government A Governação Digital na Autarquia.* 218 páginas. ISBN 972 8589 41 7 Publisher: SPI Principia

Habitat III (2017). *Nueva Agenda Urbana Español.* Secretaría de Habitat III de las Naciones Unidas. ISBN: 978-92-1-132736-6

Hall, C. M. (2011) A typology of governance and its implications for tourism policy analysis. Journal of Sustainable Tourism 19, pp. 437 – 457.

Lefebvre, H. (2008). O Direito à Cidade, Tradução Rubens Eduardo Frias. São Paulo: Centauro Editora.

Meneses, V. D. de (2017) Participação na era da informação: uma análise das TICs nos processos participativos. Mestrado em Arquitetura e Urbanismo e Design. Universidade Federal do Ceará, Fortaleza.

OCDE. (2002). O Cidadão como Parceiro, Manual da OCDE sobre Informação, Consulta e Participação na formulação de políticas públicas. MP SEGES, Brasília, 124 p. CDU 332.145+316.43

Raposo, I., Crespo, J. L., Lages, J. P. (2017) Participatory approaches in the qualification of semi-urbanised peri-urban areas: The case of the Odivelas Vertente Sul Area. In Mendes, M. et al. (Eds.) *Architecture and he Social Sciences. Inter-and Multidisciplinary Approaches between Society and Space*, Springer, pp. 151-176.

CHAPTER 10

The Potato We Need:
Public Space, Social Media and Participation in São Paulo's Batata Square

Fernanda Castilho
Paula Souza Educational Centre, Brazil
and
Richard Romancini
University of São Paulo, Brazil

ABSTRACT

The aim of this study is to analyze how social movements have been organizing public space occupation actions by analyzing the Potato Square in São Paulo, a historical place that, besides renewed recently, also acquired a new identity thanks to citizens engaged in this urban change (e.g. planting trees, organizing protests, fairs and educational booklets). The theoretical framework is based on the *placemaking* concept, particularly concerning collective rights of living, influencing meaning production processes and empowering collective spaces. Thinking about the city we need is thinking about a new urban space with active democratic participation, not only based on different demands for rights, but also on different political-economic practices (Harvey, 2003). The purpose of this paper is to observe the mobilization of social movements, highlighting the current one with strong use of social media, and what concrete actions have already been implemented in the square. We also want to observe whether these changes planned on social media contribute to the adoption of a new urban paradigm, according to the objectives and principles of the UN (UN-Habitat program). The methodology includes interviews with local residents and participants of movements such as "Potato Needs You" and the systematic participant observation of these groups on social media.

1. Introduction

Historically, Largo da Batata [Potato Square] is an urban space located in the junction of major roads of São Paulo. In addition to its symbolic value, it has also undergone several renewal processes over time, representing well the changing identity of its metropolis. In December 2016, *Veja São Paulo* magazine[iv] published an article on the possible internationalization of this space, reporting that the municipal administration had installed English signs to indicate Batata Square's location. Several activists who advocate for places with living space see the idea of turning Batata Square into a touristic spot as both positive and negative.

According to the activists, the symbolic recognition of the occupation history of the territory and its popular experiences are the main advantages of this idea, which corroborates with the guidelines of the activists who founded collectives such as *A Batata Precisa de Você* [Potato Needs You] and *Batatas Jardineiras* [Potato Gardeners]. To value the origins of the neighborhood, to organize more human occupation actions in the **public** space and to look after the patrimony are the main objectives of these activists. On the other hand, publicity (especially disseminated by media), regarding both the square and the Pinheiros neighborhood where it is located, would contribute to the distancing between real-estate speculation and its former residents, giving rise to new urban tribes and collaborating toward the place's gentrification (Hori, 2017).

The activists' activities developed a set of communicative strategies, mainly using social media, to subvert the image of the square as only a touristic or passing point, presenting it as a space for social coexistence, rescuing its origins. The pages created on Facebook are an example of how these activists communicate and organize their actions. The scheduling of activities, the dissemination of publications about the neighborhood or discussions on the inappropriate use of the square are examples of what can be observed in these webpages.

This moment is one of the most recent chapters of a long trajectory of conflicts developed in São Paulo and Brazil since the 1970s regarding the "right to the city." This expression was and is used by Brazilian urban social movements, which have achieved some victories, such as the enshrining of the right to the city in the Brazilian national law – the City Statute.[v] However, this mobilization brings up new elements, such as the participation of well-educated segments of the middle class in the so-called "urban collectives" who use the media strategically to mobilize and disseminate their cause.

Thus, the main objective of this study is to observe the strategies of media mobilization that support Batata Square and what actions were later implemented due to this mobilization. Furthermore, this study analyzes whether these planned changes would contribute to the city's adaptation to the new urban paradigm according to the objectives and principles of the UN (World Urban Campaign, 2016).

2. Old Urban Paradigm: São Paulo

São Paulo is one of the largest cities in the world, with almost 12 million inhabitants and a population density of 7.398,26 inhabitants per km² (IBGE data[vi]). Capital of the state of São Paulo, it is the largest South American city and the financial center of Brazil. Brazilians usually say that in São Paulo we can observe worldwide news, especially regarding consumption and culture, but they also point out its poor quality of life as one of the city's main downsides. As in other major Latin American cities, what prevails in São Paulo is an urban planning that neglects the human dimension, as stated by Jan Gehl: "Dominant planning ideologies – modernism in particular – have specifically put a low priority on public space, pedestrianism and the role of city space as a meeting place for urban dwellers" (2010: 3). Urban planning has focused on individual vehicular transport, with less emphasis on mass public transport, and even less emphasis on alternative means – despite the recent efforts toward the use of bicycles and electric scooters with the construction of cycle paths. The city has several types of obstacles for pedestrians, including noise and visual pollution (although the latter has improved after laws prohibiting the excess of advertisements), numerous risks of accident, such as irregular sidewalks, light poles with low and exposed cables, as well as other risks to health, such as the accumulation of domestic garbage in the streets due to the lack of public containers/collectors, two large and highly polluted rivers that cut through the city, making it smell bad and suffer from an excess of disease-transmitting insects. Unfortunately, these poor conditions are typical for city dwellers in most cities worldwide, as noted by Gehl (2010: 3).

Considering the conditions of an oppressive city, finding spaces of coexistence is a constant struggle for residents. São Paulo has some large and pleasant parks, such as Ibirapuera and Villa Lobos, among others, but considering the number of inhabitants, there is still need for more. São Paulo has approximately 12.4 m^2 per resident of public green space, but this space is not distributed equitably across the city (Welle, 2016). Hence, it has been increasingly common for the population to meet up in great avenues, such as Paulista Avenue, which is the financial center of the country during weekdays and now a coexistence space of several urban tribes and youth subcultures on weekends, especially due to the many cultural spaces located there (there is also an action by the municipal government to prohibit vehicle transition every Sunday, transforming the space into a pedestrianized street). Once again, the great squares have become important meeting places, such as Roosevelt Square and Batata Square

We chose the latter as the case study of this article precisely because it is an example of a place where the old and new urban paradigms coexist. To stay in the public space, city dwellers need to feel secure. A safe city, according to Gehl (2010), invites people to walk, as it has wide sidewalks, with adequate pavement, short walking distances, trees and attractive spaces. São Paulo has a humid subtropical climate, with mild winters and summers of high temperatures, mainly due to pollution and the high concentration of buildings. However, streets with public seats are very rare, and it is very common to observe long and narrow paths without any kind of natural or artificial coverage. These factors impact public health, as it is a city that does not invite its citizens to walk or to ride a bicycle, but encourages a sedentary lifestyle with car use.

Gehl (2010) presents a set of cities, including New York, Copenhagen and Sydney, where the government has intervened in policies to improve the human dimension. The subtitle of one chapter of his work, "First we shape the cities, then they shape us," is significant because he reminds us that decisions from the top actually impact citizens' lives and behaviors in the cities. Moreover, when do the citizens decide to resist the government decisions by the way they consider more appropriate, in a situation with no public policies have been made to dwell in a humanity way in the cities? Here, we have decisions being made from by the population or following strong social pressure.

São Paulo was built based on the functionality of an old urban paradigm, but its population is feeling the effects of this model as, "There are direct connections between improvements for people in city space and visions for achieving lively, safe, sustainable and healthy cities" (Gehl, 2010: 7). Thus, we note that groups of people have come together in "urban collectives" to resist the decisions of the public administration and to propose alternatives to occupy spaces such as Batata Square, transforming São Paulo into a *rebel city* (Harvey, 2012).

In the preface to the book *Rebel Cities – from the right to the city to the urban revolution*, David Harvey (2012) revisits Henri Lefebvre's ideas by recalling what the author wrote in his seminal essay "The Right to the City" in 1967, when Paris went through an existential crisis in the daily life of the city. Harvey highlights the importance of knowing the historical moments of cities and them theories. Currently, Brazil faces one of the greatest political crises of the democratic period following the impeachment of President Dilma Rousseff, which was understood as a political coup. Before that, in 2013, the insurgency of the population, known as the "Brazilian Spring," had already displayed the citizens' discontent at a wide range of subjects, particularly regarding urban issues in Brazil. The protesters shared "the sense that they have a right to better conditions of life that have not been realized; a right to the city they have made and that they should be able to live in ways worthy of their efforts; a right that has been violated" (Holston, 2014: 893).

São Paulo has an important role in this sense, because it is the city (together with Rio de Janeiro) with the most street demonstrations. Paulista Avenue and Batata Square are the main spaces for insurgency. Harvey also remembers the Brazilian history of fighting:

> The fact, for example, that the strange collision between neoliberalization and democratization in Brazil in the 1990s produced clauses in the Brazilian Constitution of 2001 that guarantee the right to the city has to be attributed to the power and significance of urban social movements, particularly around housing, in promoting democratization. The fact that this constitutional moment helped consolidate and promote an active sense of "insurgent citizenship" (as James Holston calls it) has nothing to do with Lefebvre's legacy, but everything to do with ongoing struggles over who gets to shape the qualities of daily urban life. (Harvey, 2012: xii)

Thereby, Harvey suspected that the urban social movements existing at the time melded into that revolt and helped shape its political and cultural demands. Harvey's explanation of the urban revolution not only concerns the intellectual legacy of

Lefebvre; what is happening in the streets (and online) is especially important to understand the new urban paradigm:

> Lefebvre's concept of heterotopia (radically different from that of Foucault) delineates liminal social spaces of possibility where 'something different' is not only possible but foundational for the defining of revolutionary trajectories. This 'something different' does not necessarily arise out of a conscious plan, but more simply out of what people do, feel, sense, and come to articulate as they seek meaning in their daily lives. Such practices create heterotopic spaces all over the place. We do not have to wait upon the grand revolution to constitute such spaces. Lefebvre's theory of a revolutionary movement is the other way round: the spontaneous coming together in a moment of 'irruption'; when disparate heterotopic groups suddenly see, if only for a fleeting moment, the possibilities of collective action to create something radically different. (Harvey, 2012:17)

In fact, Harvey's words translate well São Paulo's current moment, and can be applied to Batata Square and other places of the city. They are citizens who gather in the so-called "urban collectives" concerned with urban issues particularly created from the 2010s. These collectives aim to propose something different for the city and the spaces where they act by taking different paths with the use of new technologies and media.

3. Urban Social Movements in Brazil

3.1 Overview Through the 2000s

Tilly and Tarrow define a social movement as "a sustained campaign of claim making, using repeated performances that advertise their claim, based on organizations, networks, traditions, and solidarities that sustain these activities" (2007: 8). Thinking directly about "urban social movements," Castells characterizes them as "a conscious collective practice originating in urban issues, able to produce qualitative changes in the urban system, local culture, and political institutions in contradiction to the dominant social interests institutionalized as such at the societal level" (1983: 278).

It is also important to note that, to achieve certain results, social movements must highlight problems not always perceived by the rest of society, which contributes to the activists' protest actions. Social movements make the "invisible" issues "visible," or as Johnston notes, they establish "new frames of interpretation [...] by which people can come to see old injustices in new ways" (2014: 65). Hence, leaders of movements and activists develop themes and ideas to motivate actions and to attract new supporters.

Due to the hierarchical and undemocratic nature of Brazilian society, marked by "patronage," which is the exchange of favors between leaders and the population, social movements had little relevance until 1950. In that decade, neighborhood associations (*Sociedades de Amigos do Bairro*) emerged, which were supported by progressive sectors of the Catholic Church and which supported residents' claims, from poor and middle-class neighborhoods, regarding basic sanitation, public transportation and housing. Progressive Church sectors have worked in favela communities also, helping poor people living there to get organized and to claim their rights. However, the democratic rupture in Brazil harmed the emergent urban social movements of an autonomous character. As Earle (2017: 116) notes, "The repressive tactics of the military regime from 1964 onwards against worker, student and peasant groups quickly put down popular organizations that had emerged."

Paradoxically, however, in the midst of the political closure in the 1970s, there was a further strengthening of social movements, and this "can be seen as the *constitution of the social as a political space* in which people began to imagine alternative futures and to perceive these in opposition to the state's project for them" (Telles, 1994: 198). Explaining the specific return of urban social movements, there is need to consider the fact that the rapid population growth in peripheral urban areas provides new impetus to the claims, so that "several groups emerged to emphasize favelas, poor neighborhoods, and living conditions in Brazilian cities" (Friendly, 2017: 134). Again, the Catholic Church, but also urbanists and Marxist intellectuals collaborated with these urban social movements, helping them to produce a discourse aimed at "fostering a politics of citizenship around the 'right to have rights'" (Idem).

These movements played an important role in pro-democracy mobilizations with the creation, in 1980, of the party that would become the main Brazilian left-wing party (the Workers' Party, PT) and, in 1982, of the *Movimento Nacional da Reforma Urbana* [National Movement for Urban Reform] (MNRU), which established a proposal for "urban reform"[vii] during the Brazilian National Constituent Assembly (1986–1988). The constitutional proposals elaborated by the MNRU were diluted in the document, but the discourse constructed by the urban social movements had a strong influence on the elaboration of the Bill of June 28, 1989, which became known as the City Statute. Urban social movements then adopted Lefebvre's ideas on "the right to the city," but from a less utopian perspective (i.e. they were more concerned with the *inclusion* of marginalized groups in the *city as it exists today*) (Friendly, 2017). This more "materialistic" dimension was also the focus of activist political lobbying practices, as well as their role in government positions, in the management (mainly municipal) of leftist parties, in subsequent years.

This aspect also characterizes the emergence of another struggle front of urban social movements in the mid-1980s: the struggle for decent housing in the city's more central regions. Quite visible today due to the media coverage, the movements that occupy vacant buildings in central areas of the city, demanding their ownership and the requalification of them for popular housing, have *União de Movimentos de Moradia* [Housing Movements Union] (UMN), created in 1987, among their pioneer organizations by the joining of different associations focused on popular housing. Today, *Movimento de Trabalhadores Sem Teto* [Homeless Workers Movement]

(MTST), whose leader (Guilherme Boulos) was a candidate for presidency in the 2018 elections with *Partido Socialismo e Libertade* [Socialism and Freedom Party] (PSOL), was formed by a group expelled from PT in 2004. These and other associations are inspired by what is probably the most well-known social movement organization in Brazil, the *Movimento dos Trabalhadores Sem Terra* [Landless Workers' Movement] (MST), bringing occupation tactics to the urban context. It is estimated that there are currently 206 occupations of land and buildings in São Paulo, where approximately 45,000 families live (Santiago, 2018).

3.2 The Collectives of the 2000s: New Urban Social Movements?

Several studies, starting in the mid-2000s, have identified the emergence of "urban collectives" and are dedicated to questioning the predominant urbanism and use of São Paulo (Maziviero, 2016; Hori, 2017; Giaretta and Giulio, 2018). Sometimes, these collectives have objectives directly linked to urbanism and the placemaking of a certain space in the city (which is the case with the group "Potato Needs You"); in other situations, they develop an appropriation of the city in more diverse contexts and from more properly artistic concerns, and of performance and playfulness (as in the case of "Barulho.org," or "Noise.org," created in 2002 and aimed at using public spaces through the organization of parties). But:

> all are united around the same ideal of starting discussions about the practice of building the city through unpredictable appropriations and actions. They draw citizens' attention and attract glances at idle public spaces, forgotten by government and society, to highlight the ideal of leisure, culture and coexistence in the urban environment. (Hori, 2017: 4)

Still regarding collectives, Hori (2017) observed that those who work in the transformation of space have their actions concentrated downtown and in the southwest quadrant of São Paulo, which are the regions with the highest income, high Human Development Index, and lower homicide rates and social vulnerability of the city. Therefore, the author hypothesizes that these collectives are counterpoint to the idea of Caldeira (2000). In this case, Caldeira argues that young people from the elite were trying to isolate themselves from the city, which would characterize São Paulo as a "city of walls." However, this does not seem true, at least for the younger segments of these elites, who tend to comprise certain urban collectives. "In addition, these young people from the privileged classes were able to learn about experiences and experience the public space in other cities around the world, giving them the awareness that the city of São Paulo is lacking in quality spaces suitable for people's use" (Hori, 2017: 7).

At the same time, the educational conditions of these participants contribute to the use of technologies to organize and disseminate their proposals and actions. Therefore, Giaretta and Giulio (2018), when analyzing three city collectives whose discussions and actions focus on urban space, approached the emergence of "new social movements," which were deeply grounded on the use of technologies as they "use ICT as the main resource to organize and structure their groups, to later be able to elaborate strategies to directly influence the government's decision-making with expanded visibility of their claims in traditional media channels (TV and newspaper)" (Giaretta and Giulio, 2018: 172).

In this brief description and characterization of the collectives, we can see some important differences regarding the traditional urban social movements, which leads us to the question: Do the collectives represent *new urban social movements*? These collectives are, without doubt, significant collective actions, but, according to the definitions by Tilly and Tarrow, as well as Castells, these groups lack a longer and "sustained" trajectory. These features would define, more clearly, the contours and the nature of the demands on the proposed uses of the city by these groups. As Hori (2017) observes, some types of collective action made by the groups are closer to "cultural **animation's**" logic than to urban and political claims, being sometimes appropriated by politicos with this ludic sense too. This appropriation did not occur in the second case, which ended, contradictorily, by strengthening right-wing groups that joined the demonstrations (Earler, 2017).

Perhaps, however, collectives may constitute new embryonic forms of social movements. Thus, it is worthwhile studying them to understand the new forms of urban action and claims of cities with as many problems as São Paulo. Anyway, what is the meaning of the "right to the city" for a collective like "Potato Needs You"?

4. Batata Square

The Largo da Batata [Batata Square] is an open space area (intersected by two large avenues) of 23,000 m^2. This place is important because of its geographical location (in the Pinheiros district) as a crossing point of the Pinheiros river for the ancient Brazilian natives (Caldeira, 2015; Petrone, 1963). As a crossing point, commerce developed there, especially since 1910, with the inauguration of the *Mercado de Pinheiros* [Market of Pinheiros] in the square region. One of the best-selling products was potatoes, produced on a large scale by farmers (many of Japanese origin) in regions near São Paulo. With the overwhelming population growth (reaching rates of 400% between the 1940s and 1960s in Cotia), the populations of these more peripheral regions continued to move to São Paulo, passing through Largo da Batata (Caldeira, 2015: 23). For many years, this location had one of the busiest bus terminals, resulting in traffic and pollution problems. Avenue-widening projects have been under discussion in the government for decades.

The large number of planned expropriations to extend the Faria Lima Avenue (which intersects the square) in the project proposals of 1993 generated dissatisfaction and resistance among the middle-class residents of "Pinheiros Alive Movement."[viii] More than 10 years later, after different exchanges between governments and several popular resistances, there was the inevitable expansion of Faria Lima Avenue and an

Urban Reconversion of Potato Square was proposed in 2001, which was only "completed" in 2013.

The "Pinheiros Alive Movement" is a traditional union of the residents of the Pinheiros district. These educated middle-class people had raised awareness of the need for participation in urban management for over 15 years since 1993. It is likely that the current urban collectives in the region stem from these old movements, articulating through emerging technologies.

4.1 Potato Needs You: Occupy and Resist

The object of our analysis, *A Batata Precisa de Você* [Potato Needs You], is a collective formed by residents and visitors to Batata Square. The collective is a horizontal organization that defines itself as a "movement of citizenship and social and urban implementation."[ix] The group's proposal is to transform the space into a more human and socially friendly place. The group has carried out weekly actions toward space occupation since 2014, with meaningful results of transformative mobilization. In addition to the occupation and actions aimed at strengthening the affective relationship of the population with the space and at making improvements, the collective also claims more participatory urban governance through public power.

Another affirmative action is the collective's website, whose media content has received the support of the city of São Paulo through the "Networks and Streets" announcement of 2014, in partnership with the municipal departments of Culture, Human Rights and Citizenship and Services, during the mandate of the mayor Fernando Haddad from the Workers' Party.[x] In addition to information on the group and an open agenda of the popular events, the website has two important materials: a publication/occupation manual and a video. The manual (pdf) is very rich and extensive (66 pages), including the history of the square and information about different activism movements justified by urbanism concepts (one of the founders of the collective is an architect and activist).

Another important feature is the manual's educational dimension, as it teaches the practice of urban tactics – quick and temporary projects with change potential. The booklet describes cultural activation methods and how to make temporary furniture, explaining the importance of knowing legal instruments, including a summary of the legislation on public space use and an occupation manual with the systematization of the process carried out by the collective. The video is a mini-documentary with testimonies and images of past actions; it is very illustrative, complementing the booklet well. The development of high-quality media materials indicates that the collective understands the importance of the media as a dissemination and mobilization **strategy.**

5. Methodology

Considering that social networks play a fundamental role in the bonding of these urban collectives, according to our analyses and the consulted bibliography, in this article we mainly analyze the communication produced by the collective "Potato Needs You" and "Potatoes Gardeners" (a sub-collective of the first) on Facebook (closed group and pages). We conducted also a participant observation during one of the collective actions in Batata Square, on November 29, 2017. For the analysis of the closed group "Potato Needs You," we became members and individually collected information from all publications between August 2017 and August 2018. We created a database of 376 publications, composed of six variables: date, author, topic, comments, likes and shares. We defined four possible topics: Neighborhood (neighborhood assistance, event release); Mobilization (mobilization for works in the square, convocation for meetings); Problematization (discussion on the impacts of laws and political actions); Awareness (on urbanism, ecological and sustainable actions not necessarily linked to the square). The materials (agenda, booklet and video) were available on their website: http://largodabatata.com.br/a-batata-precisa-de-voce/.

6. The Potato Activists Communication Strategies on Facebook

In this article, due to space limitations, we mainly discuss the analysis on the Facebook closed group "Potato Needs You," which has around 6,475 people (September 10, 2018). From this expressed number of members, there were nine people whose posts are more frequent than the other's (one post per week on average) more sporadic posts. Each of these more-engaged activists plays a clear role in the group, establishing "identity typologies": the philanthropist, ecological activists, the town planner, the mobilizer of related causes (mobilizations in other squares), the participant engaged in municipal councils, the promoter of cultural proposals and so on.

Regarding interaction and participation, 89.6% of the publications obtained likes, 46% received comments and 37% were shared. We realize, however, that some members have a greater capacity for mobilization than others. In fact, the nine people (the possible critical mass) previously mentioned are the ones who best engage the others and mobilize the group for the most problematizing discussions. It is important to note that the same critical mass mobilizing the online medium coincides with the group that is also most frequently present in the square, the photos posted denote such active participation, which was also noted during the observation. The posts are never anonymous, so it is possible to recognize their authors offline.

The analysis of one year of posting resulted in 376 publications, which is a little over one publication per day, on average. The main discussion points occurred between August and October 2017 because, on September 13, the mayor of São Paulo opened works in Batata Square, which, according to the collectives, only included the

Brazilian flag mast and a few monetary banks without backrest. All the other improvements did not come from the public power but from collective actions (as shown in Figure 1). On the same date, the collective organized a resistance action to the scheduled political act. Shortly before this period, two posts generated controversy, circulating both in the group and in the pages of the two collectives. These posts are videos produced by an activist who participates in both groups. In the first post, she reports leaving her house to water the plants cultivated by the collective and realizing that City Hall had destroyed everything and that even the seedlings had been discarded. In the second post, even more controversial, she records her "meeting" with the Pinheiros sub-mayor in the square, following him with a camera in hand to ask questions about the lack of compliance with agreements settled between the collectives and himself (mentioning the destroyed plants situation). We realize that the coverage of these events resembles the alternative media that emerged on "June Days" (or Brazilian Spring). Today's collective activists use similar strategies: informality and first-person reporting, camera-phone footage, combative and questioning language, and almost instantaneous publications of events (Rekow, 2014).

Figure 1: Overview of Batata Square

Source: Google Maps

Although there is a fairly homogeneous distribution of the four categories established in the topic variable, in quantitative terms, publications classified as "mobilization" and "problematization" types had the highest number of comments, likes and shares, indicating that the meetings and collective works held in the square obtained much engagement, including discussions on the political actions and the impacts of the carried out activities, including the published reports on the changes in the square by the mainstream media. Using the categories "neighborhood" and "awareness", we based it on neighborhood literature (Mosconi et al., 2018; Tayebi, 2013; Wynn, 2016), particularly Tayebi's idea of "communihood" in which she problematizes the more classical notions of community and neighborhood (and their differences), especially considering emerging technologies. "In communihood, place is one of the main factors that defines the identity of members, which also extended to online spheres via social media" (Tayebi, 2013: 86).

Figure 2: Topics graphic

Source: Author's photos

Figure 3: Citizens and 'Potatoes Gardeners' in action

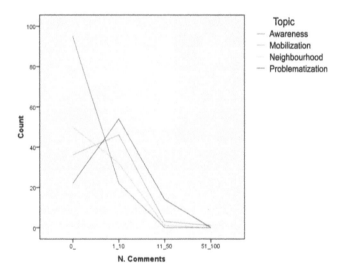

Source: Authors

Thus, we realize that the activists gather in both virtual and real spaces, with specific questions and concerns to improve an important space in their neighborhood. Furthermore, according to our hypothesis, these collectives corroborate with some of the principles for a new urban paradigm of the UN (UN-Habitat) program. The program provides 10 principles, which implies that the city needs to (1) be socially inclusive and engaging; (2) be affordable, accessible and equitable; (3) be economically vibrant and inclusive; (4) be collectively managed and democratically governed; (5) foster cohesive territorial development; (6) be regenerative and resilient; (7) have multiple identities and give rise to a sense of place; (8) be well planned, walkable, and transit-friendly; (9) be safe, healthy and promote wellbeing; and (10) learn and be innovative (World Urban Campaign, 2016).

We note that the above are, in fact, the concerns that guide the purposes of the collective "Potato Needs You." In general, the collective was very coherent in three instances: 1) the well-founded initial ideological proposition, materialized in a booklet form, which points out the high knowledge and specialized formation of the founding members in well-orchestrated face-to-face actions and in virtual activism, which contribute to the engagement process (dimensions related to all principles, but mainly with Principle 4); 2) There were ephemeral and permanent actions with effective and visible results generated by the collective and appropriated by the public authority: urban furniture, the construction of a pocket forest to recover the original Atlantic Forest, a rain garden, walking tracks (these actions adhere to Principles 8 and 9); and 3) a regular occupation of the area, as shown in Figure 1. Today, the area is visibly inhabited for different reasons and has become not only a crossing point space, but a space of rest and living for events ranging from concerts to protests, as well as being socially inclusive and engaging (as states Principle 1).

REFERENCES

Caldeira, D. (2015). Largo da Batata: transformações e resistências. PhD dissertation, University of São Paulo, São Paulo.

Caldeira, T.P.R. (2000). *City of Walls Crime, Segregation, and Citizenship in São Paulo*. Berkeley, CA: University of California Press.

Castells, M. (1983). *The City and the Grassroots: A Cross-Cultural Theory of Urban Social Movements*. Berkeley/Los Angeles: University of California Press.

Earle, L. (2017). *Transgressive Citizenship and the Struggle for Social Justice: The Right to the City in São Paulo*. Cham, Switzerland: Palgrave Macmillan.

Fernandes, E. (2007). Constructing the "right to the city" in Brazil. *Social and Legal Studies*, 16(2): pp. 201-219.

Friendly, A. (2017). Urban Policy, Social Movements, and the Right to the City in Brazil. *Latin American Perspectives*, 44(213): pp. 132-148.

Gehl, J. (2010). *Cities for People*. Washington, DC: Island Press.

Giaretta, J.B.Z. & Giulio, G.M. Di (2018). The role of the Information and Communication Technologies (ICT) in the urban 21st century and in the emergence of new social movements: reflections on experiences in the São Paulo megacity. *Rev. Bras. Estud. Urbanos Reg.*, 20(1): pp. 161-179.

Harvey, D. (2012) Rebel cities: From the right to the city to the urban revolution. Verso books.

——— (2003) The right to the city. International journal of urban and regional research, 27.4: pp. 939-941.

Holston, J. (2014). "Come to the Street!": Urban Protest, Brazil 2013. *Anthropological Quarterly*, 87(3): pp. 887-900.

Hori, P. (2017). Os Coletivos Urbanos da cidade de São Paulo: ações e reações. Paper presented at the ENANPUR, 17th, pp. 1-17.

Johnston, H. (2014). *What is a Social Movement?* Cambridge, UK: Polity Press.

Maziviero, M.C. (2016). Insurgent Urbanism: alternative modes of production and appropriation of urban space in the outskirts of São Paulo. In C. Hein (ed.) *International Planning History Society Proceedings*, V. 02, Deft: TU Delft Open, pp. 259-269.

Mosconi, G., Korn, M., Reuter, C., Tolmie, P., Teli, M. and Pipek, V. (2017), From Facebook to the Neighbourhood: Infrastructuring of Hybrid Community Engagement. *Comput Supported Coop Work*, 26(4-6): pp. 959-1003.

Oliveira, R. de C.A. and Segurado, R. (2014). Web Activism in São Paulo: New Political Practices. *Books and Ideas*, 14 July. Retrieved from URL: http://www.booksandideas.net/Web-Activism-in-Sao-Paulo-New.html

Petrone, P. (1963). *Pinheiros: aspectos geográficos de um bairro paulistano.* São Paulo: EDUSP.

Rekow, L. (2014). On unplanned urbanism: How Mídia NINJA are disrupting mainstream politics in Brazil. *Favelas@LSE*, 19 Jun. Blog Entry.

Rolnik, R. (2013). Ten years of the City Statute in Brazil: from the struggle for urban reform to the World Cup cities. *International Journal of Urban Sustainable Development*, 5(1): pp. 54-64.

Santiago, T. (2018). Cidade de São Paulo tem 206 ocupações onde moram 45 mil famílias. *G1*, 02 May. Retrieved from URL: https://g1.globo.com/sp/sao-paulo/noticia/cidade-de-sao-paulo-tem-206-ocupacoes-onde-moram-45-mil-familias.ghtml

Souza, M.L. de (2006). Social movements as "critical urban planning" agents. *City*, 10(3): pp. 327-342.

Tayebi, A. (2013). "Communihood:" A Less Formal or More Local Form of Community in the Age of the Internet. *Journal of UrbanTechnology*, 20(2): pp. 77-91

Telles, V. da S. (1994). The 1970s: Political experiences, practices and spaces. In L. Kowarick (ed.). *Social Struggles and the City: The case of São Paulo*. New York: Monthly Review Press, pp. 174-201.

Tilly, C. and Tarrow, S. (2007). *Contentious Politics*. Boulder: Paradigm Publishers.

Welle, B. (2016). Public Space in Cities – What's the Measuring Stick? *The City Fix*, March 9. Blog Entry. Retrieved from URL: http://thecityfix.com/blog/measuring-public-space-cities-sdg-habitat-indicator-ben-welle/

World Urban Campaign (2016). *The City We Need 2.0: Towards a New Urban Paradigm*. Prague, Czech Republic: UN.

Wynn, J. (2016). An Arson Spree in College Town: Community Enhancement Through Media Convergence. *Media, Culture & Society*, 39(3): pp. 357-373.

CHAPTER 11

Cities as Capitals of Innovation:
The Study of Media Organizations and Emerging Digital
Culture in Ghana

Africanus Lewil Diedong
Department of African and General Studies
University for Development Studies
Wa Campus, Ghana

ABSTRACT

The need to introduce digital technologies into newsrooms is not merely driven by the fact that Ghanaian newsrooms must catch up with their counterparts elsewhere but, more importantly, urban residents' tastes for digitized news is an increasing reality facing media outlets. Drawing on key informant interviews of leaders in print journalism, this exploratory study investigates shifts in newsroom environments and their implications for news work and trends in urban living, and how these changes can engender participatory communication among urban dwellers and rural residents. Ghana has experienced a checkered press history. The post-independence press in Africa was subjected to varying degrees of control by authoritarian regimes, which impacted news media outlets. Many news outlets in Ghana operate with limited budgets and slim readership in urban areas, yet they are pressured by trends in modern news practices to adopt new media technologies to stay in business. The investment of scarce resources in new media technologies needs to consider the current reading culture of Ghanaians, especially urban youth, who are more attracted to using digital technologies. The high cost of digital equipment and problems with internet connectivity add to the challenges that newspaper organizations must surmount to be of relevance to an emerging urban readership, which desires to acquire the most current information rapidly. Despite changes in modes of news production, it seems there is dearth of research in Africa about the nature of changes triggered by the Digital Revolution. Such changes generate debates about imbalance of access to information between city and rural residents in some African countries. Paradigm shifts in communication in newsroom environments are a response to new lifestyles of city residents; manifested mainly in consumerism and instant gratification, the ability to harness the right of freedom of expression, the monetization of news/communication as a result of the purchasing power of urban readers, and networking at individual and organizational levels. This emerging digital culture in cities appears to create a gap in communication between city residents and rural communities, whereby events and matters of interest to rural dwellers seem to be overlooked in favor of city dwellers' interests in the digitization process because rural environments may be of little economic and cultural value. This suggests unique peculiarities that require the attention of stakeholders in media and Information and Communication Technology (ICT) to isolate what is relevant in new media technologies and to place it in Ghana's unique context.

Keywords: Ghana, Newsroom Environment, New Media, Participatory Communication, Urban Living, Communities, Digital Divide

1. Introduction

Compared to rural communities, Internet business-related activities are more concentrated in the cities across Africa. In the cities, ICT is redefining the way people live in a complex and fascinating manner. It is evident from the trend of ICT's spread in Ghana, in particular, and in other parts of Africa that, if well harnessed, can significantly impact the growth and development of Ghana. In fact, the Copenhagen Declaration on Social Development recognized "that the new IT and new approaches to the use of technologies by people living in poverty can help in fulfilling social development goals" (United Nations, 1995). In Sub-Saharan Africa, the development of electronic communication systems in cities is slow even though they are witnessing rapid population growth. This might be due to the low capital investment in ICT caused by poverty. According to the World Internet Statistics, 5,171,993 (19.6%) of the 26,327,649 people in Ghana in 2015 were Internet users. Now, mobile services have become an indispensable part of the daily activities of Ghanaians. These services provide channels for commerce, email, social networking, voice communication and web browsing, among others. As of the end of 2016's second quarter, six mobile network operators (MNOs) offered such services in Ghana: MTN, Vodafone, Tigo, Airtel, Glo, and Expresso. According to the data provided by the MNOs, there was a quarter-on-quarter increase of 1.3% in the total mobile subscriptions in Ghana, from 36,138,706 in the first quarter to 36,613,987 in the second quarter of 2016 (NCA, 2016).

Institutions in Ghana, including media organizations, are embracing the use of ICT resources to transform their businesses to better meet the rapidly changing demands of their customers, albeit at a slow pace. Internet technologies constitute vital infrastructure that support public and private sector activities worldwide (Shin, 2017). While ICT is gradually influencing the lives of people and businesses in the major cities of Ghana, there are disconnected communities that are yet to experience the digital revolution. Using print media as a case, this chapter delineates some beneficial shifts arising from the evolving digital culture, particularly in the capital city Accra. This chapter explores how, with the unfolding digital culture in Ghanaian cities, there appears to be a disconnect between city dwellers and rural communities, whereby rural dwellers seem to not be participating in meaningful approaches to the digitization process. The following point made by Meadway and Mataos-Garcia (2009) needs to be underscored: extensive next-generation Internet access is crucial for lasting productivity and competitiveness, and it is also a prerequisite for sustainable growth and prosperity. This chapter is divided into seven sections: The second depicts the features of emerging communicational cities in Ghana. The subject matter for Section 3 is the emerging communicational cities in Ghana and the related issues, challenges and opportunities. Section 4 focuses on Ghanaian cities as the capitals of media innovation. Section 5 looks at the synergizing of communication needs of urban residents in Ghanaian cities, and the sixth section suggests a paradigm for synergizing communication needs of urban residents in Ghanaian cities. The conclusion of the chapter is presented in Section 7.

2. Depicting Features of Emerging Communicational Cities in Ghana

Today, one key feature that characterizes the way people and institutions interact and relate with one another in cities across Ghana, particularly in Accra, is the increased Internet access. This increase constitutes a veritable cornerstone in Ghana's efforts toward economic development. Today, the Internet is one of the key drivers facilitating competition among businesses across the world. This can create a competitive business environment in Ghana as well. The Internet has helped shape the way people, especially those in cities, communicate. A decade ago, the principal means of communication employed by people engaged in business transactions was faxing. However, email has the power to instantly transmit electronic data across great distances. This affords ease of communication and leads to reductions in the cost of business transactions. The time and money saved by individuals and institutions through paperless communication are tangible benefits of Internet applications in people's everyday activities. The ratification and adoption of an ICT policy—Information and Communication Technology for Accelerated Development (ICT4AD)—by the Government of Ghana in 2004 was a landmark step toward an environment that enables better internal communications between people and businesses as well as establish beneficial networks worldwide. The aim of the ICT4AD was to harness the full potential of ICT for the country's socio-economic development by creating relevant drives and strategies (Government of Ghana, 2003).

Although the full potential of ICT is yet to be realized, people in most cities across Ghana are already using the Internet for several purposes, including education, research, work, and personal finance (banking, stock trading) as well as for following current affairs, facilitating travel, gathering product information and engaging in transactions with online merchants (Osborn, 2012). Communication plays a vital role in how people interact and network to obtain a supply of essential objects. Marchal (2014) stated that cities are essentially unique human creations that have meaningful spatial boundaries, providing people with opportunities to empower themselves.

Today, in major cities in Ghana, symbols and signs on rooftop spaces and roads intersections as well as the skylines are testament to Marchal's apt observation. Inherent to these symbols and signs is meaning that is created, recreated, and contested in the course of human development. Marchal noted that, within the web of communication systems in cities, mobility as a practice is not just valuable but a right that's necessary to enable people to realize their potential. In cities, the interconnectedness of people near and far is valuable and has a bearing on how people make meaningful use of space.

Cities, whether large or small, are constructed by people and, thus, are cultural products. As cultural products, one can find meaning in the various material forms and shapes and geographical locations. One level of understanding culture is based on expressions, which are often grouped together as art and culture (Srampickal & Perumpally, 2009: 15). Elements of non-textual artistic expressions in the form of high-rise buildings in the major business districts of Accra and Kumasi are symbolic of the modern initiatives of any globalized city. It is worth highlighting that the attractiveness of cities, aggressively marketed in the media to attract investors and the most consumerist of city tourists, paradoxically pulls in migrants from rural areas who live in deplorable conditions in shanty towns. According to Kavaratzis (2004), encounters with the city take place through perceptions and images. Thus, marketing is mostly dependent on the creation, communication, and management of the city's image. In Ghana, examples of urban communities with large migrant populations are Nima and Agbogbloshie in Accra. In fact, the true texture and experience of major cities such as Accra, Kumasi, Takoradi, and Tamale lie in not only what is beautiful but also what's ugly about them because cities are cultural products and constitute a work in progress, as noted by Umberto Eco (1962, cited in Marchal, 2014).

It is clear that the driver of change in the process of cultural evolution in cities is the triumvirate of power, business, and media. In the case of Ghana one can say that the media does not shape the culture but that media is culture. Who dominates the space in the media sphere? What is the share and place of traditional cultural heritage and values in the media landscape? The cosmopolitan lifestyles of people—manifested in the modes of consumption of trendy goods, such as smartphones, and the building of imposing houses—are markers of civilization. These lifestyles are glamorized in the media sphere under different genres, such as narratives about celebrities, advertisements of modern estate settlements, and depictions of people's success stories. Another feature common in cities is how previously unbanked consumers can now access various financial services via mobile phones and the Internet. This factor has created ease of transferring money via mobile phones, often from well-to-do urban dwellers to family, friends, and other people and institutions with whom they communicate.

3. Emerging Communicational Cities in Ghana: Issues, Challenges, and Opportunities

Across Africa, there are inherent risks in the production and consumption processes with the flow of interdependent relations and various communicational forms across nations, as noted by Beck (2004: 25). The incidence of cyber fraud/crime (called "Sakawa" in cities across Ghana) is something that threatens Internet users. Security lapses instigated by the ICT, mostly in cities and industrial hubs, are a source of concern to users. Incidents of cybercrimes in Ghana and abroad are also a source of concern (Warner, 2011: 736; see also Danquah & Longe, 2011). For instance, a cybercrime may originate in Accra or Kumasi, while its victim is located beyond the shores of Ghana. Warner (2011) notes that some, "Sakawa boys" try to justify their nefarious activities by claiming that it is a form of payback against the West for the ills of colonialism in Africa. One Sakawa boy expressed the following on a public website:

> Am a Sakawa boy and all I can say is … Sakawa in Ghana is pay back to the white men and woman … Have we all forget about what they done to as … Taking our gold and buy we the same time. By the way I wish one of you know what Sakawa is … Everyone is saying what he like … Sakawa is not about blood money … All u have to do is to email me and I will tell u what we do before white men or woman send his money [sic]. (Kwablah, 2009)

Banking fraud cases in Ghana increased from 1,002 in 2016 to 1,418 by the following year (Bank of Ghana, 2017). The report revealed the use of phishing, vishing, card cloning and ransomware attacks, among other fraud types, indicating that, with the advancement of technology, fraudsters were also becoming more sophisticated. A study conducted in November 2016 by the African Union Commission, in partnership with an IT firm Symantec, revealed that Ghana was among the top 10 most-attacked countries in Africa (Arku, 2018).

Notwithstanding the risks, people continue to use the Internet and its related products because it is a necessity in their lives. It is in this context that Beck (1999) suggested the notion of a "*world risk society.*" In the context of the extreme global risks presented in the late 20th century, Cees (2000: 108) noted that the security risks implied in the use of digital systems are especially pressing. As the sociologist Ulrich Beck wrote, "we live on the volcano of civilisation" (1992). Philosopher John Leslie even hinted at the threat of the extinction of the human species (1996). Despite these risks, the benefits and rewards of fostering formidable communicative environments cannot be discounted. Within such spaces, a media-literate public can mount advocacy campaigns to press home their right to enjoy, for example, truly independent, free, and safe media that's devoid of undue subtle manipulations for the parochial interests of the powerful sections of the population. Therefore, effective application of ICTs can propel the pace of development in cities and make them smart. If making cities smarter leads to a range of societal problems being effectively addressed, it will not be opposed by anybody. The Amsterdam Smart City is a good reflection of the focus on smart cities in urban governance today.

This example is "a unique partnership between businesses, authorities, research institutions and the people of Amsterdam," (amsterdamsmartcity.com) to transform the Amsterdam Metropolitan Area into a smart city that promotes mobility and access to open data. Smart technologies are fundamental building blocks for strengthening private and public institutions in cities (Meijer & Bolivar, 2015). However, in Ghana, apart from the infrastructural and technical challenges of the national development planning policy, and the politicization of these, one major hurdle is the gap in the curricula of institutions of learning in the incorporation of media education courses to educate people to be competent and skillful users of ICT and derive the expected benefits.

4. Cities as Capital of Media Innovation in Ghana

In Ghana, print media institutions are some of the oldest establishments and have significantly contributed to the dissemination of news of public interest. Print media remains a unique space for creative thinking and the sharing of ideas and information to advance the course of development. Given the capacity of IT to generate and store huge data as well as the capital that results from its application, it is natural for media institutions to be interested in their use in newsrooms.

It is remarkable to observe the changes in technology occurring in news media organizations. Efforts being made to invest in the ICT infrastructure to serve as the backbone for multimedia services have facilitated people and organizations' access to the Internet. This refreshing experience in communication is happening in Ghana thanks to the pioneering work of Network Computer Systems, a private Ghanaian company. (Tevie, Quaynor & Bulley 1996). In 1995, the Network Computer Systems registered the gh.com domain name. As of the first quarter of 2016, 54 ISPs were authorized by the National Communications Authority (NCA) in Ghana (NCA, 2016). Generally, Internet connectivity in Africa is the lowest in the world. Nowadays, all countries are connected, at least at the capital city level, and the number of computers permanently connected to the Internet in Africa has increased from 10,000 in the early part of 1999 to 25,000 in January 2000 (Jensen, 2000: 25). Although the connectivity level is still the lowest globally, local cultural values of solidarity, connectedness, and interdependence allow people to access the Internet and its opportunities (Nyamnjoh, 2002; Bosch, 2018: 145).

Despite the challenges of Internet connectivity across various regions of Ghana, the situation is better in Accra because media organizations that operate in cities appreciate the benefits associated with integrating ICTs into their businesses. In print media organizations, the traditional model of heavy reliance on advertisements and newspaper circulation as the main sources of revenue is witnessing a shift to more innovative strategies, which some communication scholars describe as "mobile first" strategies (see Gicheru, 2014). With over 72% of the population owning phones, Africa is seeing an uptake rate for mobile phone subscriptions that is faster than anywhere else in the world. This growth of mobile broadband subscribers is an indication of the rising smartphone adoption rate, which has almost doubled over the past two years to reach 226 million (Mobile Economy Africa, 2016).

Mobile Internet advertising is gaining ground across the various media systems in Ghana. Businesses whose products and services are certified by the Ghana Standards Authority and the Food and Drugs Authority of Ghana clamor for space to advertise on television and on the online platforms provided by media organizations because of the returns on such investment decisions. However, though this trend is similar to the trends in mobile advertising in Europe and the US, it should not be a basis to forecast Africa's future since the market and consumption habits of countries in Africa and Europe and US could be significantly different.

Despite the lack of precise market data that could help advertisers and media organizations come up with creative strategies to meet the diverse needs of their audiences, some newspapers in Ghana, such as the Daily Graphic in 2013, have introduced a barcode module called the quick read that enables readers of the newspaper to listen to speeches and discussions or watch events by means of a smartphone. Such an innovative entrepreneurial approach is a welcome development in the face of the changing media landscape. However, newspaper readership worldwide is shrinking because of competition from electronic and social media (Barthel, 2015).

ICTs facilitate the of use of multimedia content in media organizations, thereby enabling the audience to exchange and share information and ideas in unique ways. For instance, newspapers can attract advertising for their online versions through video (Gicheru, 2014). However, the Ghanaian press is yet to fully master the process of the convergence of its media systems, a process that is already impacting the media industry in other countries, especially those in the developed world (Dupagn & Garrison, 2006; Quandt & Singer, 2009).

The momentum of countries in Africa, Asia, and Latin America toward adopting journalistic practices and novel ways of disseminating news and information through the use of ICT seems to be in line with the dominant global conception of journalism, which usually produces a homogenous and monolithic worldview that rejects or ignores non-Western experiences. However, scholars such as Wasserman and De Beer argued, "Theories about how journalism should be defined, what its relationship with society is, how it should be taught and how it should be practiced ought to be constructed within a globally inclusive, dialogic setting" (2009: 429). Technological changes seem to be having a major impact on journalistic processes such as collecting, producing, packaging and reporting news (Obijiofor and Murray, 2017: 388) not only in Nigeria and Fiji but in Ghana as well. These changes result in added pressure on city journalists in particular to be more technologically knowledgeable about news gathering and reporting to withstand competition from bloggers and other non-professionals gradually providing alternatives to journalistic content.

Undoubtedly, technology is forcing the journalists to multitask and develop their skills. It is giving a platform to multi-platform news delivery channels by media organizations so they can serve consumers who have the means to access news through different outlets. Indeed, the news media environment is dynamic. Anas Aremeyaw Anas, a multi-award winning investigative journalist, paints a picture of changes being experienced on the job in Accra:

> I started as a print journalist at the New Crusading Guide. Today we have bloggers, citizen journalists, podcasting etc. I realized that you can no longer be a print journalist only. I have to do multimedia in Germany. You cannot decide that you are going to keep idle in journalism. So if you do not upgrade yourself, there is no way you can cope with the competition. The taste of the audience has changed drastically. (Diedong, 2016: 84)

Notably, the placement of news on sophisticated platforms suggests that such news items are, to a large extent, primarily accessible to the rich (the "haves"). This question of accessibility raises the issue of news monetization, which ought to be a public good. News as a public good implies that, to the extent possible, there should be no impediments to citizens' access. In other words, irrespective of how advances in technology are pushing news delivery in major cities, it is important that low-income earners (the "have-nots") in shanty areas and rural communities are integrated into the emerging media channels to share, exchange, and project their ideas and cultural heritage worldwide. Within the perspective of Habermas's (1989) notion of the "public sphere," it is notable that the "have-nots" can benefit from the unfolding digitization process. In a democratic system, it is necessary that citizens have equal and fair opportunities to generate meaning in both traditional and new media spaces. Arguments for creating new human collaboration models through ICTs to foster more open and beneficial governance processes are globally gaining traction (Meijer & Bolivar, 2015).

5. Synergizing the Communication Needs of Urban Residents in Ghanaian Cities

Sophistication of communication in cities triggered by advances in ICT is beneficial because, if harnessed well, it can aid people living outside cities as well. However, this sophistication requires a people-centered paradigm to ensure that communication supports the development and empowerment of people in all parts of the country. Such a paradigm can reveal various approaches to and means of creating a pragmatic balance between indigenous forms of communication, especially in rural areas, and their integration with ICT to preserve and project Ghana's culture. At the international level, it appears that local communities' ways of life and cultural expressions are incorporated into ICT. In the framework of the 2015 World Summit on the Information Society Forum (WSIS), the discussion panel on Action Line 8, "Cultural diversity and identity, linguistic diversity and local content," talked about how ICTs are stimulating cultural entrepreneurship in the cultural and creative industries, particularly at the local level and in developing countries, and how new forms of media and technologies are boosting platforms for dialogue and exchange, thereby enhancing the capacities of local populations worldwide to overcome their respective challenges. At the forum, Silja Fischer, Secretary General of the International Music Council, observed, "In Africa ICTs allow a greater access to cultural goods and services but beyond access and distribution, they allow creators to engage with the audience, to co-create, and to connect with the diaspora" (UNESCO, 2015).

However, Fischer's position is contested because it is different from the ground reality. Scholars, such as Beck (2014), take a contrasting position on how ICTs are allowing greater access to cultural goods. Beck points out that all urban social categories do not have identical access to international mobility, cyberterritory, ICTs and the required resources. Except for an international kinetic elite, most people continue to live apart from planetary networks. The fact is that a common standpoint on the planet is not shared by all the urban dwellers and the intellectual and financial elites, the politico-media class, the entertainment industry stars or bloggers. The ethnologist Jonathan Friedman (2000, cited in Beck, 2014) maintained that everyone does not have "an aerial view" of the earth that allows them to see the planet as a "multiethnic bazaar." Despite the concept of a "transnationalist *vulgate*" symbolizing globally integrated city dwellers, several urbanized individuals' access to global culture is limited as they still base their collective and individual identities on territorial or local foundations. Herein lies the debate of who gets included in ICT spaces and how the limitations to accessing such spaces, particularly among poor city residents and rural communities, can be tackled. Communication has become more interactive and networked in globalized cities, such as Accra, where newspapers are taking steps to incorporate new media formats, including the use of platforms such as Facebook, Twitter and WhatsApp, to offer readers a refreshing experience and the opportunity to contribute to media content. More erudite and well-to-do people are beginning to like and follow them on their news websites. The interactive networks further benefit the literate population and elites (city dwellers). In the newspaper industry, the illiterate population has limited opportunities to use interactive voice responses to share their views and comments on important issues.

The gap between the "information-strong" and "information-weak" parts of the world will not close despite optimistic declarations of the Internet establishing democratic communication soon (Ronning, 2005: 165). There appears to be a disconnect in integrating indigenous modes of community communication with modern communication platforms to enrich intercultural discourse and increase their economic value. The economic potential of folk music and other cultural narratives and products at the village level are yet to be realized because the process of digitizing them is incredibly slow in Ghana. Unlike most artists in Accra and other cities who record and produce their own albums with the possibilities of streaming them online, folk music and artefacts, despite their richness, are yet to reap the benefits of audience monetization that ICT facilitates for business entities and individuals.

6. Suggested Paradigm for Synergizing the Communication Needs of Urban Residents in Ghanaian Cities

In Sub-Saharan Africa, the media literacy levels are dismally low and coupled with a poor reading culture (Yankah, 2015: 33). The relevance of people-centered communication in an emerging digital culture needs to be anchored on the principle of participative communication for development. It appears that "off-the-grid" communities and communities on the wrong side of the digital divide might be a part of the cultural revolution simply by using basic technology such as solar power and wireless communications. According to Darkwa (2018: 8), promoting digital culture is an environmentally sound way to achieve the economic independence of societies that have traditionally been excluded from realizing the benefits of the information economy, and it enables the preservation and advancement of indigenous cultures as well as the promotion of international collaboration and business.

The new wave of communication that's taking center stage in cities demonstrates what Castells (2007, cited in Horsfield, 2015: 262) termed a new form of capitalism marked by the globalization of core economic activities, calling for awareness on the importance of integrating the cultural expressions of rural communities into digital formats. Nyerere (1973) noted that a person's self-actualization results from meaningful social engagements. In such free social ventures, a person is not compelled to participate but does so through their own free will, and a lot can be learned from traditional media forms such as group communication, songs, and dances. In the ICT age, these are still powerful forces for the social integration and mobilization of many African communities. The ability of such information to affect other cultures via the Internet has also been previously recognized (Ansu-Kyeremeh, 2005). Hence, national communication policies need to consider this fact and ensuring that the right to communication constitutes the cultural perspectives and values of rural communities.

In Ghana, residents comprise indigenous people and others who have migrated from their villages and towns or the hinterlands to the city for economic and other reasons. Despite the changes in the spatial locations of such migrant city dwellers, they stay connected to their roots. Indigenous communication is still appealing to city residents and, in one way or another, influences their cosmo-vision. The "actor network theory" (see Latour, 2005) seems to be a plausible approach to synergize the communication needs of urban residents in Ghanaian cities. The theory, as applied to news production, espouses that technology is itself an actor in a web of journalists, sources, technicians, employees of media organizations, and audiences and users (Hemmingway, 2008). All these actors are involved in a communication production process and can exert their influence on the created products to certain degrees. Technologies play a formidable role in determining not only how media organizations produce news, advertisements, and other forms of communication according to the tastes and expectations of city residents and how these converge on diverse platforms but also how concerns are expressed about the benefits or drawbacks of their use. Who benefits from the "gig economy"/"sharing economy"? (words borrowed from Onwurah, 2017). According to Starks (2019: 21), concerns related to Internet media giants have broadened and multiplied over the past years, and these include the following:

- the sheer scale of the private user data they gather through searches and posts to facilitate targeted advertising, i.e., "if you're using their services for free, you are not the consumer, you're the product" (Taplin 2017: 167, cited in Starks, 2019);
- their vulnerability to the infiltration of material created by terrorists, pornographers, child sex abusers, racists, and other hate-speech spreaders and their tardiness in effectively removing such material; and
- their dominance in the market that limits plurality, with other online news providers relying on them as their primary route into market.

For city inhabitants to derive the necessary digital dividends from emerging converging technologies, it is proposed that the "actor network theory" be democratized to make it more inclusive, responsive, and participatory and, thereby, empower the marginalized voices in the emerging urban communication landscape. The democratic-participant model of communication, which argues for dialogue among stakeholders in the process of development, emphasizes that communication is too valuable to be left to communication professionals and technological experts. Therefore, it is necessary and appropriate to incorporate this model into the abovementioned theory to engage all the involved stakeholders in meaningful ways. Maximizing the benefits of the emerging communication trends in Ghanaian cities and addressing the concerns thereof require a re-examination of the ICT4AD policy document and factoring in a forward-looking regulatory mechanism (see 2003 Communications Act) that seriously considers the industry, citizens, and consumer interests on converging communication platforms. The issues related to the communication dynamics in Ghanaian cities in particular and the country as a whole require national discourse to bring about progressive changes in the law to support the proposed shifts in the ICT4AD policy.

7. Concluding Remarks

This chapter detailed some changes emerging out of developments in ICTs in cities, with a specific focus on the implications for the newspaper industry and the cultural expressions of rural communities. Newspapers such as the Daily Graphic have taken steps to respond to the sophisticated tastes of globalized city readers by introducing a barcode module that ensures a more expansive, exciting and interactive content with possible avenues for advertisements. The introduction of these modernizing practices is putting pressure on journalists to upgrade themselves with multimedia skills and knowledge to remain relevant to their media organizations and to their knowledgeable and discerning readers. The chapter theorized that in as much as the emerging digital culture has brought some opportunities and risks, it is debatable whether local cultural expression is actually integrated in ICTs. As the number of mobile phone and internet users continues to rise, especially in cities, cybercrime-related incidents will not immediately disappear. A plausible approach for dealing with the risks is through media literacy advocacy, which requires an "all hands-on deck" approach by all stakeholders, particularly the NCA, the telecom companies, security agencies, InterPol, the Bank of Ghana, the Ghana Journalists Association and the Ministry of Education. Planning for the integration of varied cultural expressions of rural communities into the ICT4AD Policy should be seriously considered. There is a gap in the ICT4AD Policy document regarding effective integration of cultural expressions of rural communities. It is important to note that integral human development amidst the Digital Revolution should embrace diverse cultural perspectives. In outlining its views on culture and the relevance of the concept for development, UNESCO notes: "Cultural values are continually being reinterpreted and reshaped in response to coping and adjusting to new needs and conditions resulting from social and economic changes."

REFERENCES

Ansu-Kyeremeh, K. (2005). *Indigenous communication in Africa: Concept, application and prospects.* Accra: Ghana Universities Press.

Arku, J. (2018). Ghana loses Gh¢30.1 million to bank fraud. Retrieved from https://www.graphic.com.gh/news/general-news/cyber-fraud-cases-on-the-rise-in-banking-industry-in-ghana-bog.html Accessed: 14th September 2018

Barthel, M. (2015). Newspapers: fact sheet. Retrieved from http://www.journalism.org/2015/04/29newspapers-fact-sheet/

Beck, U. (2004). *Qu'est-ce que le cosmopolitisme?* trad. de l'allemand par A. Duthoo, Paris: Aubier, 2006.

Bosch, T. (2018). Digital media and political citizenship: Facebook and politics in South Africa. In *Perspectives on Political Communication in Africa*, pp. 145-158. London: Palgrave Macmillan.

_____. (1999). *World risk society.* Cambridge: Polity Press.

_____. (1992). *Risk society: Towards a new modernity.* London: Sage Publications.

Castells, M. (2007). Communication, power and counter-power. *International Journal of Communication*, 1, pp. 238-226.

Cees, J.H. (2000). *The ethics of cyberspace.* London: Sage Publications.

Communication Act 2003 (2003). C.1.3.14, Retrieved from https://.legislation.gov.uk/ukpga/2003/21/pdfs/ukpga_20030021_en.pdf

Danquah, P. & Longe, O.B. (2011). An empirical test of the space transition theory of cyber criminality: The case of Ghana and beyond. *African Journal of Computing & ICTs.* 4(2), pp. 37-48. Retrieved from http://ajcict.net/uploads/Danquah___Longe_-

Darkwa, K. (2018, August 13). Fostering wealth creation through digital culture. *Ghanaian Times*, p. 8.

Dickson, R. & Matthews, J. (2013). Studying journalists in changing times: Understanding newswork as socially situated practice. *The International Communication Gazette*, 75(1), pp. 3-18.

Diedong, A. (2016). *Responsible Journalism and Quest for Professional Standards in Ghana*. Accra: Woeli Publishers.

Dupagn, M. & Garrison, B. (2006). The meaning and influence of convergence: a qualitative case of newsroom at the Tampa News Center. *Journalism Studies*, 7(2), pp. 237-255.

Eco, U. (1962). *L'œuvre ouverte*. trad. de l'italien par C. Roux de Bézieux, Paris: Éd. Le Seuil, 1965.

Friedman, J. (2000). Des racines et (dé)routes. Tropes pour trekkers. *L'Homme*, 156, pp. 187-206.

Gicheru, C. (2014). The challenges facing independent newspapers in Sub-Saharan Africa. Reuters Institute Fellowship Paper, University of Oxford.

Government of Ghana (2003). An accelerated policy ICT-led socio-economic development policy and plan development framework for Ghana.

Habermas, J. (1998). *The structural transformation of the public sphere*. Cambridge, MA: MIT Press.

Hemmingway, E. (2008). *Into the newsroom: Exploring digital production of regional television news*. Abingdon: Routledge.

Horsfield, P. (2015). *From Jesus to the Internet. A history of Christianity and media*. London: Wiley Blackwell.

Internet Usage Statistics (2015). Retrieved from https://www.internetworldstats.com/af/gh.htm Accessed: 13th September 2018

Jensen, M. (2000). Making the connection: Africa and the Internet. *Current History*, 99, pp. 215-245.

Kavaratzis, M. (2004). From city marketing to city branding: Towards a theoretical framework for developing city brands. *Place Branding and Public Diplomacy*, 1(1), pp. 58-73.

Kwablah, E. (2009, February 17). Cybercrime: giving a bad name to Ghana. Ghana Business News. Retrieved from http://www.ghanabusinessnews.com/2009/02/17/cybercrime-giving-a-bad-name-toghana/

Latour, B. (2005). *Reassembling the social: An introduction to actor network theory*. Oxford: Oxford University Press.

Leslie, J. (1996). *The end of the world*. London: Routledge.

Marchal, H. (2014). Communication is inherent to the new urban condition. Retrieved from https://www.cairn.info/revue-questions-de-communication-2014-1-page-7a.htm Accessed: 12th September 2018

Meadway, J. & Mataos-Garcia, J. (2009). Getting up to speed: making super-fast broadband a reality. Retrieved from https://www.researchgate.net/profile/Juan_Mateos-Garcia/publication/38296612_NESTA_Policy_Briefing_Getting_up_to_speed/links/09e41508aac9b9d03a000000/NESTA-Policy-Briefing-Getting-up-to-speed.pdf?origin=publication_detail

Meijer, A. & Bolivar, P. (2015). Governing the smart city: a review of the literature on smart urban governance. *International Review of Administrative Sciences*, 82(2), pp. 392-408.

Mobile Economy Africa (2016). Growing adoption of smartphones and other advanced services. Retrieved from https://www.gsmaintelligence.com/research/?file=3bc21ea879a5b217b64d62fa24c55bdf&download Accessed: 14th September 2018

NCA (2016). List of authorized internet service providers (ISPs) as at first quarter 2016. Retrieved from https://www.nca.org.gh/index.php/media-and-news/news/list-of-authorized-internet-service-providers-isps-as-at-first-quarter-2016/ Accessed: 14th September 2018

_____. (2016). Quarterly statistical bulletin on communication in Ghana. Retrieved from https://www.nca.org.gh/assets/Uploads/Quaterly-statistics-03-11-16-fin.pdf Accessed: 13th September 2018

Nyamnjoh, F. (2002). A child is one person only in the womb: domesticating agency and subjectivity in the Cameroonian grassfields. In R. Werbner (ed.) *Post-colonial Subjectivities in Africa*, pp. 111-138. London: Zed.

Nyerere, J. (1973). *Freedom and development*. New York: OUP.

Obijiofor, L. & Murray, R. (2017). Changes in journalism in two post-authoritarian non-western countries. *The International Communication Gazette*, 79(4), pp. 379-399.

Osborn, Q.H. (2012). The growth and usage of internet in Ghana. *Journal of Emerging Trends in Computing and Information Sciences*, 3(9). Retrieved from http://www.cisjournal.org

Quandt, T. & Singer, J. (2009). Convergence and cross platform Journalism. In K. Wahl-Jorgensen and T. Hanitszch (eds.) *Handbook of Journalism Studies*, pp. 130-144. London: Routledge.

Rønning, H. (2004). Responsible media in a situation of social unrest and the struggle for democracy. The African experience. The Annual Conference of the Finnish Media Research Association Conference (Helsinki, Finland).

Shin, D.H. (2007). A critique of Korean national information strategy: Case of national information infrastructures. *Government Information Quarterly*, 24(3), pp. 624-645.

Srampickal, J. & Perumpally, L. (2009). *Let's do media education*. Delhi: Media House.

Starks, M. (2019). The digital democratic dividend. *Journal of Digital Media & Policy*, 10(1), pp. 9-17.

Taplin, J. (2017). *Move fast and break things*. London: Macmillan.

Tevie, W., Quaynor, N. & Bulley, A. (1996). Development of the Internet in Ghana. Retrieved from http://www.isoc.org/inet96/proceedings/g6/g6_4.htm.

UNESCO (2015). Culture and ICT as drivers of sustainable development. Retrieved from https://en.unesco.org/news/culture-and-ict-drivers-sustainable-development Accessed: 14th September, 2018

United Nations (1995). Copenhagen Declaration on Social Development. A/CONF.166/9.

Warner, J. (2011). Understanding cyber-crime in Ghana: a view from below. *International Journal of Cyber Criminology*, 5(1), pp. 736-749.

Wasserman, H. & De Beer AS (2009). Towards de-Westernising journalism studies. In Wahljorgensen K. and Hanistzch T. (eds) *The Handbook of journalism studies*, pp. 428-438. New York: Routledge.

Yankah, K. (2015). Empowering Ghana through reading. *Daily Graphic*, p. 33.

CHAPTER 12

Social Media Usage within the Smart City Initiative: The Case of the Creative Village in Bandung

Eni Maryani
Universitas Padjadjaran, Indonesia
and
Detta Rahmawan
Universitas Padjadjaran, Indonesia

ABSTRACT

The concept of "creative village" in the city of Bandung, Indonesia is an effort to create qualitative changes in the slums through cultural and artistic approaches. A variety of creative endeavors transformed the village into a tourist destination and is attracting tourists, observers, and activists from different cities of the world. Visitors use digital technology and social media to share creative village information with audiences, who help by building a broader network. However, the sustainability of social media usage is not optimal. This chapter identifies and analyzes the existing obstacles and attempts to answer questions such as, why, despite having good internet connectivity, and despite the encouragement that social media can be utilized as an important promotional tool for the development of the creative economy, the creative village is failing to use social media to reach out to the broader public?

Keywords: Smart City, Creative Village, Social Transformation, Bandung

INTRODUCTION

Less-privileged city inhabitants live in slums, where they become an environmental and social issue. This issue is also the case in the city hailed as a "creative city," Bandung – one of the largest cities in Indonesia. Bandung is the provincial capital of West Java. The International Gathering on the Creative Economy in 2007 granted Bandung an award to pioneer a creative city project, which in practice also meant building a creative economy. The scope of creative industry or creative economy, defined by The Indonesian Agency for Creative Economy (BEKRAF) includes 16 sub-sectors, namely "architecture; interior design; visual communication design;

product design; film, animation and video; photography; craft; culinary; music; fashion, application and game developer; publishing; advertising; television and radio; performing Arts; and fine arts" (Utoyo & Sutarsih, 2017, p. xxvii). The creative industries were regarded as an alternative answer to the decline of industries in the manufacturing field. These industries emerged from the synergy and integration between economic, cultural and social activities that had the potential to be developed (Hermawati & Runiawati, 2015).

Various efforts were made to build a "creative village" and transform the village into a tourist destination by showcasing villagers' talents through dance, music and the arts. Paintings and graffiti were turned into visual arts. The village learned about hospitality to cater to tourists' needs. The village attracted local, regional and international tourists, observers and activists from various cities around the world. Within this context, the concept of the smart city is in line with the development of the creative economy, since digital technology is needed to spread information about the creative village to a wider audience (Pardo & Taewoo, 2011). The creative village community built a network through mainstream media and utilized social media to reach a wider audience.

Since 2014, the city of Bandung has tried to apply the smart city concept, which has been primarily aimed at synergizing technology into people's daily lives and the city's dynamics. This approach was carried out under the leadership of Ridwan Kamil, who was then the Mayor of Bandung (now Governor of West Java), and it was considered a breakthrough from the slow and confusing bureaucratic reform in Indonesia (Pikiran Rakyat, 2017a). He also aspired to make the communication between the people and the Government easier and more flexible with the implementation of various IT and the exploration of various social media data. Moreover, regarding the creative economy, he encouraged more multi-stakeholder initiatives to be developed further, as illustrated in the following statement:

> The creative economy is based on society. If you only rely on the power of the government, that's not enough. That's why we embrace business people...We embrace communities...Creativity produces works. Work produces economic value (Mayangsaria & Novania, 2015; Yusuf & Badriyah, 2017).

Unlike in more developed countries, where villages and cities are clear-cut locations, in Indonesia, villages are found inside the boundaries of a large city. Certain areas are still called *kampung/kampong* or villages even though they now lie within the administrative boundaries of the city. Some may still maintain the natural atmosphere of villages, with small houses and dirt roads, while other *kampongs* have developed into packed housing or urban residential areas. The term *kampung* is also an administrative term: a group of houses becomes a neighborhood (*Rukun Tetangga/Rukun Warga*); a group of neighborhoods becomes a *kampong*; a group of *kampongs* becomes a sub-district (*kecamatan*), and so on. This chapter identifies and analyzes the challenges and opportunities of the social transformation in the Smart City Project. Despite promises, the project failed to support the creative village in its use of social media to aid the continuity of their program. Thus, this chapter examines the factors that hindered the utilization of social media, which was supposed to benefit the promotion of the creative village as part of Bandung Smart City Project.

Literature Review

The Concept of the Smart City in Bandung

There is no universal definition of a smart city. The concept of "smart" in "smart city" includes several definitions, such as cities based on knowledge, sustainable cities, digital cities, and many others. Nevertheless, "smart city" is most often used in conjunction with the concept of digital city to illustrate the intelligence of a city (Cocchia, 2014). The idea of smart city arose with the emergence of urbanization and the penetration of ICT. In this era, the development of technology encourages the presence of economic growth, which contributes to the improvement of welfare, especially in big cities, such as Bandung. The idea of smart city tried to find ways for the city to solve its urban problems while paying attention to environmental sustainability. Components of smart cities can be analyzed through four segments – industry, education, participation, and technical infrastructure – as well as an emphasis on the concept of developing smart cities, which requires an increase in the quality of life of citizens (Giffinger et al., 2007; Shapiro, 2006). The diffusion of various aspects of the application of communication and IT in the joints of community life must be able to improve the efficiency of the performance of various sub-systems in society, which leads to an improvement in the quality of life of citizens (Batty et al., 2012).

Numerous discussions and publications related to the effort to turn the city of Bandung into a smart city were associated with the appointment of Ridwan Kamil as the Mayor of Bandung (Aritenang, 2012; Hermawati & Runiawati, 2015; Jamilah, Akbar, Gunawan, & Marantika, 2018; Mayangsaria & Novania, 2015). Ridwan Kamil, as the elected mayor for the 2013-2018 period implemented many ICT initiatives to develop and build the city in a smarter way. Citizen mobility and interconnectivity were developed by encouraging citizens to use various ICT-based facilities. He tried to implement ICT in various fields of information, education, health, transportation, job vacancies, business opportunities, and even in the city's financial and income management.

During his term, collaboration between the Government, industry, NGOs, and academics was built to meet the needs of the citizens and to create value from the city (Mayangsaria & Novania, 2015; Yusuf & Badriyah, 2017). One example is a project between the city administration and one of the leading ICT companies in Indonesia, Telkom. The company provided some of the services and infrastructure, such as CCTV surveillance solutions to analyze traffic conditions and congestion and to monitor crime-prone locations, and social media analytics to locate conversations and trending topics about the city of Bandung, as well as various applications on the city's transportation and tourism (Prahadi, 2015). Furthermore, the effort to collect data and to facilitate direct complaints and other communications between the city government departments and the citizens of Bandung via social media, as well as the Bandung Command Center program, are examples of smart city implementation in Bandung (Jamilah et al., 2018).

In the city of Bandung, the concept of developing the quality of life of citizens was inculcated by introducing the measurement of the citizens' happiness index. Furthermore, various government programs can be scientifically carried out and assessed using the increasing index of happiness among Bandung residents (Pikiran Rakyat, 2017b). This approach is in line with the idea that governments and public institutions at all levels ideally implement policies and programs that have sustainable development goals, community and community-based economic growth, and improvement in the quality of life that leads to happiness for citizens (Ballas, 2013).

Creative Cities and Villages

In 2007, the Ministry of Trade of Indonesia piloted a mapping exercise on creative industries in Indonesia. During the process, the Government started to realize that the country had large potential in culture and ideas, as well as having abundant creative and artistic talent, with a large domestic market. Since then, the concept of creative industries has been widely acknowledged (Maryunani & Mirzanti, 2015; Simatupang, 2010). Moreover, the city of Bandung, as the capital of West Java Province, is considered a model for creative industries by other cities in Indonesia. Bandung became the "creative city" because of the following factors:

- Administrative and political changes (decentralization)
- The role of universities in encouraging the growth of Creative & Cultural Industries (CCI) in Bandung,
- The city's geographical proximity with Jakarta
- The existence of a creative network (such as Bandung Creative City Forum [BCCF]) as the hub for a cultural and creative economy (Aritenang, 2012)

If the concept of "creative city" targets a city-level implementation, then the concept of *kampung kreatif* or "creative village" targets the village level and smaller communities. The concept of creative village comes from the basic assumption that creativity must be based on culture, economy, and environment that are not only innovative, but also sustainable. Artists, designers, engineers, and various creative parties who will manage creative villages are encouraged to receive input from the local community and to work together in a multidisciplinary manner (De Lorenzo, 2000).

Creative village is a community empowerment program based on local creativity initiated by the activist Rahmat Jabaril. This program is a response to the marginalization of village issues in urban development, which is dominated by the perspective of economic investment. Creative programs like this are assumed to be crucial for the synergy and development of programs between the government, the community and the private sector (Kustiwan, Ukrin, & Aulia, 2015).

In the implementation of creative city, the focus of city managers has shifted from how to help city residents build and maintain their daily lives through basic provision service and welfare, to the development of space-related city promotion and marketing (Barnes, Waitt, Gill, & Gibson, 2006). The implementation of creative city as an important factor in urban economic development has been widely criticized because of the absence of detailed instructions, especially about how the concept (which in reality should be practical) can be applied specifically at the level of urban policy. However, the complexity of urban-related policies, which also look at governance planning and the relationship between various actors, and resources (political, legal, economic) and a series of socio-spatial practices in urban areas have not been frequently discussed (Ponzini & Rossi, 2010, pp. 1040-1041).

In the city of Bandung, the effort to develop a creative village in a local community in Dago and Cicukang can be seen as a factor used to strengthen the sustainable tourism industry. The development of various places that have the potential for local creativity is supported by various forms of technology, one of which is social media. The city government encourages collaboration between existing communities, so that various creative initiatives originating from the community can be developed further (Windarti, 2016).

Method

This study uses qualitative methods with constructivist perspectives to build an understanding of the reality perceived by creative village residents in the city of Bandung. These residents have been exposed to the concept of creative ideas and various technologies, such as social media, to develop their villages. Through constructivist qualitative research (Denzin & Lincoln, 2011), the researcher informally collected data in a natural setting and tried not to disrupt the activities of the residents and the situation of the village where the research was conducted.

The cases studied were the Dago Creative Village and the Cicukang Creative Village. The uniqueness of this case study (Creswell, 2007) is the number of discontinued creative village initiatives in Bandung's Smart City Program; however, the Dago Creative Village in the North Bandung area continues to exist. Another unique aspect is the awareness of the residents regarding using digital media in developing their environment and addressing the various obstacles they face. The Cicukang Creative Village was also studied due to its unique performing arts.

In reference to the explanation above, this study used several data collection techniques that were in accordance with the data source addressed; specifically, some urban activists, city officials, residents and their living conditions, as well as various digital activities related to creative villages and Smart City Programs in Bandung. Therefore, the data collection techniques used were in-depth interviews, observations, and literature studies.

Purposive sampling was used to conduct in-depth interviews with 10 people: creative village activists, arts and culture activists, officials from the Tourism Office, observers of the Smart City Program in Bandung, residents, and visitors to creative villages. The interviews with the activists and residents are related to the initial data of the creative village initiative and its development process, as well as their experiences and judgments about the existence of creative villages. With the residents, we asked also about their participation in the creative village activities and the benefits they received. The environmental experts offered their views on the existence of creative villages as part of efforts to organize a healthier and better urban environment without marginalizing community groups and less-privileged city residents. Observers of the Smart City Program gave their views on the existence, challenges and sustainability of these programs.

Observations were carried out by studying the situation and environment of the creative village to obtain data related to the arrangement of the physical environment and its implications for the patterns of interaction and activities of the villagers. Observations were also conducted during interviews with creative village activists from the Dago and the Cicukang villages. Various activities in the Dago Creative Village continue to this day, while activities in the Cicukang Creative Village named "Cicukang Locomotive Village" were slowly disappearing in 2016. Observations at the Cicukang Locomotive Village were conducted to study artifacts and activities that still exist.

Observations were also conducted on digital activities both related to information about creative villages and various creative village activities. In addition, observations were made of Twitter accounts @kpgkreatifbdg, and by typing #kampungkreatifbandung (#BandungCreativeVillage) on Instagram and YouTube to find information on social media related to the creative village of Bandung. Further observations were made of the BCCF's official website. Information in the form of text articles, photos, images and videos from various social media were used as material for visual analysis related to creative villages. Observations of various information and digital activities were carried out from June 2018 to August 2018.

Results

Creative Villages in Bandung: Innovations with Many Constraints

The BCCF, which was inaugurated on December 21, 2008, was formed with the objective to maintain the spirit of creativity to empower the economic potential of the community, to improve the welfare of the local community, to maintain the ecosystem and as a tribute to the cultural diversity that exists in the context of the social life of the people of Bandung (BCCF, n.d.). According to the BCCF, Bandung has great potential as a creative city in terms of following the three concepts of "People, Place, Idea." Bandung has business potential and active urban communities, entrepreneurial spirit, economic value and social innovation, making it ideal as a concept city.

The Dago Creative Village is a group of local neighborhoods located in the northern area of Bandung. This area is well known as an important location in the context of trade, socialization between communities, tourism, as well as being a good location for various residential areas. Dago can also be considered one of many cultural spots in Bandung (Prasetyo & Martin-Iverson, 2013).

The Cicukang Creative Village is located more toward the center of Bandung, at the Ciroyom, Andir District, near the Bandung Railway Station. Cicukang Village consists of a row of dense houses and narrow alleys, but the inhabitants have a variety of unique creativities. One activity is musical performances in which the musical instruments are made from kitchen utensils. This show is often performed right next to the railroad tracks (Nursyabani, 2019). The label "creative village" is important because it is used by a number of urban communities in Bandung as a reaction to "the declaration of the 'creative city' policy in 2008" as a localization strategy to implement this development framework at a local level (Prasetyo & Martin-Iverson, 2013, p. 7).

Early development of the "creative village" was initiated by Rahmat Jabaril in 2000. According to our interview with Jabaril, the existence of this creative village was an attempt to change or transform urban villages. He observed that the city of Bandung and noticed that city growth trend was divided into two groups, namely the superblock (housing) group and the township group. The superblock has a limited concept of time-space, different from the urban village, for which space is an object and the people are the subject. People in the community superblock group became objects that were similarly placed in limited spaces. In urban villages, the shapes of the houses are different and varied. Space, in this context, is dynamic, can be explored, and can always be recreated. The environmental condition of the villages makes people prone to eviction. Resistance to the eviction of urban villages cannot be challenged by rejection but with creative ideas. Hence, the ideas about creative villages developed.

One resident of the Cicukang Village said that the condition of his village made him feel ashamed and inferior. The village he lived in was dirty, the population is so dense they need public space, and many young unemployed people frequently gather to drink alcohol, causing commotion by disturbing people who passed by or by fighting among themselves or with other villagers. The actions of these few members of his community had a negative psychological impact on all the residents.

According to Rahmat Jabaril, although the majority of the village residents are economically poor, they have social wealth in the form of a "gathering" or *ngariung*, a tradition that allows the residents to know about and care for each other. Through *ngariung*, the abundance of free time may be interpreted positively. However, psychologically, many people in the area do not realize the potential they have to indulge in creative and useful activities. Hence, many feel resigned and do not think that they can change their conditions. They need encouragement to know more about their potential. Their environment is obviously the center of their lives in terms of their culture, education, and economy. Thus, mapping was carried out by Jabaril in all aspects of the township: sociological, educational, gender, economic, and political. In addition, environmental and architectural mapping was also carried out in the township. Based on the mapping, the development of creative villages was born.

The BCCF carried out various programs, activities, conferences and festivals in the hope of creating a spirit of independence and a grassroots movement in various corners of the city, so residents felt the direct impact and contribution of the concept of creative economy, and to increase the number of citizens who could independently shape and apply the spirit of creative cities (ibid.). Starting in 2013, the city of Bandung planned to have 30 creative villages by the 2018. The government of Bandung expected that the development of creative villages would encourage the creation of villages that have a variety of cultural arts activities that might bring improvements in their economic sector (Pikiran Rakyat, 2013).

However, since the BCCF was established in 2013, the projects of creative city and creative village have, unfortunately, not been executed properly, which is evident from the disappearance of many creative villages; only a few places still exist today. The Dago Creative Village is one that still carries out several activities, such as painting, discussions, and art performances or events. The activities in Dago are still alive due to the existence of the creative village leaders. In addition, the structures in the village are maintained and there are several creative groups in the village.

Figure 1: Artifact in Cicukang Creative Village

Source: Author's document

In the Cicukang Creative Village, however, various activities began to fade, but some people there still hope they can receive help to enliven the activities in their village. One of the problems that hampered their activities was a conflict between residents who were active in managing creative camps and the local government. According to one resident, some local officials took credit for the development of the creative village even though the idea came from the village residents. Although this problem persisted, no one tried to build a dialog to solve the issue; thus, activities at the village slowly decreased.

The Utilization of Social Media in Creative Villages: Opportunities and Challenges

Indonesians are avid social media users. Facebook is still very popular in Indonesia, although the popularity of other social media such as YouTube and Instagram continues to increase in conjunction with the availability of higher internet penetration. In total, approximately 150 million Indonesians are social media users (APJII, 2018; We Are Social, 2019). Jakarta and Bandung have been named as cities that have very active Twitter users (Semiocast, 2012). Throughout his term as the Mayor of Bandung, Ridwan Kamil frequently expressed his opinion about how to strategically use social media to promote tourism by establishing connections, engaging persuasively and creating a sense of security for prospective travelers who want to visit the city (Rosadi, 2017). One of his breakthroughs in terms of internet infrastructure was how he successfully built various WiFi access in Bandung's mosques, parks, and many other locations, either through funding from city government or in collaboration with private parties (Lukihardianti, 2016). However, in practice, these infrastructure programs are often problematic in terms of their sustainability.

Internet access for the villagers was initially facilitated by the "RW Net program" from the Bandung city government, but then the program stopped. A villager from Cicukang Village admitted that she and other villagers eventually used their own funds (to buy *pulsa* or tokens for quota) and other resources for the needs of the Creative Village Program. Even though she had to spend her own money on internet fees, she claimed that she and the other villagers, with their limited knowledge and skills, were trying to promote the events on the internet. She emphasized that, "if there is an exhibition…we hold a number of exhibitions to display the work of our young children…we promote it in 'Braga to Braga' website, and on [other platforms] via the internet." In addition to uploading information on their activities on her personal accounts, she also posts the information in the Sundanese art communities. She claimed that their effort successfully brought visitors, and they made the villagers sell their creative works and various food at the event. For the village residents, they were very proud because, previously, there were only a few people visiting their area, but now there was a reason to maintain the cleanliness and beauty of their village.

The village residents claimed that, at first, the use of social media to promote their event was successful beyond their expectations. One interviewee revealed that, when they held an event related to the "*Karinding* (traditional music instruments) Group," many visitors came not only from Bandung, but also from outside the city. One villager said, "there were so many people who came, we were overwhelmed...."

The application used was mainly the Facebook personal account. Our interviewee said that she only used Facebook because she hoped other younger villagers could contribute by using other applications. However, many young villagers go directly to work after graduating from high school. Hence, no one had the time to take care of the creative village's social media account and the effort to continue promote Cicukang Creative Village stopped.

The use of social media with personal accounts also occurred in the Dago Creative Village. One of the creative village leaders, who was also the organizer of the Dago Creative Village, said that he mainly used Facebook, while some of his friends used Instagram, but because there was no one to maintain the village Facebook account, it was eventually closed.

Internet access in the Dago Creative Village is quite good and, according to the residents, in the past two years access has massively improved, and almost every house now has private internet access via mobile phones, but free internet access for the public is not available. The leader of this creative village tried to ask one of the state-owned internet providers to provide public internet access for creative villages as part of the company's corporate social responsibility program, but they received no response from the company.

Bandung Creative Village in Social Media

This study conducted a simple search using Google. From the results of our analysis, via a simple keyword-based search in the search engine, typing "Bandung creative village" (in Indonesian), we found various articles on only one creative village: *Kampung Kreatif Dago Pojok* (Dago Pojok Creative Village). However, there was no information center, for example, an official government website, nor was there an official website of the creative village community to provide sufficient factual information regarding the project in the city of Bandung. This absence is certainly a paradox related to the concept of Bandung as a smart city and creative city, which has a variety of technological infrastructures that is already available. Information related to the cultural and creative activities of the city was neglected; articles discussing creative villages were not updated with the latest news. This same lack applied to Twitter. There were no information centers or information updates related to creative villages in the city of Bandung.

Figure 2: Information searching on Twitter with keywords "Kampung kreatif Bandung"

Source: Author's document

On Twitter, we found one Bandung creative village account with the @kpgkreatifbdg handle, but the account had been inactive since 2012 and there was no information on whether the account was an official account or a part of the Creative Village Program in Bandung. Similarly, an information search through Instagram, which has more visual content, found the #kampungkreatifbandung (#BandungCreativeVillage) hashtag, but with only 17 posts, as in Figure 3.

Figure 3 Information searching on Instagram with keywords #kampungkreatifbandung

Source: Author's document

The information provided was unclear since there were no sufficient news sources. There were no news sources from the city government of Bandung or organizations that should have functioned to provide and disseminate information related to Bandung as a creative city that also had a creative village.

Figure 4: Information searching on Instagram with keywords #kampungkreatifbandung

Source: Author's document

The use of SEO (search engine optimization) strategies in search engines such as Google and on social media should increase the number of search results for potential visitors and display professionalism in managing the tourism business. The management of keywords will increase the satisfaction of visitors to the city and creative village customers. These keywords function in helping visitors find tourist destinations, including those related to creative villages, the description of the region in accordance to the keywords and recommendations, as well as previous visitor experiences that can lead to a better branding process by using digital media (Tolica, Gorica, Panajoti, & Pjero, 2017). In managing information, social media must always be updated to exhibit sustainable management. Ideally, a creative village's social media manager should search for responses from other social media users. In this case, there had not been any effort to build any interaction or participation between creative village managers with visitors and potential visitors.

The spread of information related to tourism in Bandung, especially related to creative villages, is certainly important for city management, which is expected to be based on digital technology and information management. Although some of Bandung's government agencies already have their own sites, as well as a variety of social media platforms, there is an insufficient synergy between the account managers. The city of Bandung has a variety of potentials in terms of infrastructure and the creative potentials of its young people and organizations such as the BCCF, but seems incapable of providing the catalysts and centers of movements related to the smart city and creative city that they promote. This lack leads to obscurity about who or what institution should be the leader of data and information management related to the Creative Village Programs, and how future strategies must be developed sustainably and consistently.

Figure 5: Official Website of BCCF

Source: Author's document

Today, many social media accounts and blogs related to the Creative Village Program are inactive and abandoned. The "Braga to Braga" website eventually also disappeared. On the official BCCF website, there was no information regarding creative villages. Social media utilization for the sustainability of Dago Creative Village was halted due to problems at the community level and the local institutional level.

Discussion

This section discusses various challenges in the socio-cultural transformation process through the development of creative villages in the city of Bandung. The social and cultural choices were made and the role of social media provided benefits; however, the content created only concerned information about activities in the creative village, and the spread of information related to the program and discussing and developing the process of transforming the urban lower classes to have a better quality of life, unfortunately, began to fade.

Since the location of the Dago Creative village and Cicukang Creative Village lies in the center of the city, the land is limited, and the housing situation is generally crowded. The village residents largely have informal jobs with many uncertainties regarding income and place and time of work. Hence, there are economic difficulties for the village residents. This situation ultimately resulted in an indifference toward their village. Village residents who are relatively young and have no jobs are vulnerable to conflicts or unlawful acts such as drinking, gambling or fighting. This condition makes it necessary to develop productive activities that can help their economy, even on a small scale.

The absence of community leaders in both Bandung's urban village causes residents to not recognize their various potentials. The people are highly dependent on prominent figures they can trust to direct them, because they are not used to acting independently and actively. They need an activist who can mingle and can be socially trusted. Through coaching by the activists, the villagers began to realize that they had untapped potential in arts and other creative skills that could possibly be productive for business in the tourism sector.

In addition to developing the residents' drive, the Creative Village Program decorated the village to look more attractive and was supportive of productive activities. The village was arranged artistically based on the diverse shapes and forms of houses and buildings; the natural and irregular arrangement of their locations enhanced the characteristic of the village. The villagers' habit of *ngariung* (gathering to chat without a specific purpose, or just to meet each other and spend their free time) was used to gradually encourage them to discuss various cultural arts activities they can display or create.

Regarding physical changes in the slums, the village residents realized that a clean residential environment is an important element to attract tourists. A massive clean-up was conducted, which was acknowledged both within the village and by neighboring villages. Consequently, the residents sense of pride and self-concept increased because they felt valued by others. Previously, they felt removed by urban development and were looked down upon by the urban community. The various decorative artworks they created made the village more interesting and entertaining to visit, plus their creative products could be sold to visitors.

To promote the existence of creative villages and all the artistic activities and creative products they produced, the residents needed tools of communication, so they used internet-based platforms, such as social media. At first, the creative villagers took advantage of the free internet access, but this facility disappeared without any notification. In effect, the village residents were unable to build a network among creative villages in Bandung or people in other cities or even other countries. The absence of free internet access forced the village residents to use their personal internet access, which was very limited.

Government institutions' social media sites or accounts that were tasked or formed specifically to develop smart city programs and support the development of creative villages were not optimally implemented. The dissemination of information that was carried out did not position the village residents as subjects who can carry out interactive communication with site visitors. Furthermore, the residents were rarely involved in broad discussions related to Creative Village Programs. The BCCF and Bandung City Tourism Office did not function as facilitators for the villagers. The constraints in using social media to develop creative villages should be addressed properly if there is to be effective cooperation between the city government, via the Tourism Office or the BCCF, with activists from the Indonesian Creative Village Network and Bandung creative village residents.

Figure 6: Souvenirs for the visitors of Dago Creative Village

Source: Author's document

CONCLUSION

The focus of economic strategies and policies based on creative classes and creative cities is often trapped in defining dimensions for a city to be called "creative." Thus, there is a tendency for policy replication without considering whether they are related to the specific aspects and contextual circumstances of the various locations where the policy is carried out (Comunian, 2011, p. 1157). This was the case in Bandung; the Creative Village Program was halted by a lack of support from the local government regarding the revoking of internet access and the lack of clarity in the program. Furthermore, many village residents used social media sporadically, and this use was not well managed, with no definitive communication strategy for promoting the creative villages. Moreover, there was a lack of necessary provision from organizations such as the BCCF, which were supposed to have functioned as the intermediaries between the Government and the creative villages.

This study found that the main problem was the unavailability of actors with the time and commitment to manage social media for each creative village. In addition, there was an internal conflict between the actors from the village and the village apparatus, which also disrupted the Creative Village Program and resulted in the unavailability of internet access for public needs. Smart City and Creative Village Program managers do not understand this need; thus, they do not provide adequate support. In addition, the citizens' request to cooperate directly with the ISPs was not given any adequate response. To address these issues, better cooperation, such as forming a special committee consisting of representatives from each sector and establishing more regular and open forums to engage with the wider public, is crucial. In general, a collaborative network that is developed and managed together is needed. Furthermore, local government support needs to be improved. For example, the Government can provide more sustainable internet access and create a regular social media training program designed to promote the Creative Village Program. Finally, there are cultural factors, internal politics, digital policy support, and voices from civil society and ordinary village residents that need to be frequently maintained to ensure that the Smart City and Creative Village Programs are sustainable.

REFERENCES

APJII. (2018). *Penetrasi & Profil Perilaku Pengguna Internet Indonesia*. Retrieved from Asosiasi Penyelenggara Jasa Internet Indonesia website: https://apjii.or.id/survei2018s

Aritenang, A. (2012). The City of Bandung: Unfolding the process of a Creative City. Retrieved 20 November 2018, from MPRA Paper website: https://mpra.ub.uni-muenchen.de/48629/

Ballas, D. (2013). What Makes a 'Happy City'? *Cities*, *32*(1), S39–S50.

Barnes, K., Waitt, G., Gill, N., & Gibson, C. (2006). Community and Nostalgia in Urban Revitalisation: a critique of urban village and creative class strategies as remedies for social 'problems.' *Australian Geographer*, *37*(3), 335–354.

Batty, M., Axhausen, K Albrechtslund, A. (2008). "Online social networking as participatory surveillance". *First Monday, Vol. 13*(3). Retrieved from http://firstmonday.org/ojs/index.php/fm/article/view/2142/1949.5. W., Giannotti, F., Pozdnoukhov, A., Bazzani, A., Wachowicz, M., … Portugali, Y. (2012). Smart Cities of the Future. *The European Physical Journal Special Topics*, 481–518.

BCCF. (n.d.). ABOUT BCCF. Retrieved 20 Agustus 2018, from http://bandungcreative.id/main/main/about_me

Cocchia, A. (2014). Smart and Digital City: A Systematic Literature Review. In R. P. Dameri & C. Rosenthal-Sabroux (Ed.), *Smart City: How to Create Public and Economic Value with High Technology in Urban Space* (hal. 13–43). Switzerland: Springer Internasional Publishing.

Comunian, R. (2011). Rethinking the Creative City: The Role of Complexity, Networks and Interactions in the Urban Creative Economy. *Urban Studies*, *48*(6), 1157–1179.

Creswell, J. W. (2007). *Qualitative Enquiry and Research Design: Choosing Among Five Approaches*. Thousand Oaks, CA: Sage Publications.

De Lorenzo, C. (2000). Integrating Public Art, Environmental Sustainability, and Education: Australia's "Creative Village" Model. *International Journal of Art Design Education*, *19*(2), 153–160.

Denzin, N. K., & Lincoln, Y. S. (2011). *The SAGE Handbook of Qualitative Research* (4th ed.). Thousand Oaks, CA: SAGE Publications Ltd.

Giffinger, R., Fertner, C., Kramar, H., Kalasek, R., Pichler-Milanovic´, N., & Meijers, E. (2007). *Smart Cities: Ranking of European Medium-sized Cities*. Vienna: Vienna University of Technolog.

Hermawati, R., & Runiawati, N. (2015). Enhancement of Creative Industries in Bandung City through Cultural Community and Public Policy Approaches. *4th International Conference on Law, Education and Humanities (ICLEH'15)*, 95–99. Paris: ICLEH.

Jamilah, I., Akbar, K. F., Gunawan, M. A., & Marantika, S. (2018). Political Communication, Social Media, and Public Sphere: An Analysis to a Phenomenon in Bandung towards Smart City. *International Journal of Social Science and Humanity*, *6*(12), 923–928. https://doi.org/10.18178/ijssh.2016.6.12.774

Kustiwan, I., Ukrin, I., & Aulia, A. (2015). Identification of the Creative Capacity of Kampong's Community towards Sustainable Kampong (Case Studies: Cicadas and Pasundan Kampong, Bandung): A Preliminary Study. *Procedia - Social and Behavioral Sciences*, *184*(August 2014), 144–151. https://doi.org/10.1016/j.sbspro.2015.05.074

Lukihardianti, A. (2016). Ridwan Kamil: 4.000 Masjid di Bandung Dipasang Wifi | Republika Online. Retrieved 7 Juli 2019, from republika.co.id website: https://www.republika.co.id/berita/nasional/daerah/16/09/20/odsq21330-ridwan-kamil-4000-masjid-di-bandung-dipasang-wifi

Maryunani, S. R., & Mirzanti, I. R. (2015). The Development of Entrepreneurship in Creative Industries with Reference to Bandung as a Creative City. *Procedia - Social and Behavioral Sciences*, (169), 387–394.

Mayangsaria, L., & Novania, S. (2015). Multi-stakeholder co-creation analysis in smart city management: an experience from Bandung, Indonesia. *Procedia Manufacturing*, *4*, 315–321. https://doi.org/10.1016/j.promfg.2015.11.046

Nursyabani, F. (2019). Bandung Baheula: Kampung Kreatif Lokomotif Cicukang dan Kisah Lamanya. Retrieved 7 Agustus 2019, from ayobandung.com website: https://www.ayobandung.com/read/2019/06/13/54910/bandung-baheula-kampung-kreatif-lokomotif-cicukang-dan-kisah-lamanya

Pardo, T., & Taewoo, N. (2011). Conceptualizing smart city with dimensions of technology, people, and institutions. *Proceedings of the 12th Annual International Conference on Digital Government Research*, 82–291. New York: ACM.

Pikiran Rakyat. (2013). 5 Tahun ke Depan, Bakal Ada 30 Kampung Kreatif di Kota Bandung.

Pikiran Rakyat. (2017a). Dirintis Sejak 2014, Pemkot Bandung Kini Punya 394 Aplikasi Smart City. Retrieved 11 Agustus 2018, from Pikiran Rakyat website: http://www.pikiran-rakyat.com/bandung-raya/2017/09/26/dirintis-sejak-2014-pemkot-bandung-kini-punya-394-aplikasi-smart-city-410270

Pikiran Rakyat. (2017b). Indeks Kebahagiaan Kota Bandung Naik. Retrieved 8 Agustus 2018, from Pikiran Rakyat website: http://www.pikiran-rakyat.com/bandung-raya/2017/09/07/indeks-kebahagiaan-kota-bandung-naik-408967

Ponzini, D., & Rossi, U. (2010). Becoming a Creative City: The Entrepreneurial Mayor, Network Politics and the Promise of an Urban Renaissance. *Urban Studies*, *47*(5), 1037–1057.

Prahadi, Y. Y. (2015). Telkom Wujudkan Bandung Smart City. Retrieved 25 November 2018, from SWA website: https://swa.co.id/swa/trends/management/telkom-wujudkan-bandung-smart-city

Prasetyo, F. A., & Martin-Iverson, S. (2013). Art, activism and the 'Creative Kampung': A case study from Dago Pojok, Bandung, Indonesia. Retrieved 20 Juni 2019, from Paper presented at International conference, Planning in The Era of Uncertainty website: https://www.researchgate.net/publication/282808753_Art_activism_and_the_'Creative_Kampong'_A_case_study_from_Dago_Pojok_Bandung_Indonesia

Rosadi, D. (2017). Ridwan Kamil ajak gunakan media sosial untuk promosi wisata Bandung. Retrieved 7 Juli 2019, from merdeka.com website: https://bandung.merdeka.com/halo-bandung/ridwan-kamil-ajak-gunakan-media-sosial-untuk-promosi-wisata-bandung-170201j.html

Semiocast. (2012). Twitter reaches half a billion accounts More than 140 millions in the U.S. Retrieved 10 Juni 2017, from Semiocast website: https://semiocast.com/en/publications/2012_07_30_Twitter_reaches_half_a_billion_accounts_1 40m_in_the_US

Shapiro, J. M. (2006). Smart Cities: Quality of Life, Productivity, and the Growth Effects of Human Capital. *Review of Economics & Statistics, 88*(2), 324–335.

Simatupang, T. M. (2010). Creative Industries Mapping Projects in Indonesia: Experiences and Lessons Learned. In *Paper for a seminar of The Importance of Creative Industries Mapping Project for Cities and Countries*. Ho Chi Minh City.

Tolica, E. K., Gorica, K., Panajoti, V. H., & Pjero, E. (2017). The Role of Internet and SEO in Branding Destinations: Case of Albania as a New Destination in Balkans. *Academic Journal of Interdisciplinary Studies, 6*(1), 45–52.

Utoyo, S., & Sutarsih, T. (2017). *Profil Usaha/Perusahaan 16 Subsektor EKRAF Berdasarkan Sensus Ekonomi 2016 (SE2016)*. Jakarta: Badan Pusat Statistik & Badan Ekonomi Kreatif.

We Are Social. (2019). *DIGITAL 2019: INDONESIA*. Retrieved from DATAREPORTAL.COM website: https://datareportal.com/reports/digital-2019-indonesia?rq=indonesia

Windarti, Y. (2016). Communities Inclusion of Urban Tourism Development: The Case of Bandung City, Indonesia. *International Journal of Culture and History, 2*(4), 189–198.

Yusuf, W., & Badriyah, L. (2017). Cerita Ridwan Kamil Kembangkan Ekonomi Kreatif di Bandung. Retrieved 6 Agustus 2019, from medcom.id website: https://nusantara.medcom.id/jawa-barat/peristiwa/yNLeVdyb-cerita-ridwan-kamil-kembangkan-ekonomi-kreatif-di-bandung.

CHAPTER 13

Living Culture of Today's Apartment Dwellers: Social Interactions, Social Media, and Urban Living in Bangladesh

Md. Aminul Islam
Department of Media Studies and Journalism
University of Liberal Arts Bangladesh (ULAB), Bangladesh
and
Naziat Choudhury
Department of Mass Communication and Journalism
University of Rajshahi, Bangladesh

ABSTRACT

In the past three decades, the pattern of social relations has gone through massive transformations in Bangladesh. Within such reality, this study explores how social media are being used to shape and reshape interpersonal relationships within real-life social networks of neighbors in urban areas in the country. It sets out not only the changing patterns of interpersonal relationships among individuals on social networks, but also helps to understand the role social media play in this process. Drawing upon Barry Wellman's networked individualism theoretical framework, data are collected from residents of eight high-rise buildings using a semi-structured questionnaire. The participants of this study are selected through snowball sampling method. The findings indicate that while the urbanization and modernization process in Bangladesh is changing relationship patterns, as seen in other parts of the world, the residents here were limiting their connections to traditional methods of interaction. Social media seem to be contributing to the maintenance of weaker ties here.

Keywords: Urbanization, high-rise buildings, social networks, social relationships, social media

INTRODUCTION

In combination with rapid urbanization and modernization, the social process and social interactions have been undergoing transformations around the world.

Bangladesh is no exception to such massive change in societal structure and functions (Khan, 2013). In the past few decades, there has been a growing trend that people in Bangladesh are moving from rural areas to urban areas for better education and job purposes, which has given rise to a new form of social relationship and social structure. With the increasing urban population, traditional forms of housing, with extended families living under one roof, have been taken over by high-rise buildings and individually owned houses. These forms of urban living conditions are shaped by the Western style, in which residents are part of nuclear families. Hence, these reconstructions of residences obviously transformed the social interactions among the residents in urban areas. Furthermore, the advent of social media may also be playing a role in social relationships within the urban context (Habib, Hossain, Ferdous & Bayezid, 2018), which this paper focuses on. Therefore, this article tries to understand the living culture of apartment dwellers in terms of their social interactions, real-life social network, sense of community and social media usage.

The idea of living in individually owned houses is gradually being replaced by high-rise buildings, which has been a dominant form of residence in the world's major cities. Mainly, the middle- and upper-middle-class population are residents of these buildings, as they are coming together to form various associations. This situation has possibly introduced new sets of social relationships. Our assumption is that the residents of these buildings are creating a new form of community that may or may not be different from the sense of community that used to exist in the past in Bangladesh.

Propelled by consistent growth in gross domestic product (GDP), increased remittance, per capita income and young workforce in recent past years, Bangladesh has been experiencing phenomenal transformations in its economy, society, and ways of life and housing patterns. Due to the rapid growth in economic outcome and increased middle-class population, the country is witnessing increased urbanization. As of 2017, about 36% of the total populations were living in urban areas of the country; whereas, in 1960, it was only 5%; and, in 2000, the percentage of urban population stood at 23.6% of the entire population (World Bank, 2018).

Bangladesh has also been experiencing growth in usage of the internet. According to data from the Bangladesh Telecommunication Regulatory Commission (BTRC), the country has 80.829 million internet subscribers, among whom the majority (75.396 million) uses it through their mobile phones (BTRC, 2018). This factor is related to the number of mobile phone users Bangladesh has. There are about 155.810 million mobile phone users in the country (BTRC, 2018). In terms of social media usage, Bangladesh has around 30 million active users (We Are Social, 2018).

The rise of social media around the world has witnessed changes in the forms of social interaction, especially in the context of urban areas (Habib et al., 2018). The reason for these changes is that the majority of the users of these media are congregated within these regions. The combination of urbanization, modernization and social media popularity has led to these changes. This is the case in a developing country such as Bangladesh also. In the past few decades, much of the Bangladeshi population has moved from rural areas to urban areas for better education and job purposes, which has increased urban populations. This factor and the rise of social media usage in urban areas of Bangladesh are contributing to the changing social interaction process.

Research on various dimensions of living in high-rise buildings has been increasingly gaining attention in the fields of human social interaction, community psychology, social psychology, sociology, public health and architecture (Verhaeghe et al., 2016; Yuen et al., 2006; Mahdavinejad et al., 2014; Wandersman & Nation, 1998; Panczak et al., 2013; Farahani & Lozanovska, 2014; Aulia, 2016; Gattino et al., 2013). Previous studies have focused on the structural features of high-rise buildings, the physical health consequences of living in such buildings, the characteristics of the neighborhoods, and the social and cultural concerns of residents of the buildings. However, most of these works have been conducted in developed countries (Gaumer et al., 2014; Verhaeghe et al., 2016; Panczak et al., 2013). Although the phenomenon of residing in high-rise buildings in the context of urban arenas in developing countries is expanding rapidly, very few studies have addressed the issues from this perspective.

Investigating the frequency, nature and intensity of social interaction of residents within high-rise buildings in South Africa, Schutte (1985) concludes that density, crowding, privacy issues, and environmental perception do not always negatively affect the social interaction experiences of the residents, as opposed to the prevailing conception. Snow, Leahy, and Schwab (1981) examined the relationship between spatial proximity and social interaction in a heterogeneous apartment. They examined also the effects of other characteristics of the apartment design upon interaction patterns among apartment residents. They conclude that initial contact and interactions are influenced by spatial proximity and other design features. Several other factors play an important role in the social life of residents of high-rise buildings. Kazemzad and Shakouri (2017) argue that the factors that play an influential role in contact and interaction include the existence of an outdoor space in the building complex, a sense of place attachment, privacy, safety, and shared social and demographic characteristics.

The rise of social media is redefining urban life and the experience of physical surroundings and contributing to the further individualization and liberalization of urban society (de Waal, 2014). There exists an association between the use of social media and interpersonal relationships, as the social media influences an individual's nature, pattern and volume of communication with family members and peers (Manjunatha, 2013; Murthy, Gross & Pensavalle, 2015). However, most of these works have been conducted in developed countries (Gaumer et al., 2014; Verhaeghe et al., 2016; Panczak et al., 2013). Social media usage in urban areas of Bangladesh has increased at a rapid rate, which is perhaps contributing to the social interaction process. Therefore, this article explores multiple dimensions of social interaction within urban living conditions, in addition to its association with the usage of social media.

2. Networked Individualism and Relationships in Apartments

Debates about the impact of new media on social relationships have existed since the mass acceptance of the technology. Putnam (2000) often expressed his concern about the decay of community that used to prevail in the past. According to him, people are becoming ever more disconnected with each other in society (Putnam, 2000). There are researchers, such as Turkle (2011), who fear the decline of sense of community due to new media. Before the new media, the alarm was raised about the fall of community due to the introduction of other media, such television (Putnam, 2000). Nevertheless, there are many scholars (e.g. Hampton & Wellman, 2003; Tseng & Hsieh, 2015) who believe that the new media helped in creating and maintaining ties by opening new channels for communication. Due to the spread of social media, especially with easy access through mobile phones, maintaining social connections is not only affordable, but also time saving. The lives of city dwellers are preoccupied with professional duties and everyday chores that occupy much of their time that used to be devoted to socialization. Hence, people rely on social media to help them connect and maintain various forms of social ties that are spread around the world and not located within specific boundaries. Connections that were difficult to nurture due to space, time and money are now outdated. This factor was envisioned by Wellman (2001) as "globalized portability". He believed, "that development of globalized portability will mean the potential availability of 'small world' interpersonal connectivity. All will be connected to all, either directly or through short chains of indirect ties." (p. 230)

Wellman's (2001) networked individualism concept is applied in this study in which "social interactions today are increasingly person-to-person" (Chua and Wellman, 2016, p. 3). The emphasis is on individuals rather than groups. Wellman (2005) argues that, "the nature of community is changing: from being a social network of households to a social network of individuals" (p. 55). From this perspective, individuals are connected to each other and not to groups. They are communicating with each other through a device. Rainie and Wellman (2012) compare networked individuals to an "operating system" that "describes the ways in which people connect, communicate, and exchange information" (p. 7).

Person-to-person communication has undoubtedly increased in Bangladesh. One of the reasons for this increase is due to heavy usage of mobile technology and social media, which is similar to other parts of the world. Within the social structure of Bangladesh, how social media are being used to shape and reshape interpersonal relationships within social networks of neighbors in urban areas is explored in this study. For instance, this article reveals where people within neighborhoods meet to socialize: Is it at a semi-public place such as a café, or in the private space of homes, and what role do social media play? This article sets out not only the changing patterns of interpersonal relationships among individuals on social networks, but also helps to understand the role social media play in this process.

3. Methodology

This section discusses the methods and procedures used to collect relevant data and to assess the relationship between neighborhood and social interactions. The study was mainly based on primary data and the results, which were drawn with the help of descriptive statistics from the collected data. In this descriptive study, data were collected from Rajshahi, a divisional city about 300km north-west of Dhaka, the capital city of Bangladesh, by using a questionnaire survey method without deliberate manipulation of variables or control over the research settings.

3.1 Sample and Procedure

We collected data from residents of eight high-rise buildings in Rajshahi city, about 300 kilometer north-west of Bangladesh capital Dhaka. We chose sample buildings randomly using a multistage random sampling method. We collected data from the respondents by using a snowball sampling method. The buildings were located in different parts of the city and had at least six stories. In most cases, the buildings were constructed within five years of this study. On average, 20 families lived in each building. The buildings were consisted of two to three blocks. Some 30 questionnaires were sent to each of the selected buildings, meaning that a total of 240 questionnaires were sent out. Of those, only 100 questionnaires were returned on the scheduled date (response rate was 41.66%). Due to various inconsistencies, we excluded responses from 16 respondents. Thus, responses from 84 residents were considered for the final analysis. Of these, six respondents did not have any social media account, meaning that 78 respondents had an account on at least one social media platform.

3.2 Instruments

We collected relevant data by using a semi-structured questionnaire. The questionnaire consisted of multiple-choice closed-ended questions on demographic features, dwelling patterns, sense of community and neighborhood, social network structure and social interaction in real-life setting, and social interaction through social media platforms. To understand the dimension of community sense, we used the Sense of Community Index (SCI) developed by David W. McMillan and David M. Chavis (McMillan & Chavis, 1986). The SCI is a 12-item scale with four subscales. It has a true-false response set and only three items in each subscale. With this index, an individual's sense of community is measured through the lenses of membership, influence, meeting needs, and a shared emotional connection. The highest possible score in the index is 12. The level of an individual's sense of community is proportionate to the score he/she achieves, meaning that the higher a respondent's score, the deeper his/her sense of community. However, we tried to understand the level of the sense of community by dividing the total score into four categories. A core score of 0-4 indicates a weak sense of community; 4.1-8 indicates a moderate sense of community; and 8.1-12 indicates a strong sense of community.

We measured the social network structure and pattern of social interaction with neighbors by using an improvised version of Lubben's Social Network Scale – Revised (LSNS-R) developed by James Lubben (Lubben, 1988; Lubben et. al, 2006). The LSNS-R is a 12-item and five-point Likert scale. Using the scale, we measured the social network structure and the pattern and frequency of social interaction in the neighborhood, mainly in different blocks of the building. However, the original version of the LSNS-R was used to measure social engagement including family and friends. The scale consisted of 12 items, and scores for each question ranged from zero to five. A score of zero indicates minimal social integration; whereas, five indicates substantial social integration. The total score is an equally weighted sum of the 12 questions. Scores range from 0 to 60, with higher scores indicating a greater level of social support and low risk of isolation. A score less than 20 indicates a person with an extremely limited social network and high risk of isolation. We tried also to understand the level of social network of the respondents by dividing the total score into three categories. A score of 0-20 indicates an extremely limited social network; 21-40 indicates a moderate social network; and 41-60 indicates a strong social network.

3.3 Data Analysis

The analysis of data focused on variables narrowly measuring social interaction in real-life and virtual settings. The analysis consisted of variables measuring the extent of the respondent's sense of community, neighborhood contacts and friendships. The responses of the 84 participants were primarily described using descriptive statistics (e.g. frequencies, percentages, and means.) We used the SPSS (version 23) to prepare and analyze the data. Statistical tests such as the χ^2-test were used to determine the significance and level of association between variables. It must be mentioned that, of the 84 respondents, only 78 had an account on at least one social media platform. Therefore, we computed the associations between social media use, real-life social network and sense of community of 78 respondents.

4. Results and Discussion

Demographic features were an important indicator for obtaining in-depth insights into the social process and the dynamics of social interaction of the members of a society. Table 1 contains data on the respondents' demographic features, including gender, age, marital status, employment, level of income and education. About half (40.5%) the respondents belonged to the age group between 46 and 55 years old. The majority of the respondents were male (64.3%) and married (85.7%). Most of the respondents earned, on average, over 51,000 Bangladeshi taka (BDT or Tk hereafter) a month, and about 90.5% respondents had at least graduate or higher level of education.

Table 1: Demographic features of the respondents

Indicators		N	%
Gender	Male	54	64.3
	Female	30	35.7
Age	18-25	4	4.8
	26-35	20	23.8
	36-45	20	23.8
	46-55	34	40.5
	56-65	4	4.8
	66-above	2	2.4
Marital Status	Unmarried	10	11.9
	Married	72	85.7
	Divorced	0	0
	Widowed	2	2.4
Employment	Teaching	38	45.2
	Doctor or Engineer	4	4.8
	Private Job/NGO	12	14.3
	Government Employee	18	21.4
	Manage a Business	8	9.5
	Retired	2	2.4
	Unemployed	2	2.4
Income Level	Less than Tk10,000	4	4.8
	Tk11,000-Tk20,000	6	7.1
	Tk31,000-Tk40,000	8	9.5
	Tk41,000-Tk50,000	10	11.9
	Tk51,000-above	52	61.9
	Others (Unwilling to say)	4	4.8
Education Level	Primary	0	0
	High school or secondary level	8	9.5

Table 1: Demographic features of the respondents		
University degree and above	76	90.5

Rapid urbanization is a new in phenomenon in Bangladesh. Triggered by a gradual decrease of land availability and an unusual rise in the cost of land, the country's skyline has changed, with an increasing number of high-rise buildings within the past couple of years. We tried to understand the pattern of dwelling in the high-rise buildings in the study area. Table 2 lists the dwelling patterns in terms of ownership of residence, number of families that live in the buildings, persons per family unit, and location of residence in the building. It is unsurprising that the majority (69%) of the respondents owned the apartments they resided in, as they were older, married and employed. In most cases, the number of families living in a building ranged between 6 and 20. Of the respondents, 54.8% lived in a building where the total family numbers ranged between 15 and 19. The majority (78.6%) of families had three to four members, meaning that most of the families had two children. The location of residence in the building of the respondents varied between the first floor and the sixth floor, but (22.6%) lived on the fourth floor; 16.7% lived on the first floor; 20.2% lived on the second and fifth floors; and 17.9% lived on the third floor.

Table 2: Dwelling patterns of the respondents			
Indicators		Frequency	Percent
Dwelling ownership	Rented	26	31.0
	Owned	58	69.0
	1-5	0	0
	6-10	14	16.7
Number of families in	11-14	13	15.5
the building	15-19	46	54.8
	20+	11	13.1
	1-2	5	6.0
	3-4	66	78.6
Persons per family	5-6	13	15.5
unit	7-8	0	0
	9+	0	0
	First floor	14	16.7
	Second floor	17	20.2
Location of residence	Third floor	15	17.9
in the building	Fourth floor	19	22.6
	Fifth floor	17	20.2
	Sixth floor	2	2.4

4.1 Social Interaction on Social Media

The populations of social media around the world are mainly young and technologically knowledgeable. In the case of Bangladesh, the same scenario prevails. According to Socialbakers, around 73% of Facebook users in Bangladesh were 13 to 25 years old, and only 2% were older than 45 years of age (Shams, 2017). Hence, the finding in this study suggest that our respondents belonged to the older age group of social media users as around 40% are from the ages of 46 to 55 years. We tried to understand the pattern of social interaction on social media in terms of the following indicators—presence of social media account, the social media platforms they had accounts on, frequency of using social media in a day, the number of friends on social media, the number of social media friends who were neighbors, and the use of social media to interact with the neighbors.

The data in Table 3 reveal that the vast majority (92.9%) of the respondents had an account on at least one social media platform. The most popular social media platform among the respondents was Facebook. However, 38.5% of the respondents had accounts on Facebook, WhatsApp, Viber and other platforms. Nearly half (46.2%) the respondents used the social media platforms several times a day. Again, nearly half (43.6%) of the respondents had more than 300 friends on social media platforms they used. Interestingly, 23.1% of the respondents stated that they had no neighbors in their social media friend list. More than half the respondents (66.7%) who had their neighbors in their friend list did use social media to interact with them.

Table 3: The pattern of social media interaction on the social media platforms of the respondents

		Frequency	Percent
Have account on social media	Yes	78	92.9
	No	6	7.1
Types of social media platform	Facebook	46	59.0
	WhatsApp	2	2.6
	Viber	0	0
	All above	30	38.5
Frequency of using social media in a day	Several times an hour	20	25.6
	Every hour	2	2.6
	Several times a day	36	46.2
	Only when needed	20	25.6
Number of friends on social media	1-50	8	10.3
	51-100	4	5.1

Table 3: The pattern of social media interaction on the social media platforms of the respondents

	101-150	8	10.3
	151-200	12	15.4
	201-250	4	5.1
	251-300	8	10.3
	301+	34	43.6
	1-50	52	66.7
Number of social media	51-100	6	7.7
friends who are neighbors	151-200	2	2.6
	None	18	23.1
Use social media to	Yes	44	56.4
contact neighbors	No	34	43.6

4.2 Social Network and Social Interaction in the Neighborhood

We tried to understand the structure of real-life social networks and patterns of social interaction. The data in Table 4 indicate that there is a significant association between social network and the number of neighbors the respondents knew by name in the same block of the building (df = 6, likelihood ratio = 16.845, p-value = .010; Chi-square = 17.650, p-value = .007); the number of neighbors they knew by name in a different block within the same building (df = 6, likelihood ratio = 26.364, p-value = .000; Chi-square = 21.277, p-value = .002); the number who had friends in the neighborhood (df = 2, likelihood ratio = 9.577, p-value = .008; Chi-square = 9.016, p-value = .011); who had a neighbor with whom they could share personal problems (df = 2, likelihood = 21.278, p-value = .000; Chi-square = 21.833, p-value = .000); frequency of face-to-face meetings with neighbors (df = 6, likelihood ratio = 19.984, p-value = .003; Chi-square = 14.567, p-value = .024); place of meeting to interact with the neighbors (df = 12, likelihood ratio = 21.479, p-value = .044; Chi-square = 22.222, p-value = .035); main mode of interaction with the neighbor (df = 6, likelihood = 15.747, p-value = .015; Chi-square = 20.188, p-value = .003); depth/strength of relationship with neighbors (df = 6, likelihood ratio = 22.551, p-value = .001; Chi-square = 16.121, p-value = .013); and the nature of exchanges and favors asked/received among neighbors (df = 10, likelihood ratio = 36.271, p-value = .000; Chi-square = 37.603, p-value = .000).

Regarding social network, almost half (47.6%) the respondents said that they knew their neighbors by name. The large majority (73.8%) had moderate social networks; with 38.1% of these knowing almost all their neighbors. More than half (57.1%) the respondents had friends in their neighborhood. Of the respondents who had a moderate level of social network, 42.9% had friends in their neighborhood. Again, the large majority (76.2%) stated that they had a neighbor with whom they could share personal problems. Only 14.3% had a strong level of social network. Just over a third (35.7%) met with neighbors face-to-face every day, and 31% met occasionally. However, only 14.3% had a strong social network. The data reveal that 27.4% of the respondents met with their neighbors anywhere in the buildings, including their own residence, the neighbors' residence, corridors, or open places. These results suggest that the level of interaction among the respondents ranges from a limited to moderate level. The respondents felt that the type of social network they maintained within the building could not be recognized as a strong network. Scholars observed that the strength of relationships became weak following the migration from rural areas to cities (Wellman & Leighton, 1979; Putnam, 2000).

Table 4: Association between social interaction among neighbors and social network

Variables	Indicators	Level of social network			Total n(% of total)		Statistics and Value	
		Extremely limited social network n(% of total)	Moderate social networkn (% of total)	Strong social network n (% of total)		df	Likelihood ratio (p-value)	Pearson Chi-square (p-value)
Number of neighbors I know by name in the same block	All	4 (4.8)	18 (21.4)	6 (7.1)	28 (33.3)			
	Almost All	2 (2.4)	32 (38.1)	6 (7.1)	40 (47.6)		16.845 (.010)	17.650 (.007)
	Half	0 (0.0)	8 (9.5)	0 (0.0)	8 (9.5)			
	Very few	4 (4.8)	4 (4.8)	0 (0.0)	8 (9.5)			
Number of neighbors know by name in a different block	All	2 (2.4)	16 (19.0)	2 (2.4)	20 (23.8)			
	Almost All	0 (0.0)	22 (26.2)	10 (11.9)	32 (38.1)		26.364 (.000)	21.277 (.002)
	Half	2 (2.4)	10 (11.9)	0 (0.0)	12 (14.3)			
	Very few	6 (7.1)	14 (16.7)	0 (0.0)	20 (23.8)			
Have friends in neighbor-hood	Yes	2 (2.4)	36 (42.9)	10 (11.9)	48 (57.1)			
	No	8 (9.5)	26	2	36		9.577	9.016

Table 4: Association between social interaction among neighbors and social network

			(31.0)	(2.4)	(42.9)		(.008)	(.011)
Have a neighbor with whom can talk about personal problems	Yes	2 (2.4)	50 (59.5)	12 (14.3)	64 (76.2)			
	No	8 (9.5)	12 (14.3)	0 (0.0)	20 (23.8)		21.278 (.000)	21.833 (.000)
Frequency of face-to-face meetings	Rarely	0 (0.0)	12 (14.3)	0 (0.0)	12 (14.3)			
	Occasionally	6 (7.1)	16 (19.0)	4 (4.8)	26 (31.0)			
	Everyday	0 (0.0)	24 (28.6)	6 (7.1)	30 (35.7)		19.984 (.003)	14.567 (.024)
	Once a week	4 (4.8)	10 (11.9)	2 (2.4)	16 (19.0)			
Place of meeting to interact	Only in the building's open spaces	5 (6.0)	27 (32.1)	6 (7.1)	38 (45.2)			
	In my house	0 (0.0)	8 (9.5)	0 (0.0)	8 (9.5)			
	In neighbor's house	0 (0.0)	6 (7.1)	0 (.0)	6 (7.1)	2	21.479 (.044)	22.222 (.035)
	In the corridors	2 (2.4)	3 (3.6)	0 (0.0)	5 (6.0)			
	Outside the building	0 (0.0)	0 (0.0)	2 (2.4)	2 (2.4)			
	In social club	0 (0.0)	2 (2.4)	0 (0.0)	2 (2.4)			
	Any places of the building	3 (3.6)	16 (19.0)	4 (4.8)	23 (27.4)			
Main mode of interaction	Face-to-face	4 (4.8)	32 (38.1)	10 (11.9)	46 (54.8)			
	Telephone	2 (2.4)	0 (0.0)	0 (0.0)	2 (2.4)			

Table 4: Association between social interaction among neighbors and social network

	Mobile phone	2 (2.4)	12 (14.3)	0 (0.0)	14 (16.7)	15.74 7 (.015)	20.18 8 (.003)
	Face-to-face, telephone and mobile phone	2 (2.4)	18 (21.4)	2 (2.4)	22 (26.2)		
The depth or strength of my relationship	Moderate relationship	6 (7.1)	12 (14.3)	4 (4.8)	22 (26.2)	22.55 1 (.001)	16.12 1 (.013)
	Causal relationship	4 (4.8)	16 (19.0)	0 (0.0)	20 (23.8)		
	Close relationship	0 (0.0)	22 (26.2)	6 (7.1)	28 (33.3)		
	Strong bonding	0 (0.0)	12 (14.3)	2 (2.4)	14 (16.7)		
Nature of exchanges and favors asked or received	Loan of items	0 (0.0)	6 (7.1)	0 (0.0)	6 (7.1)	36.27 1 (.000)	37.60 3 (.000)
	Taking care of children	0 (0.0)	4 (4.8)	6 (7.1)	10 (11.9)		
	Financial help	0 (0.0)	2 (2.4)	2 (2.4)	4 (4.8)	0	
	Ceremonies (marriage, birthday) and illness	6 (7.1)	12 (14.3)	2 (2.4)	20 (23.8)		
	None	0 (0.0)	18 (21.4)	0 (0.0)	18 (21.4)		
	All	4 (4.8)	20 (23.8)	2 (2.4)	26 (31.0)		

4.3 Social interaction and sense of community in the neighborhood

The results indicate that there is statistically significant association between social interaction and sense of community among neighbors. As shown in Table 5, there is a significant association between sense of community and the number of neighbors the respondents knew by name in the same block of the building (df = 6, likelihood ratio = 22.967, p-value = .001; Chi-square = 28.000, p-value = .000); number of neighbors that respondents knew by name in a different block within the same building (df = 6, likelihood ratio = 35.532, p-value =.000; Chi-square = 26.344, p-value =.000); had friends in the neighborhood (df = 2, likelihood ratio = 18.830, p-value = .000; Chi-square = 17.694, p-value = .000); neighbor with whom they could share personal problems (df = 2, likelihood ratio = 13.304, p-value = .001; Chi-square = 11.638, p-value = .003); frequency of face-to-face interaction with neighbors (df = 6, likelihood ratio = 25.713, p-value = .000; Chi-square = 19.598, p-value = .003); place of meeting with neighbors (df =12, likelihood ratio = 36.741, p-value = .000; Chi-square = 32.718, p-value = .001); main mode of interaction with neighbors (df = 6, likelihood ratio = 32.169, p-value =   .000; Chi-square = 25.354, p-value = .000); depth of relationship with neighbors (df = 6, likelihood ratio = 21.478, p-value = .002; Chi-square = 18.096, p-value = .006); and nature of exchanges among neighbors (df = 10, likelihood ratio = 23.763, p-value = .008; Chi-square = 23.370, p-value = .009).

The data show that the respondents who knew their neighbors by name had a moderate level of sense of community. About half (47.6%) the respondents said that they knew almost all their neighbors by name, of whom 23.8% had a moderate level of sense of community, with a similar proportion with a strong sense of community. Over half (57.1%) the respondents stated that they had friends in their neighborhood. A significant number of the respondents had a moderate level (19.0%) and strong level (35.7%) of sense of community. The data show that over two-thirds (76.2%) of the respondents shared their personal problems with their neighbors. Of these, 50.0% had a moderate and 42.9% had a strong level of sense of community. Meanwhile, 35.7% of the respondents met every day, and 31% met their neighbors occasionally. Among those who met every day, 23.8% had a strong level of sense of community. The respondents mainly met in open spaces in the building. The data indicate that there is a strong association between meeting place and sense of community among the residents of a building. Just under half (45.2%) the respondents stated that they met with their neighbors in any place of the building. Of them, 29.8% had a moderate level of sense of community, and 14.3% had a strong level of sense of community.

Regarding the main method of communicating with neighbors, the majority (35.7%) preferred to interact face-to-face every day. Half (50%) had a moderate level of sense of community, of whom 26.2% met face-to-face and 16.7% used mobile phones to communicate with neighbors. One-third (33.3%) of the respondents believed that they had close relationship with their neighbors. Half the respondents had a moderate level of sense of community, and 42.9 % had a strong level of sense of community. The respondents stated that they asked for various types of favors from their neighbors, but few (7.1%) loaned items, and only 4.8% sought financial help. Although they met every day, the respondents believed that they had a mainly moderate and, in some cases, strong sense of community among them.   These responses were related to the fact, as seen in the data, that they met mainly within the open space of the buildings and less within their own homes.

Furthermore, it is evident that they requested assistance from neighbors only in formal activities such as family parties, marriage ceremony, death of someone and celebrating, national days, New Year and academic success of children. Although the respondents requested items or financial support in rare cases, they only did so from those bounded by close relationships and trust. An interesting aspect of this research is that the respondents heavily relied on face-to-face communication, and used mobile and internet-based technologies less often for interaction purposes. Therefore, the strength of ties among residents of the buildings seemed to be weak.

Table 5: Social interaction among neighbors and sense of community

Variables	Indicators	Level of Sense of Community			Total n (% of total)		Statistics and Value	
		Week comm unity sense n (% of total)	Moder ate Com munit y sense n (% of total)	Strong comm unity sense n (% of total)		df	Likelih ood ratio (p-value)	Pears on Chi-squar e (p-value)
Number of neighbors know by name in the same block	All	2 (2.4)	14 (16.7)	12 (14.3)	28 (33.3)			
	Almost All	0 (0.0)	20 (23.8)	20 (23.8)	40 (47.6)		22.96 7 (.001)	28.000 (.000)
	Half	0 (0.0)	4 (4.8)	4 (4.8)	8 (9.5)			
	Very few	4 (4.8)	4 (4.8)	0 (0.0)	8 (9.5)			
Number of neighbors know by name in a different block	All	2 (2.4)	10 (11.9)	8 (9.5)	20 (23.8)			
	Almost All	0 (0.0)	12 (14.3)	20 (23.8)	32 (38.1)		35.53 2 (.000)	26.344 (.000)
	Half	0 (0.0)	4 (4.8)	8 (9.5)	12 (14.3)			
	Very few	4 (4.8)	16 (19.0)	0 (0.0)	20 (23.8)			

Table 5: Social interaction among neighbors and sense of community

Have friends in the neighbor-hood	Yes	2 (2.4)	16 (19.0)	30 (35.7)	48 (57.1)		18.830 (.000)	17.694 (.000
	No	4 (4.8)	26 (31.0)	6 (7.1)	36 (42.9)			
Have a neighbor with whom can talk about personal problems	Yes	4 (4.8)	26 (31.0)	34 (40.5)	64 (76.2)		13.304 (.001)	11.638 (.003)
	No	2 (2.4)	16 (19.0)	2 (2.4)	20 (23.8)			
Frequency of face-to-face meetings	Rarely	2 (2.4)	10 (11.9)	0 (0.0)	12 (14.3)		25.713 (.000)	19.598 (.003)
	Occasion-ally	2 (2.4)	12 (14.3)	12 (14.3)	26 (31.0)			
	Everyday	0 (0.0)	10 (11.9)	20 (23.8)	30 (35.7)			
	Once a week	2 (2.4)	10 (11.9)	4 (4.8)	16 (19.0)			
Place of meeting to interact	Only in the building's open space	1 (1.2)	25 (29.8)	12 (14.3)	38 (45.2)		36.741 (.000)	32.718 (.001)
	In my house	0 (0.0)	2 (2.4)	6 (7.1)	8 (9.5)			
	In neighbor's house	2 (2.4)	4 (4.8)	0 (0.0)	6 (7.1)	2		
	In the corridors	1 (1.2)	4 (4.8)	0 (0.0)	5 (6.0)			
	Outside the building	0 (0.0)	0 (0.0)	2 (2.4)	2 (2.4)			
	In club	0 (0.0)	2 (2.4)	0 (0.0)	2 (2.4)			
	Any place of the building	2 (2.4)	5 (6.0)	16 (19.0)	23 (27.4)			

Table 5: Social interaction among neighbors and sense of community

Main mode of interaction	Face-to-face	4 (4.8)	22 (26.2)	20 (23.8)	46 (54.8)	32.169 (.000)	25.354 (.000)
	Telephone	0 (0.0)	2 (2.4)	0 (0.0)	2 (2.4)		
	Mobile phone	0 (0.0)	14 (16.7)	0 (0.0)	14 (16.7)		
	Both face-to-face, telephone and mobile phone	2 (2.4)	4 (4.8)	16 (19.0)	22 (26.2)		
The depth or strength of my relationship	Moderate relation-ship	2 (2.4)	16 (19.0)	4 (4.8)	22 (26.2)	21.478 (.002)	18.096 (.006)
	Causal relation-ship	0 (0.0)	12 (14.3)	8 (9.5)	20 (23.8)		
	Close relation-ship	4 (4.8)	6 (97.1)	18 (21.4)	28 (33.3)		
	Strong bonding	0 (0.0)	8 (9.5)	6 (7.1)	14 (16.7)		
Nature of exchanges and favors asked or received	Loan of items	2 (2.4)	2 (2.4)	2 (2.4)	6 (7.1)	23.763 (.008)	23.370 (.009)
	Taking care of children	0 (0.0)	6 (7.1)	4 (4.8)	10 (11.9)		
	Financial help	0 (0.0)	2 (2.4)	2 (2.4)	4 (4.8)		
	Ceremonies (marriage, birthday) and illness	2 (2.4)	8 (9.5)	10 (11.9)	20 (23.8)		
	None	0 (0.0)	16 (19.0)	2 (2.4)	18 (21.4)		
	All	2 (2.4)	8 (9.5)	16 (19.0)	26 (31.0)		

4.4 Use of Social Media and Level of Social Network in the Neighborhood

The data in Table 6 indicate that the frequency of using social media in a day is an important indicator to understand the level of social interaction and its association with social network (df = 6, likelihood ratio = 18.688, p-value = .005; Chi-square = 17.096, p-value = .009). Nearly half (46.2) the respondents used various social media platforms several times a day. The large majority (71.8%) stated that they had a moderate level of social network; of whom 10.3% used social media only when it was needed, 35.9% several times a day, and 23.1% several times an hour. Of those who had strong level of social network (15.4%), most-used social media platforms only when it was needed.

The number of friends on social media is also an important predictor of an individual's level of social network (df = 12, likelihood ratio = 56.916, p-value = .000; Chi-square = 58.514, p-value = .000). The data show that 43.6% of the respondents had more than 300 friends on a social media platform (Facebook). Most of the respondents had a moderate level of social network (71.8%), and of these, 41.0% had more than 300 friends on social media, 7.7% had 1-50 friends, and 5.1% had 101-150 friends. Interestingly, among those with strong level of social network (15.4%), 5.1% of their friend lists contained 101-150 friends. This result indicates that those who had 101-150 friends on social media were more likely to have a strong social network in their real lives.

We tried to understand the respondents' preferred modes of interaction with their neighbors and the relationship with their real-life social network. The data indicate that over two-thirds of the respondents (76.9%) preferred not to interact with their neighbors by using social media platforms, preferring face-to-face communication instead. Of all the respondents, only 15.4% had a strong level of social network, of whom 7.7% preferred face-to-face interaction and 7.7% through social media. It is evident that there is an association between level of social network and preferred mode of social interaction (df = 2, likelihood ratio = 5.076, p-value = .079; Chi-square = 5.813, p-value = .055).

There is an association also between level of social network and frequency of interaction with neighbors on social media (df = 8, likelihood ratio = 25.610, p-value = .001; Chi-square = 24.202, p-value = .002). The data in Table 6 indicate that those who had a strong level of social network were less frequent in interacting with their neighbors on social media. Only 5.1% of the respondents used a social media platform daily to interact with their neighbors, and 23.1% never interacted that way with their neighbors.

The data in Table 6 indicate that there is a signification association between social network and the extent to which an individual sought help from neighbors who were in their social media contacts (df = 4, likelihood ratio = 17.128, p-value = .002; Chi-square = 15.405, p-value = .004). Half (51.3%) the respondents said that they sought help from neighbors in their social media contacts. Most of the respondents (71.8%) had a moderate level of social network; among whom 41.0% sought help to some extent from neighbors who were also in their social media friend list. Of those

(12.8%) who had an extremely limited level of social network, a small number of them (7.7%) did not request for help from their neighbors on social media.

There is a significant relationship between social network and the feeling of being connected with neighbors via Facebook (d = 2, likelihood ratio = 12.335, p-value = .002; Chi-square = 9.710, p-value = .008). The majority of the respondents (71.8%) said that they did not feel out of touch with neighbors when they were not on Facebook. Among those who had a strong level of social network in real life, none felt out of touch with neighbors when they were not logged onto the social media platform.

The majority (66.7%) of respondents mentioned that social media did not take away from face-to-face socialization with their neighbors. Of those (71.8%) whose had moderate level of social networks in their real life, 53.8% thought that the use of social media did not take away from face-to-face socializing with their neighbors. Furthermore, of those (15.4%) who had a strong social network in their real life, only 10.3% believed that the use of social media contributed to reduce face-to-face socialization. Thus, it is evident that there is a strong association between level of social network, use of social media and nature of socializing (df = 2, likelihood ratio = 7.578, p-value = .023; Chi-square = 7.950, p-value = .019).

The large majority (76.9%) of the respondents stated that they would meet face-to-face more often with their neighbors if there were no social media. Again, the large majority (71.8%) had a moderate level of social network, among whom 51.3% would meet their neighbors more if there were no social media. Of those (15.4%) who had a strong level of social network in real life, all wished to meet face-to-face more with their neighbors if there were no social media platforms. These results indicate that either face-to-face interaction leads to a strong level of social interaction, or that people with a strong level of social network prefer more face-to-face social interaction (d = 2, likelihood ratio = 7.258, p-value = .027; Chi-square = 4.606, p-value = .100).

The data in Table 6 suggest that social media do not play an influential role in improving relationships, as the majority (59.0%) of the respondents mentioned that social media did not improve their relationships with their neighbors. Of those (12.8%) who had an extremely limited social network in their real life, 10.3% believed that social media had improved their relationships with their neighbors. Therefore, there is a significant association between levels of real-life social network and the role of social media in improving relationships with neighbors (d = 2, likelihood ratio = 8.631, p-value = .013; Chi-square = 8.504, p-value = .014). Even though, as the data indicate, social media do not have a significant role in complicating relationships with neighbors, there is an association between level of social network, social media use and complication of relationship with the people of the neighborhood (df = 2, likelihood ratio = 9.160, p-value = .010; Chi-square = 6.747, p-value = .034). It appears from the data that the respondents still preferred face-to-face interaction over the use of any social media to maintain relationships with their neighbors. Social media were regarded as a matter of personal space, and only those close to the respondents were given permission to access that space. Although a large number of friends were included in their social media, neighbors were not there in most cases. Proximity played a role in this result. As the respondents often met their neighbors within the building premises, they felt less eagerness to maintain friendship through social media. This result indicates also the existence of moderate to weak ties among the neighbors. However, social media in this context networked as an additional venue for communication among neighbors. For these respondents, social media were a tool to maintain relationships with those residing at a distance. Hence, the sense of community among the neighbors was not compromised due to the usage of social media, countering Turkle's (2011) thesis.

Table 6: Association between social media interaction and level of social network

| Variables | Indicators | Level of social network | | | Total | | Statistics and Values | |
		Extremely limited social network n (% of total)	Moderate social network n (% of total)	Strong social network n (% of total)	n (% of total)	df	Likelihood ratio (p-value)	Pearson Chi-square (p-value)
Frequency of using social media in a day	Several times an hour	2 (2.6)	18 (23.1)	0 (0.0)	20 (25.6)			
	Every hour	0 (0.0)	2 (2.6)	0 (0.0)	2 (2.6)			
	Several times a day	4 (5.1)	28 (35.9)	4 (5.1)	36 (46.2)		18.688 (.005)	17.096 (.009)
	Only when needed	4 (5.1)	8 (10.3)	8 (10.3)	20 (25.6)			
Number of friends on social media	1-50	0 (0.0)	6 (7.7)	2 (2.6)	8 (10.3)			
	51-100	0 (0.0)	2 (2.6)	2 (2.6)	4 (5.1)			
	101-150	0 (0.0)	4 (5.1)	4 (5.1)	8 (10.3)	2	56.916 (.000)	58.514 (.000)
	151-200	2 (2.6)	10 (12.8)	0 (0.0)	12 (15.4)			
	201-	0	2 (2.6)	2	4			

Table 6: Association between social media interaction and level of social network

	250	(0.0)		(2.6)	(5.1)		
	251-300	6 (7.7)	0 (0.0)	2 (2.6)	8 (10.3)		
	301+	2 (2.6)	32 (41.0)	0 (0.0)	34 (43.6)		
Prefer social media to communicate with neighbors	Yes	2 (2.6)	10 (12.8)	6 (7.7)	18 (23.1)	5.076 (.079)	5.813 (.055)
	No	8 (10.3)	46 (59.0)	6 (7.7)	60 (76.9)		
Frequency of interaction	Several Times a day	0 (0.0)	14 (17.9)	2 (2.6)	16 (20.5)	25.610 (.001)	24.202 (.002)
	Daily	2 (2.6)	2 (2.6)	0 (0.0)	4 (5.1)		
	Weekly	2 (2.6)	12 (15.4)	2 (2.6)	16 (20.5)		
	Monthly or less	4 (5.1)	20 (25.6)	0 (0.0)	24 (30.8)		
	Never	2 (2.6)	8 (10.3)	8 (10.3)	18 (23.1)		
The extent to which go to neighbors in social media contacts for help	No extent	6 (7.7)	16 (20.5)	0 (0.0)	22 (28.2)	17.128 (.002)	15.405 (.004)
	Little extent	2 (2.6)	8 (10.3)	6 (7.7)	16 (20.5)		
	Some extent	2 (2.6)	32 (41.0)	6 (7.7)	40 (51.3)		
Feel out of touch if not logged onto Facebook	Yes	6 (7.7)	16 (20.5)	0 (0.0)	22 (28.2)	12.335 (.002)	9.710 (.008)
	No	4 (5.1)	40 (51.3)	12 (15.4)	56 (71.8)		
Think that the use of social media takes	Yes	4 (5.1)	14 (17.9)	8 (10.3)	26 (33.3)	7.578 (.023)	7.950 (.019)
	No	6 (7.7)	42 (53.8)	4 (5.1)	52 (66.7)		

Table 6: Association between social media interaction and level of social network

away from face-to-face socializing							
If there were no social media, would meet face-to-face with neighbors	Yes	8 (10.3)	40 (51.3)	12 (15.4)	60 (76.9)		
	No	2 (2.6)	16 (20.5)	0 (0.0)	18 (23.1)	7.258 (.027)	4.606 (.100)
Social media improved relationship with neighbors	Yes	8 (10.3)	18 (23.1)	6 (7.7)	32 (41.0)		
	No	2 (2.6)	38 (48.7)	6 (7.7)	46 (59.0)	8.631 (.013)	8.504 (.014)
Social media complicated relationship with neighbors	Yes	0 (0.0)	16 (20.5)	6 (7.7)	22 (28.2)		
	No	10 (12.8)	40 (51.3)	6 (7.7)	56 (71.8)	9.160 (.010)	6.747 (.034)

4.5 Use of social media and level of sense of community in the neighborhood

We tried to understand the dynamics of interaction on social media platforms and its relationship with sense of community among the respondents. Our findings, shown in Table 7, suggest that there is a significant association between sense of community and having account on social media platforms (df = 2, likelihood ratio = 4.062, p-value = .131; Chi-square = 6.701, p-value = .035); the type of social media platform (df = 4, likelihood ratio = 47.821, p-value = .000; Chi-square = 68.613, p-value = .000); frequency of using social media in a day (df = 6, likelihood ratio = 38.631, p-value = .000; Chi-square = 59.025, p-value = .000); number of friends on social media (df = 12, likelihood ratio = 23.547, p-value = .023; Chi-square = 24.767, p-value = .016); number of social media friends who were neighbors (df = 6, likelihood ratio = 34.906, p-value= .000; Chi-square = 55.931, p-value = .000); using social media to contact neighbors (df = 2, likelihood ratio = 7.645, p-value = .022; Chi-square = 6.160, p-value = .046); frequency of interaction with neighbors on social media platforms (df = 8, likelihood ratio = 31.058, p-value = .000; Chi-square = 27.010, p-value = .001);

use of social media to plan events with neighbors (df = 2, likelihood ratio = 6.391, p-value = .041; Chi-square = 6.299, p-value = .043); purpose of social media used to contact neighbors (df = 4, likelihood ratio = 19.304, p-value = .001; Chi-square = 14.296, p-value = .006); social media use, face-to-face interaction and socialization with neighbors (df = 2, likelihood ratio = 9.233, p-value = .010; Chi-square = 8.435, p-value = .015); existence of social media and face-to-face interaction with neighbor (df = 2, likelihood ratio = 7.987, p-value = .018; Chi-square = 7.525, p-value = .023); role of social media in complicating relationship with neighbors (df = 2, likelihood ratio = 7.272, p-value = .026; Chi-square = 6.191, p-value = .045); and frequency of meeting face-to-face with neighbors in social media contacts (df = 8, likelihood ratio = 28.231, p-value = .000; Chi-square = 23.842, p-value = .002).

The data in Table 7 indicate that the vast majority (92.9%) of the respondents used at least one social media platform, among whom 47.6% had a moderate sense of community, and 40.5% had a strong sense of community. Facebook was the most-used social media platform, with 59.0% of the respondents using it. Furthermore, 38.5% of the respondents said that they used Facebook, Twitter, WhatsApp or other social media platforms. Of those (43.6%) who had a strong level of sense of community, 12.8% of them used Facebook. Interestingly, of those who used all forms of social media platforms, 30.8% of them had a strong level of sense of community, which suggests that using multiple social media platforms leads to an increase in sense of community.

Table 7: Association between social media interaction and level of sense of community

Indicators		Level of community sense					Statistics and Values		
		Week comm unity sense n (% of total)	Moder ate commu nity sense n (% of total)	Strong commu nity sense n (% of total)	Total n (% of total)	df	Likel ihoo d ratio (p-value)	Pearson Chi-square (p-value)
Have account on social media	Yes	4 (4.8)	40 (47.6)	34 (40.5)	78 (92.9)			
	No	2 (2.4)	2 (2.4)	2 (2.4)	6 (7.1)		4.062 (.131)	6.701 (.035)
Have social media accounts	Facebook	0 (0.0)	36 (46.2)	10 (12.8)	46 (59.0)			
	WhatsApp	2 (2.6)	0 (0.0)	0 (0.0)	2 (2.6)		47.821 (.000)	68.613 (.000)
	All	2	4	24	30			

Table 7: Association between social media interaction and level of sense of community

		(2.6)	(5.1)	(30.8)	(38.5)		
Frequency of using social media in a day	Several times an hour	2 (2.6)	2 (2.6)	16 (20.5)	20 (25.6)	38.63 1 (.000)	59.025 (.000)
	Every hour	2 (2.6)	0 (0.0)	0 (0.0)	2 (2.6)		
	Several times a day	0 (0.0)	26 (33.3)	10 (12.8)	36 (46.2)		
	Only when needed	0 (0.0)	12 (15.4)	8 (10.3)	20 (25.6)		
Number of friends on social media	1-50	2 (2.6)	2 (2.6)	4 (5.1)	8 (10.3)	23.54 7 (.023)	24.767 (.016)
	51-100	0 (0.0)	4 (5.1)	0 (0.0)	4 (5.1)		
	101-150	0 (0.0)	2 (2.6)	6 (7.7)	8 (10.3)	2	
	151-200	0 (0.0)	8 (10.3)	4 (5.1)	12 (15.4)		
	201-250	0 (0.0)	2 (2.6)	2 (2.6)	4 (5.1)		
	251-300	2 (2.6)	4 (5.1)	2 (2.6)	8 (10.3)		
	301+	0 (0.0%)	18 (23.1)	16 (20.5)	34 (43.6)		
Number of social Have social media friends who are neighbors	1-50	2 (2.6)	24 (30.8)	26 (33.3)	52 (66.7)	34.90 6 (.000)	55.931 (.000)
	51-100	0 (0.0)	0 (0.0)	6 (7.7)	6 (7.7)		
	101-150	0 (0.0)	0 (0.0)	0 (0.0)	0 (0.0)		
	151-200	2 (2.6)	0 (0.0)	0 (0.0)	2 (2.6)		
	None	0 (0.0)	16 (20.5)	2 (2.6)	18 (23.1)		
Use social media to contact neigh-	Yes	4 (5.1)	18 (23.1)	22 (28.2)	44 (56.4)	7.645 (.022)	6.160 (.046)
	No	0 (0.0)	22 (28.2)	12 (15.4)	34 (43.6)		

Table 7: Association between social media interaction and level of sense of community

bors

Frequen-cy of interact-tion	Several Times a day	0 (0.0)	2 (2.6)	14 (17.9)	16 (20.5)	31.058 (.000)	27.010 (.001)
	Daily	0 (0.0)	4 (5.1)	0 (0.0)	4 (5.1)		
	Weekly	2 (2.6)	8 (10.3)	6 (7.7)	16 (20.5)		
	Monthly or less	2 (2.6)	18 (23.1)	4 (5.1)	24 (30.8)		
	Never	0 (0.0)	8 (10.3)	10 (12.8)	18 (23.1)		
Use social media to plan events	Yes	2 (2.6)	10 (12.8)	18 (23.1)	30 (38.5)	6.391 (.041)	6.299 (.043)
	No	2 (2.6)	30 (38.5)	16 (20.5)	48 (61.5)		
Purpose of using social media	To get in touch	2 (2.6)	26 (33.3)	32 (41.0)	6 (76.9)	19.304 (.001)	14.296 (.006)
	To avoid face-to-face meeting	0 (0.0)	2 (2.6)	2 (2.6)	4 (5.1)		
	Others	2 (2.6)	12 (15.4)	0 (0.0)	14 (17.9)		
Social media reduced face-to-face socializ-ing	Yes	4 (5.1)	12 (15.4)	10 (12.8)	26 (33.3)	9.233 (.010)	8.435 (.015)
	No	0 (0.0)	28 (35.9)	24 (30.8)	52 (66.7)		
In absence of social media, face-to-face meeting	Yes	2 (2.6)	27 (34.6)	31 (39.7)	60 (76.9)	7.987 (.018)	7.525 (.023)
	No	2 (2.6)	13 (16.7)	3 (3.8)	18 (23.1)		
Social media has comp-	Yes	0 (0.0)	16 (20.5)	6 (7.7)	22 (28.2)	7.272	6.191
	No	4	24	28	56		

Table 7: Association between social media interaction and level of sense of community

		(5.1)	(30.8)	(35.9)	(71.8)	(.026)	(.045)
licated relation -ships							
Frequen -cy of meeting face-to-face	Several times a day	0 (0.0)	0 (0.0)	6 (7.7)	6 (7.7)		
	Daily	0 (0.0)	2 (2.6)	0 (0.0)	2 (2.6)		
	Weekly	2 (2.6)	10 (12.8)	16 (20.5)	28 (35.9)	28.23 1 (.000)	23.842 (.002)
	Monthly or less	0 (0.0)	20 (25.6)	4 (5.1)	24 (30.8)		
	Never	2 (2.6)	8 (10.3)	8 (10.3)	18 (23.1)		

As mentioned previously, there is a significant association between sense of community and frequency of using social media in a day. The data in Table 7 show that 43.6% of the respondents had a strong level of sense of community, among whom 20.5% used social media several times an hour, 12.8% several times a day and 10.3% only when in need. On the other hand, of those (51.3%) who had a moderate level of sense of community, 33.3% used social media several times a day. Sense of community is not only associated with frequency of using social media, but also with number of social media friends. Of the respondents, 43.6% had a strong sense of community, among whom 20.5% had more than 300 friends in their social media contact list. Of those (51.3%) who had a moderate level of sense of community, 23.1% had more than 300 friends on a social media platform (Facebook). The majority (66.7%) of respondents had 1-50 friends in their social media contacts who were their neighbors, among whom 33.3% had a strong sense of community, and 30.8% had a moderate level of sense of community. Social media seemed to play an influential role in social interactions among the respondents. The data show that 56.4% of the respondents used social media to contact their neighbors. Of these, 23.1% had a moderate level of sense of community, and 28.2% had a strong level of sense of community.

The majority (61.5%) did not use social media for planning events with neighbors, among whom 38.5% had a moderate level of sense of community, and 20.5% had a strong level of sense of community. Social media had become an important tool for contacting others. The large majority (76.9%) of the respondents said that they used social media platforms for getting in touch with neighbors, and 5.1% for avoiding face-to-face communication. Of those (43.6%) who had a strong sense of community, 30.8% believed that social media platforms were not taking away from face-to-face socializing with neighbors. The large majority (76.9%) mentioned that, if there were no social platforms, they would meet face-to-face more with their neighbors. Of those, 39.7% had a strong sense of community, and 34.6% had a moderate level of sense of community. The majority (71.8%) of the respondents thought that social media did not negatively affect their relationship with their neighbors. The data indicate that the respondents in this study were casual users of social media, occasionally using them, and mainly for entertainment purposes and less for maintaining or strengthening relationships, especially with their neighbors. The existence of social media did not contribute to creating problems in relationships, nor was it helping in bonding relationships.

5. Conclusion

Although the urbanization patterns are bringing changes to the relationship structures, social media seem to be contributing to the maintenance of weaker ties. The neighbors emphasized interaction through traditional methods of communication (face-to-face), rather than through digital devices. The respondents were reluctant, however, to allow other residents to enter their personal domain of social media. For the respondents, social media are used only when needed, and mainly for entertainment. While the urbanization and modernization process in Bangladesh is changing relationship patterns, as seen in other parts of the world, the residents here were limiting their connections to traditional methods of interaction.

The results of this study indicate that the level of social network and social interaction ranged between limited and moderate. The respondents felt that the type of social network they maintained within the building could not be recognized as a strong network. Although there is a significant association between social interaction and sense of community among the neighbors, the population mainly had a moderate sense of community. The results from the analysis of the data suggest that the ties among the residents of the buildings seemed to be weak. More precisely, the level of ties among the neighbors ranged between moderate and weak. Furthermore, our results indicate that the respondents in this study are casual users of social media, mainly using them for entertainment purposes, and less for maintaining or strengthening relationships, especially with their neighbors. The existence of social media did not contribute to creating problems in relationships, nor did it help in bonding stronger relationships.

5.1 Implications of the Study

The findings of the study have implications for understanding multiple dynamics of rapidly increasing urbanization in a developing country such as Bangladesh. The study generates insights into real-life social interactions, sense of community, neighborhood and the role of ICTs in social interaction in residential high-rise buildings. These findings can be a base for studying the structure of society, social interaction and communication in Bangladesh.

5.2 Limitations of the Study

The main limitation of this study is the size of the sample. Moreover, it was conducted in only one divisional city of the country. To obtain a clearer understanding of social interaction in high rise building in urban settings, further research should be conducted with a larger sample size and in more cities.

5.3 Future Research

With expanding urbanization and more residential high-rise buildings being constructed in cities, there is a need for further research to determine the livability of cities and the effects of high-rise residential living. Therefore, we suggest more studies be conducted on the social and health consequences of living in high-rise buildings in Bangladesh.

REFERENCES

Aulia, D. (2016). A Framework for Exploring Livable Community in Residential Environment. Case Study: Public Housing in Medan, Indonesia. *Procedia – Social and Behavioural Sciences, 234*, pp. 336-343.

BTRC. (2018). Internet Subscribers. Retrieved October 25, 2018 from http://www.btrc.gov.bd/content/internet-subscribers-bangladesh-january-2018

Chua, V. & Wellman, B. (2016). Networked Individualism, East Asian Style. *Oxford Research Encyclopedia of Communication.* Retrieved April 20, 2018, from http://communication.oxfordre.com/view/10.1093/acrefore/9780190228613.001.0001/acrefore-9780190228613-e-119

de Waal, M. (2014). The Future of the City: a Smart City or a Social City? In The City as Interface: How New Media Are Changing the City, Rotterdam, Netherlands: nai010. Retrieved April 2018 from http://www.thecityasinterface.com/read-first-chapter/

Farahani, L.M. & Lozanovska, M. (2014). A Framework for Exploring the Sense of Community and Social Life in Residential Environments. *International Journal of Architectural Research: Archnet-IJAR, 8*(3), p. 223.

Gattino, S., Piccoli, N.D., Fassio, O. & Rollero, C. (2013). Quality of life and sense of community. A study on health and place of residence. *Journal of Community Psychology, 41*(7), pp. 811-826.

Gaumer, E., Jacobowitz, A. & Brooks-Gunn, J. (2014). Building Ties: The Social Networks of Affordable-Housing Residents. *Cityscape: A Journal of Policy Development and Research, 16* (3), pp. 47-68.

Habib, A., Hossain, F., Ferdous, T. & Bayezid, K. (2018). Social Networks and Social Ties: Changing Trends Among Urban Dwellers in Bangladesh. *Open Access Library Journal, 05*(05), pp. 1-12. doi: 10.4236/oalib.1104604

Hampton, K. & Wellman, B. (2003). Neighboring in Netville: How the Internet Supports Community and Social Capital in a Wired Suburb. *City and Community, 2*(4), pp. 277-311.

Kazemzadea, M. & Shakourib, R. (2017). Enhancing Social Interaction in Residential Complexes (Case Study): Esfahan. *Space Ontology International Journal, 6*(2), pp. 1-8.

Khan, M. (2013). Social Changes in Contemporary Bangladesh. *Journal of the Asiatic Society of Bangladesh (Hum.), 58*(2), pp. 263-276

Lubben, J. (1988). Assessing social networks among elderly populations. *Family & Community Health: The Journal of Health Promotion & Maintenance,* 11, pp. 42-52.

Lubben, J., Blozik, E., Gillmann, G., Iliffe, S., von Renteln Kruse, W., Beck, J.C. & Stuck, A.E. (2006). Performance of an abbreviated version of the Lubben Social Network Scale among three European Community-dwelling older adult populations. *Gerontologist, 46*(4), pp. 503-513.

Mahdavinejad, M., Sadraie, A. & Sadraie, G. (2014). Social Sustainability of High-rise Buildings. *American Journal Of Civil Engineering And Architecture, 2*(1), pp. 34-41.

Manjunatha S. (2013). The Usage of Social Networking Sites Among the College Students in India. *International Research Journal of Social Sciences, 2*(5), pp. 15-21 .

McMillan, D.M. & Chavis, D.W. (1986). Sense of community: A definition and theory. *Journal Of Community Psychology, 14*(1), pp. 6-23. doi: 10.1002/1520-6629(198601)14:1<6:aid-jcop2290140103>3.0.co;2-i

Murthy, D., Gross, A., & Pensavalle, A. (2015). Urban Social Media Demographics: An Exploration of Twitter Use in Major American Cities. *Journal Of Computer-Mediated Communication, 21*(1), pp. 33-49. doi: 10.1111/jcc4.12144

Panczak, R., Galobardes, B., Spoerri, A., Zwahlen, M. & Egger, M. (2013). High life in the sky? Mortality by floor of residence in Switzerland. *European Journal of Epidemiology, 28*(6), pp. 453-462.

Putnam, R.D. (2000). *Bowling Alone: The Collapse and Revival of American Community.* New York: Simon and Schuster.

Rainie, L. & Wellman, B. (2012). *Networked: The new social operating system.* Cambridge, MA: MIT Press.

Schutte, C.D. (1985). Social interaction at a high-rise, high-density urban flat complex. *South African Journal Of Sociology, 16*(3), pp. 104-110. doi: 10.1080/02580144.1985.10558304

Shams, S.R. (2017). Social media trends usages in Bangladesh. *The Asian Age.* Retrieved October 30, 2018 from https://dailyasianage.com/news/46958/social-media-trends-usages-in-Bangladesh

Snow, D., Leahy, P. & Schwab, W. (1981). Social Interaction in a Heterogeneous Apartment: An Investigation of the Effects of Environment upon Behavior. *Sociological Focus, 14*(4), pp. 309-319. doi: 10.1080/00380237.1981.10570404

Tseng, S.F. & Hsieh, Y. (2015). The implications of networked individualism for social participation: How mobile phone, E-mail, and IM networks afford social participation for rural residents in Taiwan. *American Behavioral Scientist, 59*(9), pp. 1157-1172.

Turkle, S. (2011). *Alone together: Why we expect more from technology and less from each other.* New York: Basic Books.

Verhaeghe, P., Coenen, A. & Van de Putte, B. (2016). Is Living in a High-Rise Building Bad for Your Self-Rated Health? *Journal of Urban Health, 93*(5), pp. 884-898.

Wandersman, A. & Nation, M. (1998). Urban neighborhoods and mental health: Psychological contributions to understanding toxicity, resilience, and interventions. *American Psychologist, 53*(6), pp. 647-656.

We Are Social. (2018). Digital in 2018: World's Internet Users Pass the 4 Billion Mark. Retrieved October 25, 2018 from https://wearesocial.com/blog/2018/01/global-digital-report-2018

Wellman, B. & Leighton, B. (1979). Networks, neighborhoods, and communities: approaches to the study of the community question. *Urban Affairs Review, 14*(3), pp. 363-390.

Wellman, B. (2001). Physical place and cyber place: The rise of networked individualism. *International Journal of Urban and Regional Research, 25*(2), pp. 227-252.Wellman, B. (2005). Community: From Neighborhood to Network. *Communications of the ACM, 48*(10), pp. 53-55.

World Bank. (2018). World Development Indicators. Retrieved September 17, 2018 from http://databank.worldbank.org/data/reports.aspx?source=2&series=SP.URB.TOTL.IN.ZS&country=

Yuen, B., Yeh, A., Appold, S., Earl, G., Ting, J. & Kwee, L. K. (2006). High-rise Living in Singapore Public Housing. *Urban Studies, 43*(3), pp. 583-600.

Notes on Contributors

Dr Bhakti More is an architect and academician with over two decades of experience in the design industry and academia. Currently she is an Associate Professor at School of Design & Architecture, Manipal Academy of Higher Education Dubai Campus. She pursued her architecture studies at L.S.Raheja School of Architecture Mumbai, India and doctoral studies from University of Salford, Manchester, UK. Her area of interests are urban planning and social cohesiveness, evolution of cities and sustainability practices. Dr Bhakti is a co-ordinator for Conservation and Environment Students Club that has received awards for 'Best Green Campus Audit' and 'Best Sustainable Action project' from Environment Agency Abu Dhabi. She has initiated Mentorship Programs for university female graduating students 'Her Tomorrow Begins Today' as part of D&I Initiative 'Manipal Beyond Gender' and is a recipient of Prof.Indira Parikh 50 Women in Education Leader's Award.

Kapil Kumar Gavsker works as senior Assistant Professor in Department of Applied Geography, School of Regional Studies and Earth Sciences, Ravenshaw University, Cuttack, Odisha (India). He has Post Graduate degree in Geography from Dr. B.R.Ambedkar University, Agra (Uttar Pradesh), M.Phil and Ph.D in Regional Studies from University of Hyderabad, Hyderabad. His research interests lie in urban planning, urban and regional development, environment and heritage studies etc. He has several quality publications to his credit in various journals including *Economic and Political Weekly*; *Annals- National Association of Geographers, India*; *International Journal of Research in Geography*; *Journal of Asian Profile*; *Indian Geographical Journal; International Journal of Environment, Ecology, Family and Urban Studies* etc. He has participated and presented research papers in several national and international conferences, workshops, seminars and webinars. He is life member of important professional societies including The Geographical Society of India, Kolkata (India); The Institute of Indian Geographers, Pune (India); and The Association of Socio-Economic Development Studies, Lucknow (India).

Marcus Breen was born in Melbourne and educated at The University of Queensland, The Australian National University and Victoria University, Melbourne. Since 2014 he has been a full-time faculty member in the Communication Department at Boston College, where he is Director of the Media Lab. He has taught at The University of Melbourne, The University of North Carolina at Chapel Hill, Northeastern University and Bond University, Australia. After a career in journalism, he was director of the cultural industries program at the Centre for International Research on Communication and Information Technologies (CIRCIT) in Melbourne before consulting for Multimedia Victoria in the Victorian Department of State Development. Later he worked for Gartner, consulting in the US, Mexico and the Caribbean on telecommunication policy, new media and regulation. His books include Uprising: The Internet's Unintended Consequences (2011), and Rock Dogs: Politics and the Australian Music Industry (1999). As editor Missing in Action: Australian Popular Music in Perspective (Vol. 1, 1987), and Our Place Our Music: Aboriginal Music. Australian Popular Music in Perspective (Vol. 2, 1989). He is editor of the International Journal of Technology, Knowledge and Society.
Boston Media Theory is a collection of his interviews with Boston academics and researchers available on You Tube.
https://www.youtube.com/channel/UC9OkPztazE5WDuF4PQ-lYdA

Pierre Depaz is an educator, artist and programmer from France. He is currently lecturing at NYU Berlin and Sciences Po Paris. His research focuses on the multiple way's computers are attempting to represent and interface with human concepts and emotions. His academic research revolves around how software systems create representational frameworks for inter- and intra-personal organization, while his artistic practice includes digital games, computer simulations, interactive installations, networked performances and experimental web projects, and has been exhibited in NYC, Paris, Cairo, Abu Dhabi, Brussels and Berlin.

Nicolas Grefenstette is a landscape architect and urban planner. His academic background in cultural and human geography at University College London (UCL) and his experiences living and observing cities across Europe, Asia and the United States have lead him to complete his graduate studies at Cornell University in Ithaca, New York, where he focused on the reclamation of industrial and underutilized urban land. He currently works for Starr Whitehouse Landscape Architects and Planners, where he designs public space in New York City.

Rodrigo Paraizo is a professor with the Department of Form Analysis and Representation of the School of Architecture and Urbanism (FAU) and the current vice-coordinator of the Graduate Program in Urbanism at the Federal University of Rio de Janeiro (2018-2020). He joined the Urban Analysis and Digital Representation Lab as one of the Lab's supervisors in 2010. His research experience includes digital representation of architecture and the city and the use of databases to record cultural objects.

He works primarily in the field of digital heritage, studying, creating and developing digital interpretative environments to visualize the history of the city of Rio de Janeiro. Publications include articles in IJAC and IEEE Multimedia, and conferences as SIGraDi and eCAADe, and the organization of books on digital representation and heritage management and conservation. Current research deals with the use of locative media such as augmented reality and hybrid spaces in architecture and their effects on urban life, and the use of games and rule-based environments as a framework for the representation of urban heritage.

Marina Lima Medeiros is an Architect and Urbanist that learned how to program and now works as a virtual and augmented reality researcher. She holds a master in Urban Design (2014) from Federal University of Rio de Janeiro in Brazil. Currently she is doing her PhD at Graz University of Technology and works in VRVis Research Center in Austria.

Marina has experience in urban and landscape design for public sector, and also worked in Usina CTAH, a non-profit organization in a social housing participatory project in São Paulo and worked as assistant professor in Ibirapuera University in Brazil. Her curious mind and interest for social causes have led her to cross-disciplinary activities. In the past years Marina engaged in urban design workshops around the world, taught augmented reality, robotic and interactive design for different audiences and participated in hackathons, maker events, art exhibitions and public interventions.

As a researcher she worked in the Research Group NOAH – Habitat Center Without Borders of the University of São Paulo and in the Urban Analysis and Digital Representation of the Federal University of Rio de Janeiro. At VRVis she works developing virtual reality applications for industries and public sectors. Publications include papers in IEEE ISMAR workshops, World Conference on VR Industry, and conferences as SIGraDi and eCAADe. Her research is focused on how virtual and augmented reality can improve the understanding of urban spaces and how those innovative technologies can be used in participatory design processes.

Dr. Surhita Basu is working at present as Assistant Professor in the Department of Journalism and Mass Communication at Women's College, Calcutta of University of Calcutta in India specializes in online media and international communication. Her doctoral thesis on online international journalism was analysis of online news on Arab uprising. A gold medallist at her masters' program on Mass Communication and Videography, Surhita started her career in online magazines and creative writing. Soon she shifted to academics, teaching at various universities of Delhi, Tamilnadu and West Bengal. Apart from earning a second master's degree in English literature, Surhita has also completed a diploma in Information Communication Technology Application and various courses on social media, web 2.0 and data journalism. Teaching new media and online journalism in various universities of India over a decade, she has carried forth multiple research projects in related area. Her works have been published internationally by Asia Pacific Media Educator, Media Asia, Global Media Journal, Cyber-psychology: Journal of Psychosocial Research on Cyberspace, Journal of Global Communication and other renowned publications.

Surhita has been the coordinator and trainer of various international journalism workshops, training journalists from Africa and Afghanistan and journalism students from France. She has also worked with UPI for their university collaboration project. She has presented papers in numerous international conferences including conference of Asian Media Information and Communication Centre and World Congress of International Institute of Sociology. Her research interest includes online media, virtual identity, politics of knowledge, political communication and development communication.

Dr. Francesca Savoldi is a Researcher at at CICS-NOVA – Research Centre in Social Sciences - NOVA University of Lisbon. With a background in human geography and urban planning, her work has engaged with topics concerning cities their urban communities, public participation issues and their relationship with communication technology. Her postdoctoral research moved on towards the studies of port cities at the time of the technological and logistics revolution, and their impact on local communities. She has a PhD in Geography and Territorial Planning. Her area of specialisation: Human Geography (NOVA University of Lisbon, 2018). She holds a BA in Urban Planning from the Polytechnic of Milan, as well as a master degree in GIS and Remote Sensing from the Univesity of Alcalá de Henares (Madrid).

Dr. Sadia Jamil is a postdoctoral fellow at Khalifa University of Science and Technology, Abu Dhabi. In July 2015, she has received her PhD degree in Journalism at the University of Queensland, Australia. She also holds postgraduate degrees in the disciplines of Media Management (University of Stirling, Scotland) and Mass Communication (University of Karachi). Dr Jamil is currently serving IAMCR as the Co Vice-Chair of Journalism Research and Education Section. As postdoctoral research fellow at Khalifa University's Department of Humanities and Social Sciences, Dr. Jamil is part of the team for Khalifa University (جامعة خليفة) research project: "Cultural Determinants of Digital Skill Levels among Internet Users in Abu Dhabi." It is the first-ever #DigitalDivide study to be conducted in the UAE & one of very few to be conducted in the MENA region.

Dr. Jamil has published and edited collections on freedom of expression, media freedom, safety of journalists, data journalism, ethnic media and digital divides. Her most recent books include 'the Handbook of Research on Combating Threats to Media Freedom and Journalists' Safety' (IGI Global, 2019), 'Ethnic Journalism in the Global South (forthcoming, Palgrave MacMillan) co-edited with Dr. Anna Gladkova, and 'Discrimination, Gender Equality and Safety Risks in Journalism' (forthcoming, IGI Global) co-edited with Professor Baris Coban, Professor Bora Ataman and Dr Gifty Appiah-Adeji.

To date, Dr Jamil is the recipient of a number of international awards and scholarships including: The University of Queensland's Centennial Award (2010), UQ's International Postgraduate Research Support Award (2010), the Norwegian UNESCO Commissions' and Oslo Metropolitan University's conference scholarships (2015-2018), IAMCR's travel grant award (2019), Union Insurance's Cairo Air Crash Journalists Victim Memorial Gold Medal (2007) and Daily Jang's and The News' Sardar Ali Sabri Memorial Gold Medal (2007).

Email: sadia.jamil@ymail.com, sadia.jamil@ku.ac.ae
Facebook: https://www.facebook.com/sadia.jamil.948
IAMCR's Journalism Research and Education Section Facebook page: https://www.facebook.com/JRE000/

Yvonne Hoh Jgin Jit is a lecturer at Universiti Tunku Abdul Rahman Universiti Tunku Abdul Rahman (UTAR) in Malaysia, as well as a PhD student at the University of Malaya, also in Malaysia. Her PhD research focuses technology and surveillance culture, specifically the normalization and use of surveillance in Malaysia. Her research interests are in surveillance, media and politics, online alternative media as well as film studies.

She has previously presented papers about the development of surveillance studies and the need for the study of this area in Malaysia as well as normalization and acceptance of surveillance by Malaysian social media users. She graduated from City University of Hong Kong with a Master of Arts in Media Cultures, with her research about alternative radio in Hong Kong and political activism through online radio. It was also in Hong Kong that her interest in surveillance and cities began and eventually formed the basis of her PhD research. Surveillance studies is still a relatively new area of study in South East Asia and she hopes that in the future, it can be developed into an important course for students interested in the study of cities, communication and technology.

Amira Firdaus is a Senior Lecturer at University of Malaya's Department of Media and Communication Studies. Amira is currently the Deputy Director of UM's faculty training outfit, the Academic Enhancement & Leadership Development Centre (ADeC), where she founded the Unit for Leadership and Wellbeing (LeadWell), offering workshops and training on happiness and wellbeing for university faculty. Amira's multi-disciplinary interests span across the fields of positive psychology, higher education, ageing, organizational studies, ADHD/ADD as well as media and communication. Her current interests in the latter revolve around positive communication, positive/constructive journalism, digital ethnography and also the use of technology in teaching and learning (T&L) and student supervision. Earlier in her academic career, Amira's own doctoral research touched upon the city as a place-based locality for news production in digital and networked news spheres (see Network Newswork: Media Globalization and Digital Journalism in Malaysia, 2018, Routledge, Taylor and Francis). Amira holds a PhD in communication from the University of Melbourne, Australia, and currently sits on the international editorial board of the journal Digital Journalism.

Lucinda Caetano is architect and member of the College of Specialties in Urbanism at the Portuguese Architects Order. She has graduated from the FAU of at the Federal University of Rio de Janeiro, with equivalence from the FA of the of Porto. She is Master's in history and Art Criticism from the EBA / UFRJ, with equivalence from the FCSH of Nova University of Lisboa, Postgraduate in Archeology and Heritage from the FCSH of Nova University of Lisboa.

She is currently a collaborating researcher from CIAUD, FA of the University of Lisbon; PhD fellow at the Foundation for Science and Technology and scientific reviewer at the magazine kult-ur - interdisciplinary magazine on the culture of the city, at Jaume I de Castellón University - with ISSN 2386 -5458.

She has experience in Public¯Administration, in Brazil and Portugal, in the areas of heritage and urban rehabilitation, urban management and planning and she was professor from Degree in Architecture at Instituto Superior Manuel Teixeira Gomes de Portimão, as well as having taught by invitation at the Faculty of Architecture at the University of Lisbon. Publications include articles in scientific journals and conference papers, as well as participation in books on governance; sustainability and public participation in the territorial process.

José Crespo is the Assistant Professor at the Lisbon School of Architecture, Lisbon University (FA.ULisboa) and researcher in the Research Center for Architecture, Urbanism and Design (CIAUD). His main research is focused in urban governance, public participation in urban planning, and architecture.

Fernanda Castilho is Postdoc at the School of Communications and Arts, University of São Paulo (ECA/USP). Professor at Centro Estadual Paula Souza (State Center Paula Souza), Fatec Barueri. She has a master's degree and a PhD from the University of Coimbra, Portugal. She has taken part in several international research projects and her most recent research interests are: genre and media, fan studies, transmedia, new methodologies and popular culture. E-mail: fernandacasty@gmail.com

Richard Romancini is a adjunct professor of the Department of Communications and Arts, School of Communications and Arts, University of São Paulo (CCA/ECA/USP). He has a master's degree and a PhD in Communication Sciences from the ECA/USP Graduate Program in Communication Sciences. His research interests are educommunication, research methodology and communication history. He is the author of thebook História do Jornalismo no Brasil (History of Journalism in Brazil - Florianópolis: Insular, 2007), and papers in scientific journals. Email: richard.romancini@gmail.com.

Africanus Lewil Diedong holds a PhD in Social Communications from the Gregorian University in Rome, Italy. He is an alumnus of the Ghana Institute of Journalism. He is a Senior Lecturer at the Department of African and General Studies of the University for Development Studies, Ghana. He has been teaching in the Department since 2007. Dr. Diedong is the Vice Dean of the Faculty of Integrated Development Studies and the Editor of the Ghana Journal of Development Studies. He is a member of the Society of African Journal Editors. His membership to professional associations include: Communication Educators Association of Ghana, International Association for Media and Communication Research and Catholic Association of Media Practitioners in Ghana. He is a former fellow of the International Study Commission on Media, Religion and Culture and a recipient of an International Award for Excellence in Communication.

His areas of research include: Media and Democracy, Media Ethics and Journalism Education, Development Communication, Media-Religion-Culture, Community Radio Broadcasting, Media Education and Pastoral Communication. He is the author of a book (2016): Responsible Journalism and Quest for Professional Standards in Ghana. Dr. Diedong has authored several book chapters and papers in peer-reviewed journals and newspapers and magazines in Ghana and overseas.

Eni Maryani is a Head of Centre for Study of Communication, Media, and Culture, Padjadjaran University. She earned her doctoral degree in Communication Science at University of Indonesia. Her works has been published in several well respected Journal, such as International Journal of Public Relations Review (review), Malaysian Journal of Communication (mjc), Journal of Communication Science (JIK Atmajaya), and Journal of Communication Study (JKK Unpad), the Jurnal Komunikasi Ikatan Sarjana Komunikasi (jkiski). Her research subject is media industry, digital media, and gender in media and communication. She actively involved in community networking of digital literacy in Indonesia (Japelidi) and Institution of Indonesia for humanity (IKa) that focused to human right issue, and social transformation. She also a member of International Association for Media and Communication Research (IAMCR) and International Communication Association (ICA).

Detta Rahmawan is a lecturer and researcher at the Department of Communication Management, Faculty of Communication Science, Padjadjaran University. He obtained his master's degree on Cross-Cultural Communication and Media Studies at Newcastle University, UK, with scholarship from Indonesian Ministry of Education and Culture. His works has been published in several well respected journals in Indonesia, such as Indonesian Journal of Library and Information Science (Edulib UPI), Jurnal of Communication Science (JIK Atmajaya), and Jurnal of Communication Study (JKK Unpad). Detta teaches several subjects on communication technology and digital media industry. Aside from teaching and research, he also actively involved in several community service on digital literacy and youth empowerment. His works mainly focused in digital media industry and digital activism.

Md. Aminul Islam is a faculty member at the Department of Media Studies and Journalism, University of Liberal Arts Bangladesh (ULAB). He received his master's degree in Mass Communication and Journalism from the University of Rajshahi, and his bachelor's degree in Mass Communication from the same university. He also received a Post Graduate Diploma in Journalism (New Media) from the Asian College of Journalism, Chennai, India. His research interests include social network analysis, cyberpsychology, communication in healthcare, and interrelations between social interaction, psychology and mental health. Currently he is working on communication in healthcare with special focus on impact of social network and doctor-patient relationship on health outcomes. Emails: aminul.islam@ulab.edu.bd (office) / aminulbd@protonmail.com (personal).

Naziat Choudhury received her master's from the University of Calgary, Canada and her PhD from Monash University, Australia. She is currently an associate professor at the Department of Mass Communication and Journalism, University of Rajshahi, Bangladesh. Her research interests include intercultural communication, mHealth services and social and cultural aspects of social media and internet use. She is currently working on social media in the context of China. Email: naziat96@yahoo.com.

Disclaimer:
The views expressed in every chapter are the responsibility of the named author(s). Neither the publisher nor the editor can be held responsible for errors or for any consequences arising from the use of information contained herein.

Lightning Source UK Ltd.
Milton Keynes UK
UKHW020940060421
381461UK00001B/12